FORMS OF INTUITION

15°

FORMS OF INTUITION

AN HISTORICAL INTRODUCTION
TO THE TRANSCENDENTAL AESTHETIC

by

RICHARD A. SMYTH

1978

MARTINUS NIJHOFF / THE HAGUE - BOSTON

This book is dedicated to
Elizabeth Smyth
and to the memory of
Ralston Smyth

ISBN 90 247 2001 X

78-9600

TYPESET IN THE UNITED KINGDOM

TABLE OF CONTENTS

CHAPTER ONE

THE ELEMENTS OF KNOWLEDGE

I. THE NATURE OF TRANSCENDENTAL PHILOSOPHY

An introduction to Kant's transcendental aesthetic requires a look at the general character of transcendental philosophy. Kant introduces the subject in his *Critique of Pure Reason*, saying, "I entitle *transcendental* all knowledge which is occupied not so much with objects as with the mode of our knowledge of objects in so far as this mode of knowledge is to be possible *a priori*. A system of such concepts might be entitled transcendental philosophy." [1] Events very quickly proved to Kant that this explanation itself required some explaining. What happened sheds some light on his concept of transcendental philosophy.

Several branches of traditional philosophy can be described as having a direct concern with objects. In particular, general metaphysics or ontology is the science that supplies the basic concepts and principles that apply to all objects whatsoever. Kant's explanation of his new transcendental philosophy might easily be taken to say that it deals with our knowledge of objects, but does not concern itself at all with the objects of knowledge. Several of Kant's most devoted students did read him in this spirit and they concluded that an ontology is not supplied with the new philosophy. Acting in good faith on the basis of that assumption, they attempted to supplement Kant's system with the missing chapters on metaphysics. In response to Fichte's work Kant very forcefully made the point that a metaphysics *is* included in his system of transcendental philosophy and that he had worked out such a metaphysics himself in the *Critique of Pure Reason*.

---

[1] Immanuel Kant, *Critique of Pure Reason*, trans. Norman Kemp Smith (New York, 1965), p. 59. Subsequent references to the first *Critique* in the text will designate the page of the original edition of 1781 ("A") or of the revised edition of 1787 ("B").

The misunderstanding arose out of the very special and very oblique approach that Kant takes to metaphysics. The philosophical conclusions that he reaches about objects are drawn from his investigation of our possible knowledge of objects. Transcendental philosophy does not abandon or ignore any of the traditional areas of philosophy; it simply employs a strategy of indirection in developing those areas. Conclusions about possible objects of cognition are to be sought in a careful inquiry into the possibilities of the cognitive representation of objects. This strategy will strike some as a peculiarly round-about procedure and will strike others as the kind of re-description of problems that is to be expected of philosophers. Those in the first group should know that Kant had good reasons and ample precedent for his transcendental approach. Those in the second group should know that the most important pioneers of the method were not philosophers.

In the first place, the language that has been quoted in which Kant defines his discipline is borrowed almost word-for-word from his predecessor Lambert, and Lambert had also made a number of specific suggestions about inferences from logic—which concerns itself with a certain type of possibility in representations—to metaphysics.[2] The general idea that at least a part of metaphysics can be based upon logic was a commonplace in Kant's day. For example, the great schoolmaster of German rationalism, Christian Wolff, had devoted several sections of his *Ontologia* to a consideration of the logical relationships between *veritas transcendentalis* or metaphysical truth, and *veritas logica* or logical truth.[3] To be sure, we will see that there are very significant differences in the details of the idea in Wolff and in Kant, but nevertheless the general idea is not different.

Kant's thought is that we should replace the direct investigation of the nature of things with an indirect approach through a study of the representations of things. From the earliest times Pythagoreans and Platonists have borrowed philosophical inspiration from mathematics. The field of mathematics in Kant's century provided a methodological perspective that may well have been more decisive in his mind and in Lambert's mind than anything they could have discovered in earlier philosophers. Mathematicians had become accustomed to the idea that inquiries concerning certain types of mathematical objects can only be conducted indirectly through a study of

---

[2] Johann Lambert, *Anlage zur Architectonik* (Riga, 1771; reprinted Hildesheim, 1965), p. 120. The part called "Das Ideale der Grundlehre" opens: "Ich werde mich zu denjenigen Hauptstucken der Grundlehre, welche vielmehr unsere Vorstellungsart der Dinge, als die Dinge selbst betreffen, . . ."

[3] Christian Wolff, *Philosophia Prima sive Ontologia* (Frankfurt and Leipzig, 1736), reprinted in *Gesammelte Werke*, Second Series, Vol. III (Hildesheim, 1962), section 495ff.

their possible representations. These objects are ones which need not and perhaps cannot be "given directly"; they can nevertheless be classified and studied through an investigation of their possible representations in equations. They are objects which the mathematician sees that he must suppose to be possible as a condition for the possibility that the equations represent anything at all, or for the possibility that the equations represent something for at least some of the possible solutions to the equations. The mathematician, failing to have any direct insight into the possibility of certain objects, relies instead on indirect arguments which relate these objects, by way of their representations, to other objects which *are* given directly, or which are supposed to be given directly. Among the many types of objects which mathematicians had come to think of in these terms are the so-called "transcendental numbers". Conceivably in this case as in so many other cases there is an echo of the mathematical terminology in Kant's use of the term. In any event, the absolute necessity for a transcendental turn had become evident prior to Kant in the area of mathematics and had become evident for reasons which play a decisive role in transcendental aesthetic.

The influence of Hume on Kant's approach to metaphysics forms one of the best-known episodes in the history of philosophy. Kant credited Hume with having wakened him from a "dogmatic slumber". We can certainly understand how a philosopher who already possessed the idea of a transcendental approach in philosophy would have been galvanized into action by Hume's results. Hume argued that our ideas of the metaphysical aspects of things are not given directly in experience. He based this conclusion on what he could report after a careful examination of what we do in fact experience. He added other and independent considerations to deliver a final conclusion that was distinctly hostile to the very possibility of any future metaphysics. Suppose for the moment that these notorious conclusions had come to the attention of a man who was so favorably disposed to metaphysics that he would devote a long life to providing the metaphysical foundations of this discipline, of that discipline, and of almost every other conceivable discipline. Kant did that. So suppose that our philosopher had already perceived that some aspects of the world cannot be grasped directly but can only be approached indirectly and through a transcendental inquiry into how such aspects can possibly get represented. If such a philosopher had never yet troubled himself about the possibility of causes, substances, and the like metaphysical objects, but if he realized their importance for metaphysics, then we can well imagine that he would have been stimulated into action by Hume. Now, one point that is revealed by an examination of the historical background to Kant's transcendental aesthetic is that Kant had had the idea of a way to reply to Hume even before he had received the challenge. The psychology of his situation is manifest. The one who will become most excited on hearing the question is the one who thinks he knows how to answer it.

We have ample reason to conclude that Kant did have the idea of a transcendental philosophy before he encountered the challenge from Hume, or, at least, before he was wakened by the challenge. In the first place we must consider the fact that the transcendental aesthetic is encorporated into the *Critique* as an integral part of transcendental philosophy. That is a significant fact because the main conclusions in the aesthetic were already derived in Kant's earlier study of our world-concept, a study in which he considers those aspects of things by virtue of which they are co-ordinated with one another as existing parts of this actual world we find ourselves in. His inquiry deals mainly with space and with time as the ways in which things are co-ordinated through the form of the world, and it proceeds to its conclusions by way of an examination of our representations of space and time. These arguments form the main substance of the transcendental aesthetic and we will be studying them in detail in due course. The important point to notice at the moment is that these results of Kant's inquiry into our representations of space and time had been published before the time at which the challenge from Hume had been acknowledged by Kant.

One might challenge the signicance of this point on the grounds that the arguments of the aesthetic do not form a proper part of a transcendental philosophy or do not form an integral part of it. There are objections at various levels of profundity that can be developed along those lines, and some of them are based upon considerations that need not concern us now. As an example of the type of view that can be safely set aside, the views of Norman Kemp Smith were those of an eminent Kant-scholar and a harsh critic of the transcendental aesthetic. He objected to Kant's introduction of these earlier arguments into the *Critique* on the ground that their defective and shoddy quality prove that Kant had not attained a clear conception of his own transcendental standpoint at the time the arguments were devised. The only effective or convincing answer to this type of objection comes with the presentation and defense of the arguments themselves. They are good arguments. Kemp Smith's judgment cannot be sustained.

A second kind of objection deserves a closer look while we are attempting to bring the general idea of a transcendental philosophy into focus. Let us agree that transcendental philosophy does seek to derive metaphysical conclusions from a study of the possibilities of representation. Let us also agree that transcendental aesthetic is a proper part of this general project. Still, we may wonder whether it is an integral, or a possibly self-subsistent, part of transcendental philosophy. We can imagine a mini-Fichte who would say, "Surely the transcendental aesthetic, at least, requires supplementation before it will yield results for metaphysics." And in this case Kant himself might be thought to have supplied the "something else" in his transcendental analytic, where he deals with the metaphysical categories of substance, cause, and the rest. On this view we may wonder whether Kant had taken the transcendental turn before he had developed his account of the categories.

The persuasiveness of this view comes in part from our own tendency to collapse the problems of metaphysics into the problems of the theory of categories. P.F. Strawson's recent essay in descriptive metaphysics, *Individuals*, is typical of the trend to subsume the discussion of our representations of the world, of space, and of time, as "forms of pure intuition", under the discussion of metaphysical concepts or categories. If more than one recent commentary on Kant has followed the same fashion, the precedents which can be claimed for the fashion are very ancient indeed. The common definition of metaphysics follows Aristotle's conception of his "first philosophy" and identifies metaphysics with the science of being. If we accept this identification of metaphysics, then we find the first suggestion that the representations of metaphysics are all conceptual or categorial representations in Aristotle himself. For example, he says in the work that has come to be called his *Metaphysics*, "And indeed the question which was raised of old and is raised now and always, and is always the subject of doubt, viz. what being is, is just the question, what is substance?"[4] It follows that if Kant did not accept this collapse of the study of being into the theory of the categories, that very fact will have a certain importance for our understanding of his position and for our understanding of the history of metaphysics.

The transcendental analytic deals with categories that are "pure concepts of the understanding". These concepts are one of the two major types of representation that are to be found in Kant's doctrine of the elements of knowledge. The transcendental aesthetic deals with our representations of space and time as what Kant calls "forms of intuition". These pure intuitions are a species of the second major type of representation and, as intuitions, they are a non-conceptual element in our knowledge. It is a distinctive trait of Kant's transcendental analysis of knowledge, as contrasted, say, with logicians in the schools of Aristotle or of Strawson, that Kant's analysis does not reduce to conceptual analysis. Provided that we retain Aristotle's first thought about metaphysics as a science of being, rather than his second thought about it as a science of substance, we can say that the transcendental

---

[4] *The Works of Aristotle*, trans. W.D. Ross (Oxford, 1954) Vol. VIII, *Metaphysica*, Book Zeta, 1028b.

aesthetic is an essential and integral part of any argument from transcendental premises to metaphysical conclusions. Kant does not believe that the way things can be conceptualized has anything to do with their being or their being one, as objects of knowledge. Whenever we are concerned with the presuppositions of existence or uniqueness in our representations, we will discover that we are concerned with those "forms of intuition", rather than with "pure concepts of the understanding"—such as the concepts of substance. And, of course, in order for our inquiry into the possibilities of representation to yield conclusions in a science of being, we must be concerned about just those presuppositions. Having in mind the classical definition of metaphysics, and knowing that the transcendental aesthetic is concerned with the element of form in our knowledge, we will get a correct sense of Kant's priorities from an ancient metaphysical maxim which he repeated on numerous occasions: *Forma dat esse rei*—It is the form that gives the being of things. One of our tasks in coming to understand the aesthetic is to see how Kant was able to infuse that old maxim with a new vigor.

The arguments of the aesthetic are not merely an adjunct for the conclusions Kant reaches in metaphysics. They are sufficient by themselves to establish a number of interesting metaphysical conclusions—though these are, to be sure, conclusions which tend to be taken for granted by contemporary thinkers. To illustrate the historical importance of Kant's deductions, we only need refer back to the passage from Aristotle that has just been cited. Immediately following those lines that identify the study of being with the study of substance, Aristotle continues, "For it is this that some assert to be one, others more than one, and that some assert to be limited in number, others unlimited. And so we also must consider chiefly and primarily and almost exclusively what that is which *is* in *this* sense." Aristotle's reference to the historic debates about the one and the many supplies just the examples one needs to have in mind when considering whether there are any metaphysical issues that can get settled through the arguments of the aesthetic or whether, on the contrary, every metaphysical conclusion must depend upon the outcome of an analysis of our categories of understanding. One position which emerges from the transcendental aesthetic is a rather strong form of pluralism in regard to the possible objects of scientific knowledge. The version of pluralism is strong because, as Kant will argue, we are not only justified in taking the possible objects of knowledge to be many, we are justified in taking the many to be infinite or "unlimited" in number. Furthermore, Kant gives this conclusion as independent of any assumption about whether the objects of knowledge can be regarded as substances, and, if so, what kinds of things substances are. The reason why I emphasize the point that the aesthetic is self-subsistent in regard to this conclusion has nothing to do with any desire to draw a polemical contrast between Aristotle and Kant, or Strawson and Kant. It has to do with a very basic issue concerning the possibility of a scientific knowledge of things: Can we suppose that the number of things under discussion can be multiplied—even perhaps multiplied to form an infinite population—without creating implications about any corresponding changes in the ways the objects must be conceptualized? In a later section in this chapter I will return to this problem as it relates to the possibility of inductive knowledge in the factual sciences and I will show how this problem becomes a concern for Kant in the aesthetic. It is an aspect of the problem of induction which is frequently neglected in contemporary discussions, where it is never satisfactorily explained how we are able—as it were—to come out short in the concepts we have of the objects. For the moment, I am content to rest the case for the independence of Kant's pluralistic conclusion on an observation about its relationship to the pure science of mathematics. Kant regards the infinistic version of pluralism as indispensable to any account of the possibility of our purely mathematical knowledge of the world. But pure mathematics does not presuppose any categorization of things as substances. This observation is bound to suggest the type of difference between Kant and Aristotle that separated Aristotle from some of his predecessors. The Pythagoreans, for example, invoked elements in metaphysics that Aristotle would not himself categorize as substance. However we will see that the issues that separate Kant and Aristotle over the difference between forms of intuition and categories are far deeper than those that divided the latter from the Pythagoreans or the Atomists.

The dimensions of one of these issues is suggested by a remark that Aristotle quotes from the Pythagoreans with evident approval: "Evil belongs to the class of the unlimited." The veritable Medusa's head for ancient metaphysicians was everything unlimited, inexhaustible, or infinite. The infinite turned their hearts to stone, but it does not petrify Kant. Why? The answer to this question confronts us with a second reason for suspecting that Kant had had the idea of a transcendental turn in philosophy before he had ever encountered the scepticism of Hume. It was the mathematicians who discovered the secret for conquering the Medusa's head of the infinite. We cannot face the thing directly. The secret is to strike out for the thing while studying its reflection in our representations. That is to say, among the objects that the mathematician cannot understand the possibility of directly are those which cannot be given directly, because the mathematics of these objects assumes an infinitization in the domain of the objects. In such cases the only approach is transcendental, and, as Kant will say, the mathematician's understanding of the conditions under which these objects are possible is entirely dependent upon his understanding of the conditions of the possibility of representing the objects. But if the possibility of progress in modern mathematics depended upon the conquest of the infinite and if that conquest involved reflection by mathematicians on the possibilities of representation in mathematics, there is reason to suspect that Kant was fully aware of these precedents as he formulated his own idea of a transcendental philosophy.

The fact that a dim awareness, at least, is involved in his very conception of a transcendental philosophy is suggested by a remark that he makes in the same paragraph in the *Critique* in which he introduces the idea of a transcendental philosophy. Elsewhere, to be sure, there is mention enough of Hume, but here, where he is citing a reason for investigating the possibilities of our representations rather than going directly to the things themselves, he does not allude to Hume's observation that the causal connection is not to be grasped directly in the things we experience. Instead, the reason he cites is that the nature of things is inexhaustible. We will see from the transcendental arguments of the aesthetic that Kant was perfectly capable of making the relevant connections between that remark, the point which has just been made about the possibility of progress in pure mathematics, and a corresponding point about the possibility of a mathematicized science of nature.

The decisive fact for an understanding of Kant's transcendental turn is that his immediate predecessors in metaphysics, notably Spinoza and Leibniz, had already commenced Kant's revolution. We will find that the transcendental aesthetic is a dense work and a valuable work because it compresses so much of the work of these forerunners. More often than not the relevant analyses or arguments were first prepared by philosophers who believed that the intellect of man can grasp the being of things directly through positive concepts, direct judgments, and express reasonings. In Kant's terminology, these philosophers who have not worried about the possibilities of representation and who have not consciously taken a transcendental turn in philosophy are transcendental realists rather than transcendental idealists. A transcendental realist is one who believes that the being of things can be grasped directly through concepts furnished by the intellect. One of Kant's major conclusions in the transcendental aesthetic decides against this belief. As a consequence, when Kant employs the analyses and arguments of the transcendental realists, these ideas and arguments take on a novel and unfamiliar form. Probably the most important and certainly the most striking example of this sea-change is what happens to Spinoza's argument from the concept or definition of God to the monistic conclusion that there is only one substance. We will see that Spinoza's argument is formally valid within the logical framework in which it is presented by Spinoza. Still later we will see that in the transcendental aesthetic Kant turns this valid argument on its head and that, by doing so, he is able to reach the transcendental conclusion that certain representations that can be treated in the geometrical manner cannot be general concepts. This conclusion, in turn, is a vital step in his defense of the possibility of a metaphysical pluralism in the objects of scientific knowledge. A chunk of Spinoza's reasoning—in effect—is used by Kant to protect him against the dread heresy of Spinozistic monism. The sole point I wish to make about these connections at the moment is this: a person might well be familiar with the argument in Spinoza, familiar also with its counterpart in the aesthetic, and yet if he had not grasped the way in which transcendental philosophy simply moves the fulcrum-point to a new ground, he might easily overlook the historical connection between the two.

Spinoza's reasoning from the concept of God supply a good illustration of the other type of argument which Kant inherited. I mean the type of argument in which the transcendental turn has already been taken, whether implicitly as with Spinoza himself, or whether explicitly as with Leibniz and Lambert. Spinoza's *Ethics* records a profound novelty in the history of thought: it sets out from a concept or definition of God. We are better able to appreciate the dimensions of this accomplishment if we recall to mind some common assumptions that had been built up over the long centuries of patient reflection and hard thinking about metaphysical topics. From the days of Duns Scotus it had been granted on all sides that if a metaphysician desires to encompass both God and God's creatures in a general science of being he must be prepared to concede that no distinction of beings is more comprehensive than the distinction of infinite and finite.[5] In applying this distinction the metaphysician understood as a matter of course that in seeking to conceive the being of God he seeks to conceive something that lies on the first side of the distinction. Now there is no difficulty in conceiving God vaguely or indeterminately, or even analogically in His Own determinate nature. But what Spinoza audaciously proposed was to base his reasoning on a definition of God; that means he proposed to formulate a distinct or determinate conception of the very things that God is. An examination of Spinoza's way of dealing with this task will show that he conforms to the spirit of modern mathematics in its conquest of the infinite. An essence, historically, is an object of simple apprehension through an act of the intellect. These acts of

---

[5] Cf. Efrem Bettoni, *Duns Scotus* (Washington, 1961), p. 132.

direct apprehension are concepts of the understanding and through such concepts the understanding grasps what the thing is that confronts it. But the mathematical infinite is not an object of simple apprehension, and no mathematician of any consequence has supposed that it is. It is grasped indirectly as something that conforms to a given law, or as something generated by some specified operations. The particular operation which is most essential to Spinoza's definition of God is an operation of "second-order generalization" over the properties of things. Kant is a conceptualist and, as such, he regards the properties of things as being, in effect, ways of thinking about things or ways of getting things represented. Accordingly, in the context of Kant's own way of looking at things, Spinoza's solution to the problem of conceptualizing an infinite being involves thinking about our ways of representing things. However, the approach is only implicitly transcendental in Spinoza's definition itself, because one could perfectly well interpret it as signifying a commitment to an extreme form of metaphysical realism.[6]

Spinoza's definition of God had been taken up and examined by Leibniz, particularly as the concept served as a basis for Spinoza's ontological proof of the existence of God. The special question that Leibniz raised—a question that he rather prided himself on being the first to raise—is how we are to guarantee that what Spinoza attempts to conceive through his definition is indeed a possible object of definition. In proposing a solution to the problem about the possibility of Spinoza's God, Leibniz gives an explicitly transcendental foundation to Spinoza's proof. Leibniz explicitly saw what Spinoza saw at least implicitly. Namely, he saw that Spinoza never in fact proposed to do what Anselm, Scotus, and the rest would have condemned as a preposterous absurdity; Spinoza does not in fact set out from a direct apprehension of what God is. Accordingly, Leibniz interprets his own demand for a proof of God's possibility as a request for a proof that the required operation of summation when performed upon the representations of the different things which God is will yield a representation that is a logically possible representation. By describing an intellectual operation which preserves logical consistency and by arguing that the operation only need be applied to partial concepts of God that are themselves simple and, hence, that are themselves logically possible, Leibniz convinces himself that he has a solution to his problem. The "solution" is explicitly transcendental in the sense that it bases our alleged knowledge of the existence of God—a knowledge which would be metaphysical, if it were knowledge—on a proof of the possibility of our representation of God.

---

[6] "Metaphysical realism" is used here to describe the position which ascribes a real being to things that are not concrete particulars.

Kant views this alleged knowledge as "transcendental illusion". The concept of transcendental illusion is an important one in Kant's discussion and is used by him to distinguish the real gains of transcendental aesthetic and analytic from the illusory gains of transcendental dialectic. The concept of transcendental illusion is built around the type of proof which has just been considered. Transcendental illusion is what results from every effort to gain metaphysical insight into the natures of things from a study of the formal and merely logical conditions of representation. (A59–A64) Since the time of Kant the implied distinction between the mere appearance of knowledge and the reality of knowledge has been an identifying mark of those philosophies that embody his conception of a transcendental turn. The distinction is not the ancient and familiar Platonic distinction between illusion and reality. Instead, Kant's distinction takes this classical division from the science of being and repeats the division at the level of our representations of objects. Just as the Platonic dialectic was intended to free the minds of men from their engagement with mere appearances and to lead them to an engagement with the really real, so the Kantian dialectic has a serious positive purpose. Kant seeks to lead us from the pretensions and the illusions of metaphysical knowledge to the "one, true" metaphysics.

How is Leibniz's proof of the possibility of God typical of a process that results in the false and uncritically accepted opinions of a seeming metaphysics? It would be absolutely incorrect to say that Leibniz had not had the idea of a transcendental turn in philosophy, and it would be absolutely incorrect to say that he had made no advance in knowledge beyond Spinoza. As to the first of these two points, Leibniz's investigation of the being of God is distinctive just because he sets out quite deliberately from a study of the conditions for the possibility of the representation of God. That was the source of his pride, and his seeming metaphysics becomes a transcendental metaphysics at this point precisely because it argues for metaphysical conclusions from transcendental premises. It is very important for the reader to have a clear grasp of what Kant had defined transcendental illusion to consist in. The reason that transcendental illusion and only transcendental illusion was created in Leibniz's proof is because Leibniz uncritically identified the conditions for the possibility of representing objects with the merely logical conditions for the possibility of representing objects. In every single case, and by its very definition, transcendental illusion is a deception which is produced by a faith in general logic as a source of metaphysical insight. Transcendental illusion—one might say—is what always results from the attempt to do transcendental analytic without doing transcendental aesthetic first. The truth of this characterization of transcendental illusion should become more and more evident as we go forward with our study of the transcendental aesthetic, but for the moment we can work from Kant's characterization of transcendental illusion as what results when we treat the formal conditions of the possibility of knowledge as though these, by themselves, contained the conditions for the possibilities of the objects of knowledge. Now the formal conditions of possibility are the conditions set forth by general logic as the conditions to which our concepts and judgments must conform. Hence, we can say that, according to Kant, a purely conceptual analysis of the possibilities of knowledge will yield only the fraudulent pretense of knowledge. This point deserves to be underscored all the more because of the direction which has been taken by several contemporary philosophers who have invoked the name of Kant but who deploy transcendental deductions that more closely resemble those of Kant's predecessors. The chief negative conclusion that Kant establishes by his dialectical study is that the way to metaphysical truth is not along the broad and well-beaten path that had been tramped out by Leibniz, Wolff, Baumgarten, and countless others. There is no direct route from the ordinary truths about the logic of concepts to metaphysical truth because the conditions for the possibility of representations are not merely logical or conceptual conditions. The results that Kant reported in the transcendental aesthetic are what shattered his faith in general logic or the mere study of our concepts as a source of metaphysical insight.

If it is true that Leibniz had anticipated the transcendental turn in philosophy, then it is also true that his knowledge represented an advance upon earlier knowledge. How is this possible if what he attained was transcendental illusion? The answer to this question will carry us up to one of the most important distinctions in the Kantian philosophy, but to understand the necessity of the distinction we must return to Plato's original distinction between illusion and reality. There are many versions of what happens as our mind passes from its preoccupations with illusions to a vision of the really real. Transcendental dialectic should be compared to the healthy and robust version of Plato's metaphysical dialectic—the version that insists upon the positive conclusions that the Platonist seeks in regard to the appearances. Undoubtedly there is another, unhappy type of Platonism and the reader may even be inclined to assign this version to Plato himself. This second type of dialectic is a flight and a retreat from the world of appearances to the world of pure forms. This interpretation of Plato's intent stresses that the form is entirely different from the appearance and stresses that the subject matter of knowledge is always only the form. This view denies that we rise to a comprehension of being for the purpose of coming to a better understanding of this world of appearance and of becoming. It denies that there *is* any knowledge of appearances. If the reader has this conception of Platonic dialectic in his mind, then to understand the function of the Kantian dialectic he must replace it with a conception of a happier and more robust form of Platonism. This type of Platonism does not despair of coming to an understanding of the world of appearances. On the contrary, it holds that one of the functions of the theory of forms is precisely that of explaining how it is possible for us to have a kind of knowledge that we manifestly do have. This view stresses that the world of forms is not simply a different world from our familiar world of appearances. On the contrary, the relevant form is in each case what it is that we do know in knowing the appearances. The metaphysical underpinning of this explanation is a domestication of these otherwise alien or estranged forms; the form is no alien in this world of illusion; the form is simply what the illusion is—to the extent that the illusion is anything at all or has any definite way of being.

The reference to these two familiar versions of Platonism has not been made with any intention of re-kindling the ancient controversies in the interpretation of Plato. My purpose has been to call attention to the "this-worldly" version of Platonism in order to make it clear that something has not necessarily been disposed of when it has been declared an illusion. Kant's dialectic does not simply dismiss the illusions of Leibniz and Wolff. The dialectic is intended to expose what the actual knowledge is that is contained within the transcendental illusions of these men. Where Wolff pretends to derive transcendental results from the truths of general logic, Kant does not dismiss his conclusions as though they were nothing or as though they had no truth in them. The conclusions drawn in this way from the conditions under which we can conceptualize things are illusions that contain real knowledge. Kant's assessment of what this seeming knowledge is—to the extent that it is— is that it is analytic knowledge.

The concept of what is analytic in our knowledge brings us down from the most general idea of a transcendental inquiry to the first and the most important specification of that idea in the *Critique*. We will see in the next section how the idea of a transcendental philosophy begins to assume a much more definite shape in connection with the distinction between analytic and synthetic knowledge. This is the distinction that makes Kant's idea of a transcendental philosophy so entirely different from the same general idea that many others had had before him. And in later sections of this chapter we will see how the ancient Platonic insight into the importance of the element of form returns at the level of the transcendental investigation of knowledge. If the reality of knowledge that is contained in the illusions of Kant's predecessors is the reality of analytic knowledge, the being of this knowledge is given by the forms of thought. If there is another type of knowledge whose reality is that of synthetic knowledge, the being of this synthetic knowledge is only given by the forms of intuition.

II. KANT'S ANALYTIC-SYNTHETIC DISTINCTION IS DIFFERENT FROM OURS

The distinction to which we now turn is supposed to be among the most frequently discussed and the best understood items from the Kantian tradition. Historians who have occupied themselves with the difficult and often treacherous business of recovering the thought of a past epoch learn to distrust these easy translations of the ideas of one period into the ideas of another. I therefore begin by posing a question that will strike some English-speaking readers as an odd, an unnecessary, and perhaps even as an obfuscating question. Did Kant anticipate our contemporary distinction between analytic and synthetic propositions? In asking this question, I am not concerned with whether Kant succeeded in giving some ideal or perfect formulation of the distinction. Of course he did not—even Hempel, who is a clearer writer and who had the advantage of a better education in logic, never reached perfection in formulating our distinction. I am concerned with the rather more basic issue of whether our distinction is even in a line of descent from Kant's or, indeed, whether it has any other direct connection with Kant's. The conclusion for which I will argue is that the founders of the modern discussion of the analytic-synthetic distinction are more to be honored and more to be trusted for their accuracy in logic than for their accuracy in the history of philosophy. Many students of Kant's writings have been aware of the problems here, but clear information on the point is difficult to communicate in the presence of the background noise. What is worse, there have even been a few recent works on Kant that set out from the explicit assumption that our distinction is family-related to the distinction that the logical positivists developed to account for the possibility of mathematics and the impossibility of metaphysics. But far from being the same, these distinctions do not even have the same general subject matter. The evidence that will establish this difference will also suggest that Kant had something better in mind.

It is well known that there has been a substantial and a continuing criticism of our distinction between analytic and synthetic propositions.[7] The contro-

---

[7] A sample of the recent arguments will be found in *Analyticity*, ed. J.F. Harris and R. Severens (Chicago, 1970).

versy has raised questions about whether our distinction can be drawn in a clear way and about whether such a distinction, if it could be drawn, would have any value. It is less well known that Kant was the first major critic to line up with the opponents of our distinction. The evidence for his disaffection deserves to be reviewed, if only for the light that it sheds on the relations between his thought and ours. But perhaps the most undisputed point with which to begin is a point about something that Kant did not do.

The controversies over our analytic-synthetic distinction have clarified many of the things that need to be done in order to formulate our distinction in a clear manner. It is generally agreed today that a necessary condition for any satisfactory account of analytic statements is an adequate treatment of the logical syntax of our statements. Very briefly, the reasons that persuade us to this conclusion are as follows: First, if one wishes to specify exactly what it means to say that a statement is analytic, one must supply some explanation of what it means for a statement to be a logical truth. The class of logical truths is itself one of the important subclasses that we hope to catch within our class of analytic statements. But the problem of defining logical truth is tantamount to the problem of adopting or of constructing some adequate general theory of deductive inference.[8] And the logical syntax of statements is their logical form or is simply what they are—to the extent that the deductive logician has any interest in what they are. Secondly, one wishes to be able to specify the property of analyticity in such a way that one can say that the direct or immediate deductive consequences of an analytic statement are themselves analytic. Thirdly, one wishes to be able to define the analytic-synthetic distinction in such a way that it applies to all statements, or at least to all true statements, and not just to those statements that have some special logical form.

The point of general agreement today is that Kant did not supply any adequate treatment of the logical syntax of statements. In the next section of this chapter I will be arguing for a more charitable interpretation of one of Kant's remarks on this subject than has usually been offered, but that only amounts to a qualification of the agreement. The standard and usual assessment was stated many decades ago, when Yorck described Kant's logic as a "sandbank" in the broad stream of modern logic. Whether or not we agree that Yorck was entirely fair to Kant in assessing his role in the history of logic, the thrust of his criticism is sound. Hence, we can all agree that if Kant's

---

[8] The reason for this assertion is the assumption that if we are in possession of the concept of logical truth, then the concept of a valid deduction can be defined by the logical truth of the conditional assertion formed from the premises and conclusions of the deduction.

distinction is a forerunner of our own, it is defective on each of the three counts mentioned in the last paragraph. In the first place, Kant gives us no adequate general theory of deductive inference. His theory of deduction does not appear to cover more than the traditional syllogistic. Secondly, as one of his correspondents noted, Kant's distinction appears to be drawn in such a way that immediate inferences from analytic judgments will yield synthetic judgments. Thirdly, Kant appears to draw the distinction in such a way that he limits it to statements that have a subject-predicate form. Each of the first two points presupposes the truth of this third point. The latter will strike some of his readers as so obvious that it does not even require proof. In truth and in fact his distinction does not make any presupposition about the form of judgments, as we will discover in just a moment. But if we review the three points against the background of the assumption that Kant intended to formulate our contemporary distinction, we are forced to say that Kant's writings have no very great significance to the more advanced and sophisticated levels of contemporary discussion of the distinction. One author has even gone so far as to imply that in the light of our improved, modern understanding of these matters, we should be prepared to reformulate the question which sets the problematic for the *Critique*: "How are synthetic *a priori* judgments possible?" The properly phrased question would be "How are unobviously analytic statements possible?" The presumption here is of course the same as one that animates a certain attitude toward primitive art—the attitude that views the primitive as a defective forerunner of the modern and that sighs for the savage's lack of mastery of basic modern techniques.

I assume that Korner speaks what is in our mind about the distinction between the analytic and the synthetic when he discusses what was in Kant's mind in the following terms: "An analytic proposition, being only about the meaning of terms, does not give us any other information." He adds—and again I take him to be commenting at the level of our own informal understanding, "All analytical judgments must be a priori since they merely elucidate the meaning of their terms and are thus logically independent of judgments describing sense-experience."[9] More recently, Bennett has attempted to reconstruct Kant's meaning in the following way, "A sentence is analytic if and only if on its normal construction it says something true solely by virtue of the meanings of its constituent terms."[10] As a final illustration, we might recall Arthur Pap's *Semantics and Necessary Truth* which contains a detailed discussion of Kant's distinction and of its alleged history down to the

[9] S. Korner, *Kant* (Bristol, 1955), p. 20.
[10] Jonathan Bennett, *Kant's Analytic* (Cambridge, 1966), p. 6.

present.[11] Pap regards analytic propositions as ones whose truth can be established by appeal to definitions and to principles of logic alone. In summary, then, we can say that the views of Bennett, Korner, and Pap illustrate a contemporary consensus on the relationship between Kant's distinction and our own distinction.

What is the analytic and synthetic distinction a distinction of? One is tempted to answer that it is a distinction that divides the class of all judgments, or all propositions, or all statements, or all of whatever one thinks could be a premise or a conclusion in an argument. However, Bennett and Pap call attention to the fact that such an answer cannot be correct, if we wish to avoid a contradiction in the things we are inclined to say. We must limit the class of things to which the distinction applies. The contradiction arises from the combination of four assumptions: first, that every analytic proposition is true; second, that no inconsistent proposition is true; third, that no inconsistent proposition is synthetic; and fourth, the disputed assumption that every proposition is either analytic or synthetic. These four do indeed give us a contradiction and one way to avoid the contradiction is indeed to limit the distinction to true propositions. Another way to avoid the contradiction is to introduce two sets of distinctions in place of one: analytic truth and synthetic truth; analytic falsehood and synthetic falsehood. However, this second solution rescues the larger field at the expense of an extra bit of terminology and it still calls upon us to acknowledge that we are contemplating a distinction between types of truth. Now, since Pap realizes that Kant's views would also be inconsistent if Kant were to maintain the same four assumptions, he feels justified in saving Kant from inconsistency by rejecting the assumption that for Kant every judgment is either analytic or synthetic. He concludes that what Kant had in mind was a distinction between types of truth—and perhaps also, though this is altogether less important, a distinction between types of falsehood.

The historian of philosophy who is called upon to evaluate Pap's reconstruction receives a distinct surprise. The first point which he will notice is that Pap's conclusion amounts to an hypothesis about what should be found in the texts and that the historical evidence does not support the hypothesis. The point is not that Pap's historical evidence is insufficient; Pap does not offer any evidence for his conjecture. The point is rather that the historical evidence supports an entirely different hypothesis about Kant's distinction. We will see directly that Kant's distinction, unlike our own, is a distinction of types of knowledge, rather than a distinction of types of truth. The second

---

[11] Arthur Pap, *Semantics and Necessary Truth* (New Haven, 1958).

point which the historian will notice is that Pap's interpretation of Kant once seemed to be plausible on purely philosophical grounds, but that it no longer can seem to be plausible—or, more precisely, that it no longer can seem to be plausible for the reasons that once appeared to be persuasive. At one time it seemed that the distinction of analytic and synthetic truths is important because the distinction clarifies the nature of mathematical truth and leads to a new, positive, and detailed reconstruction of mathematics which puts the whole discipline for the first time on a sound foundation. This second point is the more important point for readers of the transcendental aesthetic, because if philosophy had really made this advance in the understanding of mathematical truth, the transcendental aesthetic would be largely superfluous. From Plato to Kant philosophers had associated the fate of metaphysics with the possibility of mathematics, but the intended reconstruction of mathematics would effectively breach the connection of the two. Mathematics will go to the side of the analytic, leaving metaphysics behind, alone and defenseless, with its synthetic truths that allegedly can be known *a priori*. The transcendental aesthetic will have been seriously—perhaps fatally—wounded, because the aesthetic provides a transcendental explanation of mathematical knowledge as synthetic and *a priori*. Let us consider the details of the proposed reconstruction.

The first step involves isolating a familiar class of logical truths within the broader class of analytic truths. If we start from Pap's informal specification of analytic truths as those that can be established by appeal to rules of inference and to definitions, then we can imagine that our idea of the logical form of propositions has been made concrete and explicit through a specification of the logical terms in propositions. The narrower class of logical truths will comprise that class of analytic truths that can be established using the rules of inference and definitions of logical terms alone. In due course we will see that Kant had a different conception of definitions and of rules of inference from the usual modern view, but those differences can safely be ignored for the moment. It is also true that Kant conceived of logical terms in a somewhat different way, but the account of the differences is unfortunately, but unavoidably, technical. (The interested reader deserves an account of what Kant's logic might look like, if it were presented today; the best that I am able to offer is the brief outline contained in an appendix.) The reader is asked to suppose that the first step has been taken and that an account of logical truth is in place before us.

The second step in the reconstruction of mathematics involved a truly prodigious expenditure of effort aimed at the reduction of mathematical truths to logical truths. This reduction can be represented as having two phases. What is called the "weak reduction" of the one to the other involves showing that the terms of ordinary mathematics can be defined as logical terms. The "strong reduction" of mathematics to logic will then involve the exhibition of the principles of mathematics as deductive consequences using only truths of logic and definitions as premises. If the strong reduction can actually be brought off, it clarifies the nature of mathematical truth by showing that it is nothing but analytic truth. As we have already indicated, Kant's motive was diametrically opposed to this; he sought to clarify the nature of metaphysics by separating it decisively from logic and by reviving its ancient associations with mathematics. The modern attempt to show that mathematics reduces to logic has been deliberately conceived as a way of freeing the science of mathematics from any taint of an association with metaphysics.

Was the desired marriage of mathematics and logic ever in fact consummated? The union was announced in a variety of places but the book which will always stand as a monument to efforts to consummate the marriage is *Principia Mathematica* by Whitehead and Russell. The work is a splendid failure. Of the two main reasons why it is a failure, one is incidental to an understanding of Kant's aesthetic, but the other is absolutely central and lies on the direct route to an appreciation of the contents of the *Critique*. The successful strong reduction must be prepared to show that whatever is a mathematical truth can be derived as a conclusion in the system, and that everything that is contained among the premises of the system is a truth of logic. Any system of the *Principia*-type is essentially incomplete in respect to the derivation of mathematical truths.[12] This discovery has great intrinsic importance, but little direct bearing on our understanding of what Kant thought. The point that is central is apparent from within the *Principia* itself, and concerns the character of its assumptions. In many cases Russell and Whitehead had to settle for something less than a derivation of the desired mathematical truth. In these cases what they actually derive is, in effect, the hypothetical statement that makes the assertion of the given mathematical truth conditional upon the assertion of one or the other of several special assumptions. If anyone wishes to derive the mathematical truth, he must add to the logical truths these other assumptions. Two assumptions that can be added for this purpose are the axiom of infinity and the axiom of choice.[13]

---

[12] Kurt Gödel, "Über formal unentscheidbare Sätze der Principia Mathematica und verwandter Systeme" *Monat. Math. Phys.* Vol. 38, p. 173. Discussions that are more accessible for the general reader will be found in Jean Ladrière, *Les Limitations internes des formalismes* (Paris, 1957); and E. Nagel and J.R. Newman, *Gödel's Proof* (New York, 1958).
[13] I have deliberately simplified the discussion at this point by abstracting from certain features of the P.M. system that have no bearing on the present argument.

Alonzo Church (from whom I borrow the terminology of weak and strong reductions) has observed that the two special axioms are not principles of pure logic. He concludes that the strong reduction of mathematics to logic has not been established in the *Principia*, but that a plausible case can be made for weak reduction on the basis of what is contained in that work. These are judicious conclusions and are undoubtedly defensible, but our special interest in Kant's aesthetic requires us to go behind the second conclusion. The normal course of the work of mathematicians gives them occasion to introduce terms by definitions—definitions that are a part of ordinary mathematical practice rather than a part of the logical reconstruction of mathematics. These ordinary mathematical definitions are quite regularly of a form that involves assumptions about the existence and the uniqueness of things that are picked out in the definition. Prior to Kant, Lambert had noticed this point and had made it the basis for an objection to Wolff's treatment of definitions in mathematics. Lambert objected that the axioms and the postulates have different logical roles in mathematics and that the job of the postulates is to enable the mathematician to be able to justify his definitions in respect to their assumptions about existence and uniqueness of the defined entities. The relevant postulate shows how the required object or objects can be given in a way that will satisfy the defining description. We will see that Kant not only assimilated this important point; he converted the point into a major motive for his analytic-synthetic distinction.

Lambert's observation shows that it can be very misleading to separate discussion of strong and weak reduction in the *Principia*. The work does not establish strong reduction because the axiom of infinity is assumed and is even assumed in contexts where the ordinary mathematician would not have anticipated the need for such a strong assumption. But the appearance of the assumption in these contexts is symptomatic of the fact that the *Principia* embodies an ingenious discovery by Russell—a discovery that allows him to evade the consequences of Lambert's insight. Russell discovered a way of displacing the existence-assumptions that Lambert had called attention to as a feature of mathematical definitions. These assumptions are not eliminated by Russell's way of introducing mathematical terms; they are simply displaced to a different part of the system where they can be collected together in special assumptions such as the axiom of infinity. This being the case, the only fair conclusion is either that the case for weak reduction is no stronger than the case for strong reduction, or that the terms which Russell has defined using the vocabulary of logic are not precisely the same as the corresponding terms that are ordinarily introduced by mathematicians. In either case, we do not have any good reason for thinking that truths about, say, the square root of x are radically different from truths about, say, the cause of x. The alleged clarification of mathematical truths as analytic is philosophically implausible on almost every count.

The customary interpretation of Kant's analytic-synthetic distinction is wrong because it interprets him as proposing a distinction in types of truth rather than in types of knowledge. The interpretation is not credible or belief-worthy on the basis of the historical evidence. Kant firmly rejected the possibility of drawing any philosophically interesting distinctions in types of truth. This attitude is implicit in the discussion of truth at the beginning of the transcendental logic, in his lectures on logic, and elsewhere. Truth, he says in these passsages, must always consist in an agreement between a judgment and its particular object, since a judgment true of one object may be false if it is referred to a different object. The implied suggestion is that every true judgment refers to some object or other and, hence, that there are no "empty" judgments that are true. There are also indications that Kant would not describe our paradigms of analytic truths—these are undoubtedly truth-functional tautologies, such as either P or not P—as true judgments. What is decisive and explicit is that Kant rejects the proposed distinction of types of truth when it is proposed as a rendition of his own distinction. In his reply to Eberhard, Kant says that his critic "speaks ... of metaphysical truth and its proof in opposition to logical truth and its demonstration." After acknow-ledging the unrelated case in which we speak of "poetic truth"—i.e., truth in which there is no necessary relation to an object, Kant continues, "Where, however, we have to do solely with the objective grounds of the determination of judgment, no one has made out a distinction between geometrical, physical or metaphysical truth and logical truth."[14] No one can argue that these remarks are perfectly transparent. In particular, Kant makes use of a concept of objective reasons that will require some discussion and elucidation. But equally, no one can argue that the main thrust of the passage is not perfectly clear.

III. AN INTERPRETATION OF KANT'S DISTINCTION

What Kant says in his reply to Eberhard appears to be contradicted by things that he says in other passages. For example, one bit of evidence is contained in the section of the *Critique* called "The Highest Principle of All Analytic Judgments", where Kant says, "If the judgment is analytic, ... its truth can always be adequately known in accordance with the principle of contradic-tion." (A51) It certainly follows from this that all analytic propositions are

[14] *Gesammelte Schriften* (Berlin, 1922), XI, p. 41.

true and that they form a subclass of the set of true propositions. Since Kant's analytic-synthetic distinction is clearly intended to frame an exhaustive division, one is tempted to suppose that the remaining truths are all synthetic, and that Kant—whether he will admit it or not—is himself committed to a distinction in the class of truths. But a moment of reflection will show that there is not necessarily any contradiction in the two passages. Bennett and Pap contract the distinction from the field of all propositions to the field of true propositions (admitting that there may be a corresponding distinction in the class of falsehoods). If we contract the distinction from the class of true propositions to the class of propositions that are known to be true on the basis of evidence that is present, then we avoid any contradiction between the two passages. The distinction then becomes a properly transcendental distinction—taking transcendental distinctions to be distinctions in the elements of our knowledge of objects.

Before considering the evidence for this proposal, we should consider very briefly the major difference between these two classes, the class of true propositions and the class of propositions that are known to be true. The first point to notice is that Kant's idea of truth is explicitly the idea of a relational aspect of judgments. Truth, as he so frequently says, is a characteristic that our judgments have by virtue of their relationship to their objects. At the risk of laboring the obvious, one might compare his conception of truth to the idea of fatherhood. We cannot conceive of a man who is a father without conceiving him as having a paternal relationship to someone or something. The particular kind of father we conceive him to be will be determined by the particular type of paternal relationship we have in mind, whether it be natural, conventional, legal, or even symbolic. We have just seen that Kant does not admit any corresponding diversity in types of truth, and we will see that the reason for that is that he does not admit any diversity in the type of relationship which propositions must have to objects in order to be true.

Where truth involves a relationship between the judgment and its object and is therefore implicitly dyadic, knowledge for Kant is essentially triadic. It involves a relationship between three things, an act of judging, the object of the judgment, and the objective grounds for the judgment. Knowledge consists of objectively grounded true judgments, and it is this class—rather than the class of true judgments—that is divided into the analytic and the synthetic. Furthermore, I will be arguing in just a moment that Kant's reflection on the relationship of objective grounds or reasons is what provoked his distinction. Plainly, if these points are to be weighed in a serious fashion, something needs to be said about the relationship of objective reasons. Three main points must be borne in mind about the way this relationship is conceived in Kant's analysis of knowledge. First, we are in the realm of rational appraisal language when we refer to this relationship; we are not in the realm of psychological description when we speak of the reasons for a judgment. The reason is what justifies the judgment, not what causes the judgment. Indeed, we will discover that the entire domain of the transcendental elements—and in that domain I mean to include the element discussed in transcendental aesthetic—is a realm of that which belongs to us *by right and in a manner that will sustain a critical review*. The realm of transcendental elements is not a domain of matters of fact. This first point is so very fundamental to the understanding of the aesthetic that we will find ourselves returning to it and returning to it, until we have seen from a variety of angles what momentous significance it has for the structure of Kant's transcendental arguments and deductions.

The second point to keep in mind is that Kant's definition of knowledge and his distinction between knowledge and justified true belief rest on a distinction between objective reasons and reasons that are not objective. The latter are called "merely subjective grounds of judgment or belief". When we speak of a belief as having a reason or being justified, our locution is always ambiguous. Sometimes if I say that my belief that Q is justified, I mean that there are reasons which justify my believing that Q or my judging that Q. These are subjective reasons. Where I have subjective reasons for what I am doing in believing that Q, and where Q happens to be true, I have justified true belief. On other occasions, if I say that my belief or my judgment that Q is justified, I mean that there are reasons for what I believe or for what I judge—namely, there are reasons for Q. These are objective reasons; they are reasons that determine how Q is in truth related to its object. The difference of the two can be clearly seen if we suppose that Q is a judgment of the effect that John Smith has a Ford automobile. Suppose that John Smith is my friend, that he is known to me as someone who is not a natural liar, and that he seems to be serious in telling me that he has a Ford. In these circumstances I have subjective grounds for my judgment that Smith has a Ford. What this means is that if anyone tries to criticize me for what I am doing in believing that Smith has a Ford, he criticizes me unjustly. But, of course, I do not have objective reasons in those circumstances. Knowledge, in the sense in which the first *Critique* defines it, is a product of human understanding, and—as was said many centuries before Kant—the mark of the man who understands what is the case is that he can provide the reasons why it is the case.

The difference between these two types of justification is not only important for an understanding of what Kant means by knowledge in the first *Critique*, the difference is also important for an appreciation of a strategy that Kant employs again and again in his transcendental inquiries. The point of the strategy is to take advantage of the fact that a subjective justification of a belief is weaker than the objective justification of a belief (and the justification of the hope that Q is weaker than both). That means that, wherever we can analyze a problem as calling for no more than a justified belief, we have a strategic advantage. Sometimes, in order to be able to make the exchange of problems, we must be prepared to show that there is no objective justification of the denial of the belief that is to be justified subjectively. The objective justification of the denial, if it could exist, would be stronger and would—so to speak—overrule the justification of the conduct of the believer. A problem of this type arises in Kant's second *Critique* in connection with his justification of our belief that we are free, and, thus, that we can do what we ought to do. One part of Kant's task is to show why there can be no possibility of an objective demonstration that our actions as practical agents are all determined by causes and that in truth we are not free. At first glance Kant's strategy will appear self-defeating, for, if his opponent cannot know that we are not free, by the same token Kant can have no insight into our understanding of our nature as free agents. In the sense of *knowledge* that is investigated in the first *Critique*, Kant can claim no knowledge of our freedom. In reality, Kant's strategy is extremely clever, because within the context of practical reason— that is, within the context in which human conduct is commanded, appraised, and criticized—knowledge is not necessary: justified belief is sufficient in all such contexts. Now the question about freedom comes up in specific context of a critique of practical reason itself and *all transcendental critique*—whether the discussion concerns knowledge, as in the first *Critique*, or whether it concerns our pure, practical awareness of our moral obligations, as in the second *Critique*—*involves the rational appraisal and criticism of the elements in question.*

Here is where my second point about Kant's conception of knowledge joins hands with my first point. The domain of transcendental elements is a domain of things that belong to us by right and of actions that we are justified in performing. In this domain the demand for an objective justification is not justified because the inquiry only purports to establish conclusions concerning the possibility of knowledge. Heidegger and others have objected to Kant's first *Critique* in a way that reflects a profound misunderstanding of the underlying strategy of the work. They complain that Kant sets out to account for the possibility of synthetic knowledge *a priori* without ever establishing that in fact we possess such knowledge. But Kant's strategy is not to argue from a fact to a possibility—that would require as a first step a metaphysical understanding of the self as a cognitive being. Heidegger attempted to supply what he took to be the missing metaphysics of the self as cognitive agent and thus repeated in a new and original form the old error of Fichte. The Kantian strategy is not to argue from fact to possibility; the strategy is to argue from a demonstration that a certain concept or judgment is valid or is mine by right to the conclusion that the representation must therefore be possible. The assumption underlying the employment of the strategy is that *in certain circumstances we can more easily establish a right than a fact.*

The reason why this strategy is effective in the investigation of knowledge is that most of the central and perplexing philosophical questions about knowledge concern the possibility of knowledge and they are not seriously altered by a change in the facts about who knows what and when. For example, I said earlier that in certain circumstances I can be subjectively justified in my belief that John Smith has a Ford—meaning only that if someone criticizes me for holding the belief he makes an unjust attack on my conduct. Let us imagine that my circumstances are altered by the appearance on the scene of my friend Peter. Peter knows John much better than I do and assures me that no one like John Smith would ever be found in a Ford. The two things to notice about my new situation are, first, that Peter is offering me an objective reason, based on the nature of our friend, why he does not have a Ford, so that it will be very difficult for me to come to any conclusion in the matter. I must ask myself whether anyone can have the kind of insight into the motives of another to be able to know that such a person would never buy a Ford. I am bound to wonder about this, because my friend John—it will be recalled— gave me his personal assurance that he does have a Ford. I must also ask myself whether Peter has the correct insight into the particular nature of John, and since, as Kant says, the natures of things are inexhaustible, I can anticipate a certain amount of difficulty here also. The second point I will notice in my new situation is how easy it is for me to dispose of Peter's criticisms of my belief. All that I need to do in that regard is to alter my belief so that it agrees with his. If he questions my conduct, I will tell him that he is my new authority on the psychology of John Smith. If Peter detects no irony in my reply, he will be more than satisfied; he will be flattered.

If one of the great philosophical sceptics about knowledge had appeared on the scene instead of my friend Peter, my situation would have been entirely the reverse. First, it would not be so easy to dispose of the criticism by altering my belief. No philosopher who had his doubts about my judgment that John Smith has a Ford would be put off so easily. If I adopt the belief that John Smith does not have a Ford, the philosopher will pursue my beliefs into their new form. That is because his doubts—however they are derived—concern the possibility of the knowledge that I have about John Smith and not the particular facts that are related to that actual bit of knowledge. But secondly, a conclusion about what I *can* judge can be derived from a knowledge of what my rights and responsibilities are in the conduct of thought, and there is nothing in this area that cannot in principle be made manifest to me. To say that a thought is mine by right or, conversely, to say that I have an obligation not to claim something to be knowledge only makes sense if I can be conscious of possessing the thought as a thought which I am justified in having or, conversely, if I can be conscious of my obligation to reject the thought as unjustified. That is, you cannot justifiably criticize me on the basis of standards of conduct that were necessarily and in principle hidden from me at the time that I engaged in that particular bit of conduct. My dispute with Peter is not one that is in principle subject to closure: The mysteries of the Smith psychology may continue to be hidden from us, or the full laws of commercial psychology may continue to elude us. But in the area of criticism and where the question concerns whether I lived up to my full set of obligations, everything that can have a bearing on the matter must have been capable of having been made manifest and plain to me—and plain even in its systematic bearing on what I did. This feature of principles that can be applied to the criticism of my conduct gives a striking characteristic to the disciplines that set forth the systems of such principles. These systems can change, and indeed Kant says that they do change, but, nevertheless, they must at any given time present an appearance of being so complete that nothing in them could be altered or removed. But when he says this, and he says it frequently and about a variety of such systems, he is of course, only communicating what is contained in the idea of such a system, as a system of the principles that I must be capable of becoming conscious of.

What has just been said about the principles that guide us in the formation of our judgments is closely related to a third point to be made about Kant's concept of knowledge. The class that is distinguished into the analytic and the synthetic was described as the class of judgments that are known to be true on the basis of the present evidence. The point is, however, that this class should not be taken to be constituted on the basis of the psychological facts about what any individual is actually aware of judging on any given occasion. Instead, the class is constituted by the existence of reasons which stand in an objective relationship to the given judgment. A judgment will belong to this class of what is known by the individual whether or not the individual has any actual awareness of the given judgment. My third point is one that can be put as a linguistic observation and a linguistic caution: This class of transcendental elements is picked out in the language of pure rational appraisal rather than in the language of psychological description; the necessary warning therefore is that the associations of the ordinary English terms are not a safe guide to Kant's meaning. Anyone with a nose for linguistic obscurantism should be sniffing vigorously at this stage in the interpretation. Such remarks about language are so frequently used to mask something that has gone soft and rotten in the discourse. But there are two facts that will be confirmed by subsequent argument and that should lessen these concerns about whether the language of the interpretation is losing its structure or is being systematically deformed and distorted. The first fact is that in this case as in the vast majority of cases Kant's language conforms to a set of philosophical conventions that were worked out and that became established over a long period of time for the express purpose of facilitating the exact expression and communication of ideas. We will see that Kant took his obligation not to engage in obscurantism extremely seriously indeed. The second fact is that Kant's meaning can be expressed in ordinary English. The difficulty and the source of my warning does not reflect any impossibility in that regard. The difficulty is, first, that there are a few occasions (as with *analytic* and *synthetic*) when his words do not correspond to the English on a simple one-to-one basis. This is the easiest source of difficulty to deal with, but unfortunately it is also the exception rather than the rule. The second, more common difficulty is that Kant's effort at accuracy of thought requires us to make a selection from among a variety of different ways in which the English term is used in ordinary discourse. Since the use that is selected is not always the more common or obvious use, we must battle the tendency for these other associations to push themselves into the center of attention.

The class which is picked out in accordance with my first observation about Kant's concept of knowledge is the class described in the language of rational appraisal as the judgments that are known to be true on the basis of the present evidence. The very same class picked out in accordance with my second general observation is described in the language of psychological description as the judgments that can be known to be true on the basis of the present evidence. The same concept underlies each description; it invites us to consider "that which is present as evidence for a judgment or as objective ground of the judgment." The sense of this phrase and the lines of our subsequent inquiry will be clearer if we consider briefly the two main species of objective reasons. These are demonstrative evidence, and the evidence of what is present to the senses.

In both cases there are legitimate questions that must be answered as to how something can be said to be present as evidence and yet be described in the language of pure rational appraisal—devoid of any suggestion as to the actual state of awareness of the individual and of any suggestion as to the way in which the objects of the senses have actually acted on the observer. The question of what it means to say that something is present as empirical evidence or as evidence that is present to our senses is one that I mark out now as legitimate and as one to which we will return after we have acquired some of the relevant background in Kant's aesthetic. The question of what it means to say that something is present as demonstrative evidence is a more immediate concern, because it relates to the line of reflection that brings Kant to his analytic-synthetic distinction. If we restrict reasons or grounds for knowledge so as to eliminate the merely subjective reasons for judgment, we are left with objective grounds. If we restrict objective grounds so as to eliminate the direct testimony available through our senses, we are left with demonstrative grounds and the judgments that are known in this way through the use of our reason are judgments *a priori*. These form the judgments that had from the time of Aristotle to the time of Kant been held to constitute knowledge in the strict, proper and scientific sense. Such knowledge is associated with a "true" understanding, where, as was said previously, the mark of the man who truly understands is that he can present in words the reasons for what he knows and can thereby explain why what is true is true. Now up to this point in my discussion of Kant's analytic-synthetic distinction, I have simply been calling attention to three features of a proposal about the field of Kant's distinction. As we turn to consider the evidence that favors this interpretation, the existence of these prior distinctions between types of reasons will play an important role in the argument.

Why should we suppose that the class of things that are either analytic or synthetic is the class of what is known rather than the class of judgments that are true? The first reason is extraordinarily simple and relates to the familiar distinction between *a priori* and *a posteriori* judgments. When Kant introduces the distinction, he calls attention to something known to philosophers from the time of Aristotle. Now the distinction between *a priori* and *a posteriori* was never understood to apply to judgments as true; it has always been understood as applying to judgments as they can be known to be true on the basis of some ordering of the present evidence. It follows immediately that the analytic-synthetic distinction must have the same extension or a narrower extension. The reason that this is obvious is that Kant has no sooner made his analytic-synthetic distinction than he concludes that each judgment of either of those two kinds must be either *a priori* or *a posteriori*. But if he conceived his new class as wider than the older class, he would realize that his conclusions are invalid.

Nobody can suppose that the distinction between the *a priori* and the *a posteriori* was an original distinction of Kant's. On the contrary it had a perfectly clear and definite sense in his day. As Lambert says, "The words *a priori, a posteriori*, indicate a certain ordering according to which one thing is before or after another in a series. . . . They generally refer to the order in the nexus of our knowledge. For where we must have the premises before we can draw the conclusion, the premises precede the conclusion and the latter follows *a priori*."[15] It is worth remarking that the term *a priori* does not mean "that which is first" or that which is before something else; it means almost the opposite of that. What Lambert is suggesting, as he speaks about an "order" in our knowledge, is a distinction of judgments on the basis of a relational feature which certain judgments have in certain specific contexts. On the one hand, the judgment may be related to evidence which consists of certain other judgments which stand in a logical relationship to the given judgment such that one can get the latter from these other judgments. In these cases, the given judgment is *a priori*. On the other hand, the backing or evidence for what is justified may not consist in other judgments. In these cases, Lambert makes the additional assumption that the evidence or the ground for what we know must be given by what we experience. In these latter cases the given judgment is called *a posteriori* or empirical.

Lambert and Kant both see the obvious point that if one is classifying judgments relative to some ordering of reasons or ground, the classification changes as the particular ordering changes. For example, I may know from direct evidence of my senses that when the foundation of my house is removed, the house falls; or I may know the same proposition *a priori* and as a result of my scientific understanding of why houses that are unsupported fall. (Kant's physics is not our direct concern, so we can ignore the amusing counter-example in the plans that were published as Operation Skyhook— plans for putting buildings in stationary orbits.) Having in mind the variability of these classes, Lambert went on to characterize a class of "absolutely *a priori*" judgments, or judgments for which the reasons are judgments that do not themselves rest on what has been experienced. Motivated by a set of considerations that will become apparent directly, Kant borrows the very old terminology in mathematics applied to equations that are pure and equations that are affected, and uses this language to get at the same distinction that Lambert had noticed. (Kant explains that he reserves the term "absolute" for a different, unrelated purpose.) Pure *a priori* judgments are those *a priori*

---

[15] Johann Lambert, *Neues Organon* (Leipzig, 1764), I, p. 412.

judgments in which there is no admixture of anything empirical in the evidence on which the judgments are based.

We have viewed a series of distinctions that had been in place long before Kant's birth—distinctions all based upon types of evidence for judgments. Kant's analytic-synthetic distinction should be perceived as a refinement of this tradition. Thus, sometimes we know on the basis of other judgments that can be produced as evidence. This gives us the concept of the *a priori*. But, sometimes when we know what we know on the basis of other judgments, those other judgments are merely definitional. This gives us the concept of analytic judgments. If the class of analytic judgments is subtracted from the class of objectively grounded judgments, what remains is the class of synthetic judgments. Some synthetic judgments will be *a priori* and some will be *a posteriori*. The puzzling question is how there can be pure *a priori* judgments that are synthetic.

Before indicating the steps which lead Kant to this question, I should insert a remark about the philosophical tenability of the Kantian distinction. Because the distinction is drawn in the field of knowledge, and as that field is defined in the language of rational appraisal, the distinction has strengths that cannot be matched by a distinction drawn in the class of truths. The key to this analysis lies in the fact that Kant's distinction is only applied retrospectively, or to judgments for which the evidence is present. In the case of both distinctions the step that will draw the most sceptical attack as we try to get clear about the distinction will be the explanation of what is to count as "merely definitional". But in the case of Kant's distinction we only need agreement on our logical theory to secure agreement on the application of his analytic-synthetic distinction. The reason for this is that what has no presence as a part of the existing nexus of knowledge cannot be alleged as a reason for the given proposition. In the case that the given judgment is analytic, the specific logical question is whether some premise or some set of premises can pass the test of being "merely definitional." The necessary rules of logic for sorting out definitional premises from other *given* premises are purely formal rules of definition. These are rules that propose specific and precise logical issues. For example, does the given premise, taken as definition, satisfy the principle of non-creativity, or does it add to the deductive strength of the system? Does the given premise satisfy the principle of eliminability or does it not have a form that would permit the elimination everywhere in the system of the term that is allegedly being defined? The best opinion of contemporary logicians is that these rules of definition should be regarded as having the same status as, or a similar status to, the rules of deduction in logic.[16] The modern

---

[16] Alonzo Church, *Introduction to Mathematical Logic* (Princeton, 1956), pp. 76–77.

distinction between analytic and synthetic poses much more complex questions about what can count as a definition, because the classification does not simply turn on the logical role or function that is being performed by premises that can be assumed to be present as evidence. The philosophical consequences of this difference are enormous.

At the outset of this section Kant was quoted as saying that "If the judgment is analytic, . . . its truth can always be adequately known in accordance with the principle of contradiction." Kant clearly intends to call attention to a way of finding out that certain judgments are true. But if these propositions must already belong among the class of judgments that are known to be true, then the passage would seem to have no point. Does this not show that there are analytic judgments which are not known to be true, and that it is a mistake to take his classification as retrospective? My reply to this question is that it presupposes some bad philosophy and some bad history. First, the philosophical point is that the question presupposes, incorrectly, that there is only one way to talk about knowledge, and that that one way to talk is in the language of psychological description. In truth, we frequently use the language of rational appraisal to describe what someone knows. This is what occurs in those charming domestic scenes in which husbands and wives argue with each other over whether one of them knows something that he or she has just denied knowing: The first person reports on what is in fact in his mind at the time. The second person replies on the basis of a rational appraisal of the evidence that is present to the first person. ("You do too know that today is my birthday.") If the first person was not thinking of that evidence or did not connect it to the given judgment, he was justified in denying that in the psychological sense he knew the thing that he denied knowing. What these examples prove is that questions about what we do know can sometimes be settled by a review of the available evidence. Consequently, it made sense for Kant to propose a criterion for settling such questions.

Next, there is a historical point to notice about the quotation from Kant. What he says is not simply that if a proposition is analytic it can be known in a certain way; he says that it can be *adequately* known. The latter is a technical expression and puts Kant's remarks in the context of earlier rationalist doctrines. Christian Wolff observed: "Descartes proceeded no farther than to clear and distinct ideas; Leibniz added adequate, which I afterwards found he had taken from the celebrated Dominican monk and subtle philosopher, Valerianus Magnus."[17] These rationalistic distinctions will be studied in more detail in the next chapter, but for the moment it suffices to know that they give rise to the very distinction we have been concerned with between

---

[17] Christian Wolff, *Logic* (London, 1770), p. lxx.

that which I am committed to and that which I am aware of as something I am committed to.

It is worth remarking that a similar technicality from the earlier tradition appears in that familiar passage in the introduction to the *Critique*, where Kant first set forth his distinction. In the course of a rather detailed analysis Pap calls attention to the fact that the word "covertly" has a crucial role in determining what Kant means, and Pap complains that Kant never does explain what it means. Pap's sense of grievance is real and is understandable, but it also should be said that logic books that were available in Kant's day contained a section on the topic of covert inferences. As Lambert explains in his work on logic: "The premises of an argument can be hidden in a discussion and can go unnoticed; in such cases it is a matter of getting out these premises and drawing the conclusion."[18] Again, what we confront is a point that turns on the supposition that one can know a proposition and can be unaware of the support for it, even though the evidence is already present.

If we had a more accurate historical understanding of the genesis of Kant's distinction, we would realize why these expressions from the rationalist tradition occur so often in Kant's formulation of the distinction and in his related discussion of it. We cannot get a firm grasp of that genesis unless we are prepared to distinguish between the historical context in which Kant was motivated to formulate the distinction and the quite different historical context in which he rather suddenly and abruptly was awakened to its philosophical import. Kant credited Hume with alerting him to the importance of the question about the possibility of synthetic judgments *a priori*. But historians of philosophy are beginning to get a better understanding of the degree to which German philosophers of the Enlightenment remained isolated from the influence of British empiricism that was so strong everywhere in France.[19] Whatever the truth of that general observation, we can discover in Kant's notes and reflections evidence that associates the genesis of his distinction with his strong and growing doubts about characteristic doctrines of the rationalists.

The evidence suggests that Kant had particular doubts about the leading philosophical principle of the rationalists, the principle of sufficient reason. He also had doubts about the way in which that principle had been applied to give a characterization of human knowledge. Thus, one immediate corollary of the principle (if it does not count as an alternative version of the principle itself) is the belief that all our knowledge is really *a priori* knowledge. In

[18] *Neues Organon*, I, p. 157.
[19] Cf. Klaus P. Fischer, "John Locke in the German Enlightenment," *Journal of the History of Ideas* Vol. XXXVI, No. 3, July–Sept. 1975.

Baumgarten, for example, we read passages in which the principle is interpreted to mean that whatever we do know *a posteriori* we can know *a priori*. While Kant is very far from accepting any such outcome, we have seen that he does make use of the common rationalist terminology as he lays the groundwork for his own analysis of knowledge. This language is no longer well understood, and yet an understanding of a set of terms which have a very special meaning from within that historical context is indispensable for any sensible discussion of the central passage in the introduction to the *Critique*, where Kant sets forth his distinction between the analytic and the synthetic.

First, it should be understood that he follows the standard philosophical practice of his day when he speaks of the *subject* of the judgment; the practice is exemplified in Baumgarten's *Metaphysics* where a subject of a judgment is defined as the object of the judgment or the *materia circa quam*.[20] Kant notes himself in a comment on the passage that what is called in German the subject of a judgment is the object. The seond point to notice is that Kant follows a rationalist tradition of long standing, according to which our concept of the subject matter is identified with whatever reason or ground we have for our judgments about the object. This usage would seem to us like a confusion of a term and a proposition or a definition, but there was no such confusion in the minds of these authors. For example, Wolff had defined a reason as "that through which one can understand why something is . . ."[21] His subsequent discussion of the principle of sufficient reason makes explicit his association of our concept of the subject with the reason for judgments about the subject, "For as long as a thing has a reason why it is, one can know it, that is, one can conceive it . . ." And again, he writes, "Whatever is not conceivable does not allow of being explained intelligibly."[22]

I have already remarked that the followers of Leibniz and Wolff gave a strong reading to the principle of sufficient reason. For example, Gottsched interpreted it to mean that we can always give a sound demonstration of any true proposition.[23] On such a reading of the principle the word *reason* can be defined more specifically as applying to the middle term of a syllogism in the first figure, which is the logical form of the argument that was thought to be required for the production of reasons or the display of understanding. The word is given this definition in Lambert's *Organon*, for example.[24] If we then

---

[20] *Gesammelte Schriften*, XVII, p. 79. Cf. Johann Adelung, *Grammatisch-Kritisches Wörterbuch* (1773): "in die meisten Fällen in Deutschen der Gegenstand".
[21] Christian Wolff, *Vernunftige Gedanken von Gott, der Welt, und der Seele des Menschen* (Frankfurt, 1736), p. 15.
[22] *Ibid.*, p. 36.
[23] J.G. Gottsched, *Erste Gründe der Vernunftlehre* (Leipzig, 1766), p. 56.
[24] *Neues Organon*, I, p. 156.

say that we have an adequate and complete concept of some subject matter, we mean that we are in a position to demonstrate and thus to explain the truth of every true judgment about that subject matter. The common understanding of the rationalists was that the leading principle for all such demonstrations must be a definition which makes explicit in its defining term everything that is contained in our concept of that subject. When Kant explains analytic judgments by reference to what is contained in the concept of the subject, he uses these terms "concept" and "subject" in a manner that is consistent with the earlier usage and in a manner that indicates that he has in mind these earlier accounts of our *a priori* knowledge. In particular, he is asking us to consider the judgment in relation to a certain kind of reason or ground for the judgment—a reason which consists in our concept of the subject matter of that judgment.

There are any number of passages which should make it clear that when Kant classifies a judgment as analytic or synthetic he does so on the basis of a relationship between that judgment and something which lies outside that judgment and is its reason or ground. The conventional way to read Kant's intentions brings him closer to the formulation of our modern distinction, but it requires us to ignore the difference between our concept of the subject of a proposition and the subject-concept within the proposition. The customary interpretation asks one to suppose that when Kant classifies judgments as analytic or synthetic he does so on the basis of a property that judgments, or true judgments, have in themselves, by virtue of their internal composition, and without regard to the existing reasons for the judgment. These are the choices: First, either the concept of the subject is construed as that which supplies us with a type of ground for the given judgment, or the concept of the subject is construed as a term within the given judgment. Secondly, either the predicate of the given judgment is construed as what is thought about the subject in the given judgment—as the whole conceptual content of the judgment, or the predicate is construed as a second term within the given judgment and as a part of what is thought about the subject in the judgment. Finally, either the distinction itself is construed so that it can be applied to any judgment that is known to be true, or the distinction is construed so that it can be applied to any true judgment whatsoever—provided that the judgment has a subject-predicate form. That is, either we restrict the distinction to judgments that have a certain type of external complexity or we restrict it to those that have a certain type of internal complexity. In the final reckoning, it will not be our habits or prejudices that decide between the alternatives; it will be the weight of historical testimony.

Among the passages that suggest that Kant makes his distinction on the basis of the relation to reasons or grounds, there is one in particular which sheds a clear light on the genesis of Kant's idea and reveals the three main elements from which it sprang. The passage is one that undertakes to explain why the rationalist critic, Eberhard, had failed to grasp the nature of the difference between the analytic and the synthetic. Kant says that Eberhard's failure "is based on the fact that the logical relation of reason and consequence is confused with the real relation."[25] There are three ingredients which turn up in Kant's explanation of this remark; each must be considered with some care. The first is a conceptual point about the nature of the relation of reasons to the things for which they are reasons. "A reason, taken generally, is that through which something else, that is, something *different*, is determinately posited. . . . The reason, therefore, must always be something other than the consequence. He who can produce as a reason nothing but the given consequence shows that he knows (or the matter has) no reason!" Thus Kant's first remark is simply that the relation of reasons is contained in the relation of diversity or non-identity. Although this observation begins the important process of pulling apart the reasons-relation and the relation of deductive consequence (as the latter is defined in most systems of formal logic), Kant's point can hardly be contested. If I ask you why the three medians of a triangle all pass through a point, you do not supply me with a reason if you reply that the three medians of a triangle all pass through one point. If you were to reply in that fashion, I would immediately suppose that you had not heard the question or had not understood me to be requesting a reason.

The second ingredient in Kant's thinking is an ancient and important classification of types of identity or diversity. Kant continues, "This difference is either merely *logical* (in the mode of representation) or *real* in the object itself." The distinction which he makes use of here belongs with a large cluster of contrasting terms that appear in his discussion of the transcendental elements of knowledge: logical objects as contrasted with real objects; logical essences as contrasted with natures or real essences; logical possibilities as contrasted with real possibilities; and identity in the object (*Identität*, as when we say "the objects are identical—*identisch*") as contrasted with unity in the object (*Einheit*, as when we say "the objects are one and the same—*einerlei*.") The entire cluster has special interest for us, because the underlying distinction between intuitions and concepts is what gives to each of the contrasts its transcendental significance and its real or metaphysical definition. That does

[25] *Gesammelte Schriften*, XI, p. 34–35.

not mean that we cannot get a preliminary understanding of what is involved in these contrasts; on the contrary, there are two ways to approach the generic contrast between what is real and what is merely logical.

First, we can take advantage of the fact that the distinction is not new with Kant. As a consequence, there is a nominal or merely logical definition of the concept of what is real that is justified by the way philosophers had previously understood the concept, and that does not need to be justified by appeal to a disputed distinction between intuitions and concepts. What is real is what is as it is independently of the way it is represented as being *in any finitely specifiable set of representations of it*. The italicized phrase has already been motivated by my remarks about how the natures or real essences of things are inexhaustible. Later, we will see that the question of whether the representations contained in a given representation are finite (and therefore can be present in the given representation through our spontaneous acts) or infinite (and therefore not ones that can derive their validity from acts that we have performed) is taken to be decisive in the argument about whether there must be intuitions as well as concepts. And the conclusion that our knowledge contains intuitions as well as concepts will be taken to be decisive in the argument about whether the objects of knowledge can be real objects or are merely logical objects. The same conclusion will have a bearing on the closely related argument about whether the objects of knowledge constitute a manifold of objects that have real diversity or whether the objects have only a logical non-identity.

One way to understand the nominal definition of what is real is to take it as the suggestion that, where what is represented is real, changes in the representations do not necessarily mean changes in the way a thing is which is represented. This leads directly to a second observation that may help to clarify the drift of Kant's thinking as he proposes a distinction between logical and real identity (or logical and real difference). If we think very pragmatically about these two kinds of identity, we can understand the force of the concept of real identity to be given by a principle of inference that is employed in deductive reasoning. Our common sense belief is that, so long as there is no real difference in the objects represented in two representations, changes in a judgment that result from replacing one of those representations by the other will not alter the truth of the given judgment. For example, and here I deliberately choose an example that some philosophers have thought controversial, if nine is in reality identical to the number of the planets, and if it is necessary that nine is greater than seven, then it follows that it is necessary that something that is in reality the number of the planets is greater than seven. On this way of looking at such inferences, they are always valid, provided that we bear in mind that the principle is valid because of the way it explicates our concept of real identity through a practical principle or rule for the logical transformation of our representations, and provided therefore we take care to ensure that in the conclusion of the inference we make it clear that the object which is picked out as the subject matter of the transformed representation is an object with a real identity. Some logicians prefer to regard the given example and others like it in a different light. They deny that it is an example of a valid deduction; hence, they cannot admit that the principle of substitution provides a pragmatic clarification of the difference between real identity and any other form of identity. However, Kant's distinction can be approached by them in another manner. They will admit the existence of a principle of substitution—all of the rules of deductive logic can be reduced to principles for substitutions and replacements of representations. Hence, since they do not admit that the principle is valid in the given example, they must envision restrictions on the application of the principle. The type of object that is represented by representations to which they restrict applications of the principle is what we have nominally defined "real" to cover. This explanation leaves to them the task of working out the restrictions that they feel to be suitable, and that will then give them a pragmatic familiarity with Kant's idea of what is real and what is merely logical.

The first of the three ingredients in Kant's reflections was the obvious conceptual point that the reasons-relation involves a diversity in what it relates. The second ingredient was the old and familiar distinction between logical and real difference. The third point—predictably—combines the first and the second points. Kant concludes, "Now it is a real difference which is required for synthetic judgments." What the passage as a whole shows is that for Kant every synthetic judgment has a relation to a reason, and that for Kant the characteristic difference between the analytic and the synthetic is in the nature of this relationship. In every synthetic judgment there is a real difference or real non-identity between what is represented as the reason for the judgment and what the judgment itself represents. It seems clear that Kant could have come to this distinction through reflection on the rationalist principle that everything has a reason, or that every true judgment can be given a sound, first-figure demonstration based upon an adequate concept of its subject matter. That is, he would have come to this distinction if David Hume had never written a line. But before indicating what I think was the crucial step in Kant's actual course of reflection, I should interrupt the purely historical analysis in order to comment on the philosophical import of the distinctions that have just been introduced. These remarks will make it clear that once Kant had arrived at his concept of synthetic judgments he could easily relate the concept to Hume's problems. The reader will in fact have a better grasp of the sense and the import of the lines from Kant that we have just been discussing, if we stop to make that connection.

Kant formulates his distinction between types of knowledge in order to be able to propound his famous question, "How are synthetic judgments *a priori* possible?" The *Critique* is designed to give the answer to that question. Now, if we do not have the correct understanding of Kant's analytic-synthetic division, it is not easy to see any *direct* connection between this problem and any problem that was discussed by Hume. In fact, the usual explanation of this connection is that Kant asks his question precisely because he *does* have a problem that Hume did not have: Kant believes that metaphysical judgments are possible and Hume does not. Kant believes that metaphysical judgments are pure synthetic *a priori* judgments. Therefore, Kant asks how they are possible and Hume does not. This analysis is an almost hopeless mixture of truth, half-truth, and falsehood. The truth is that Kant and Hume had different opinions about the possibility of metaphysics. The half-truth is that the question which defines Kant's objectives is about the possibility of metaphysical statements. Metaphysical *and* mathematical judgments are pure synthetic *a priori* judgments. Kant says that the proper question or the *exact problem* of the *Critique* is how synthetic *a priori* judgments are possible. Only a lazy or self-indulgent thinker would fail to distinguish those two classes. Finally, the falsehood in the analysis is the suggestion that Hume did not attempt to provide an answer to precisely the question that Kant has asked. For when we realize that a synthetic *a priori* judgment is one that has been classified on the basis of its relation to reasons, where (because the judgment is *a priori*) the reasons are other judgments, we will see matters in their true perspective. From a purely philosophical perspective, and setting aside any prejudice that we have to classify on the basis of the things related rather than on the basis of the relationship of the things related, we can see that there is no substantial or important difference between the question that Kant has asked about the relata, which is based upon a classification of judgments as relata, and a corresponding question one might ask about the nature of the relationship, and which would be based upon a classification of the relationship as a form of reasoning. As a matter of historical fact, Kant did not look at matters in this way, and we can say precisely why he did not choose to do so. He held the belief, as we will see, that all the acts of the understanding can be reduced to the one act of judgment. This belief certainly dictated the way in which he formulates the problem for the *Critique*, but my point is that someone who believes that the grand distinctions in formal and transcendental logic are distinctions in forms of reasoning rather than distinctions in forms of judgments, can formulate a question which is indistinguishable from the one propounded by Kant. Instead of asking how things which enter into a certain type of relationship are possible, we ask how the corresponding relation is possible. When Kant's question is put in this form it becomes the question about how synthetic reasoning is possible. It is easy to see how a purely analytic, or deductive, form of reasoning is possible, since we can analyze the reasoning as proceeding according to principles that merely re-arrange our ways of representing things and that do not presuppose any real difference in the objects of the representations. When we consider the possibility of synthetic reasoning, on the other hand, we confront genuine puzzles.

There are two main forms of synthesis in judgments. Hume had given very detailed explanations of how both are possible. The act of understanding in which the first type of synthesis is achieved can be called *abductive* (though it should be noted explicitly that this is not Kant's term for the act in question). The characteristic of this act of the understanding is that it combines or associates together different representations as representatations of *one and the same* object, even though the objects of the different representations are *not really identical* and the representations cannot be combined on the basis of the principles of deductive logic alone. Hume gives an account of how ideas or judgments can be combined in this way, but his account appeals to the psychological principles of association. When Kant considers Hume's account of this type of combination of ideas, he rejects the account because the type of association of ideas in which he is interested is a lawful and legal association (*Verbindung*) rather than a merely factual connection of thoughts. The lawful association of ideas or of judgments is one in which the combination has validity as a representation of what is real. Kant affirms that this synthesis must conform to the principles of a transcendental logic.

The act of understanding through which the second type of synthesis is achieved can be called *inductive*. There are several different aspects to the problem of induction, but the act in question has one peculiarity that marks it off from any mere abduction or any mere synthesis in concepts. The peculiarity should figure prominently in any definition of induction. The odd thing about induction is that the same ideas are combined in the premises and the conclusion, even though the objects that are represented in the conclusion are not the same as the objects that are represented in the premises and even though the validity of the reasoning cannot be accounted for by an appeal to the formal laws of deduction alone. Any account of the validity of the reasoning should be able to explain how this connection of the ideas in a manifold is possible, as an association of ideas that preserves their validity despite the diversity of the objects represented. Readers of Hume will be aware that he does not overlook the problem of induction, but Kant was forced to reject his solution as uncritical and as involving an appeal to our natural psychological tendencies. No such solution can account for our use of rational language in discussing the validity of representations. Kant proposes instead an account of the appearance of a manifold or a diversity in the real objects of representations on the basis of an alleged synthesis in intuition. The basis for his explanation is laid in the transcendental aesthetic, *where he deals with the question of how there can be an apparent multiplication of the entities that are represented without the necessity for any corresponding multiplication in the way the objects must be conceived.*

The result of this comparison between Kant's problems and Hume's problems is to confront us once again with the step that was historically decisive in Kant's fashioning of a transcendental doctrine of elements. The point from which the step was taken was a point in the rationalist's analysis of knowledge rather than a point in Hume's analysis of knowledge. We even have a note in Kant's hand that marks the place in Meier's *Logic* where the divergency occurs. Meier asserted the reigning doctrine about the possible elements in knowledge, when he wrote, "All our representations are concepts." Kant inserted in the margin, "Not all!", and we can be sure that in entering his protest he had in mind his own doctrine of elements. Kant distinguishes between concepts and intuitions, defining the latter as that through which the judgment is referred to or cites the testimony of its object We cannot fully understand the work for which his analytic-synthetic distinction was proposed until we have probed this aspect of his doctrine of elements. If we bring together two themes—one from the remarks that have just been offered and one from an earlier section—we can anticipate one of the directions of Kant's reflections.

We have just seen that the traditional concept of reality is the concept of something that is independent of our representations of it. While the way in which we think may well come to depend upon the way things really are, the identity of what is real is not affected by our acts of thought. To be sure, Kant specifies the principal act of thought to be an act of conception or judgment (he says, by the way, that those two come to the same thing) rather than the act of inference, which was under discussion when we introduced the concept of the real. But general point remains sound. That is, what is real is what cannot be attributed to a thinker's own spontaneous activity in conceptualizing things. That is the first point to bear in mind. The second point goes back to the earlier discussion of the general motives for adopting a transcendental approach in philosophy. We saw that Kant accepts the Leibnizian view that what is real, both in mathematics and in metaphysics, is inexhaustible. An inexhaustible diversity can involve the qualitatively infinite, where the diversity is a manifold of different aspects of a given thing; or the in-exhaustible diversity can involve a quantitative infinity, where there is a mere numerical diversity of given things. In either case, when we come upon that which is inexhaustible, we have come upon that which serves as a mark of that which cannot be attributed to a thinker's own spontaneous activity in conceptualizing things. The combination of those two points suggests the following line of transcendental reflection, or reflection on the possible elements in knowledge. We know that where there is an infinitization of the subject matter of some representation, this subject matter does not reflect our capacity to perform successive acts in which we mark out, distinguish, or otherwise bring to concepts this unlimited diversity. Hence, we know that, if there is a representation which can be shown to be valid as a representation of something that is real and if in addition the representation is valid only if it presents us with an infinite manifold, then we can conclude that some of our representations are not concepts. Kant's belief that he could supply examples of such representations and could prove their validity, furnished him with one of his two main reasons for denying Meier's claim that all our representations are concepts. He classifies these other representations as intuitions and he assigns to the intuition the task of providing our synthetic judgments with an appeal to evidence that goes beyond any conceptual ground and basis for the judgment.

Until he was prepared to admit the existence of this non-conceptual element in our judgments, his question about the possibility of synthetic *a priori* judgments made no sense. By the same token, once he had realized the necessity of this step and had divided the elements of knowledge into in-tuitions and concepts, he had arrived at the point of a revolutionary analysis of the possibility of knowledge. We can gauge the revolutionary potential in Kant's situation by taking advantage of the general equivalence that has been proposed in this section between the problem of the synthetic *a priori* judgment and more familiar problems about forms of non-deductive reason-ing. This correspondence permits us to translate the puzzle about the way in which an infinite manifold can be present in the objects of knowledge into a puzzle about induction. The advantage we gain is that each of us can see the general lines which the solution must take and can see the revolutionary potential of the solution. Now we have just anticipated the Kantian conclusion that our power to conceptualize the given realities has definite limits. When our intellectual competence is brought before the higher court of criticism, a verdict will be rendered that limits the scope of that competence. If there is a representation of an infinite that is valid, it is not merely conceptual.

Here is the situation into which Kant's reasoning has brought him and it hardly seems a situation that can explode into revolution. But we might well have begun by asking the corresponding questions about induction: How can we perform an induction that is valid, if the induction involves sampling the contents of an urn, if the number of balls in the urn is finite and if the validity of our form of induction depends upon the presupposition that we are sampling from an infinite population? When the issues are drawn in this fashion, we all can see the lines of the solution. We conduct the samplings with replacement—putting the balls that we draw back in the urn and mixing them up. We thereby achieve an infinite population *by letting the numerical differences between the members of the sample depend upon our way of constituting the sample.* When this has been done, we must re-describe the members of the population we are sampling. Instead of sampling balls *per se* statisticians will say that they are now sampling observations of balls. In Kant's language we say that they are sampling appearances of balls.

These terms might suggest to the unwary that there is something peculiarly mental about the members of the population or—with Kant's term—that there is something unreal or illusory about them. Of course that is not the case, and we can see from the outcome of Kant's reflection why it is not the case. The validity of our conceptualization of the characters, properties and relationships of the members of the population is unaffected, because even though the numerical differences between the members depend upon our way of picking out the members and of taking testimony from them those numerical differences do not depend upon our way of conceptualizing the members. The appearances are appearances of something that is real, and our deductions about the objects depend upon the way the objects are found to be as we examine the sample. The upshot of this analysis is that, if we distinguish between our way of referring to the objects that can serve as evidence for our judgments and our way of describing or conceptualizing the way those objects are, the ancient metaphysical question about whether what is real is one or is many undergoes a revolution in which the answer will follow from the transcendental inquiry into our way of informing ourselves about the realities.

These remarks about our situation in framing inductions over infinite populations have not—to be sure—been intended as a description of the actual circumstances that prepared Kant for revolution. They have been intended to help disclose the philosophical import of his situation. Our next task is to survey the historical details of his call for a revolution in philosophy. In this section we have been exploring the considerations which caused Kant to reject the leading principle of rationalism—the principle that the reason for the truth of what we know is disclosed to us through our complete concept of the subject matter of the judgment. Kant's dissatisfaction with the rationalistic dogma is reflected in the distinction he makes between what is analytic and what is synthetic in our knowledge. In the next section we will pursue the historical consequences of his rejection of the principle of sufficient reason, but we will discover that Kant believed that these consequences become more vivid and more comprehensible when they are set out in the light of a metaphysical version of the principle of reason. One of the interesting changes that Kant made between the first and the second editions of the *Critique* reflects that belief about how to convey an initial understanding of his critical purposes. The metaphysical version of the principle we have discussed in this section and in connection with the origins of the analytic-synthetic distinction is a formulation that tells us about the conditions under which the possible objects of knowledge are what they are and are different from every other thing. In the preface to the second edition this principle comes under review in the course of Kant's disclosure of the possibility for a Copernican revolution in philosophy.

IV. KANT'S COPERNICAN REVOLUTION

In the preface to the second edition Kant tries to clarify our understanding of our metaphysical commitments by comparing them to the underlying presuppositions of logic, geometry, physics and Copernican astronomy. He starts from the observation that any discipline enters "the sure path of a science" only when it has certain presuppositions—presuppositions that serve to specify a subject matter, or what we would call today a "domain of objects" for the theory. These assumptions have the apparently counter-intuitive result that they fix in advance of any actual inquiry certain matters which one might suppose that it is precisely the task of the inquiry itself to establish. The procedure of the understanding in such cases has an undeniable air of paradox about it—else Kant could hardly dare claim that the procedure contains a revolutionary potential in metaphysics. Nevertheless Kant believes that in each of the disciplines that has just been mentioned, and most particularly in Copernican astronomy, we can see that reason has employed this procedure.

But before we turn to his discussion of these cases and before we turn to his analysis of what is possible in metaphysics, we should be clear about what the procedure amounts to. The problem of specifying what some object is or what the members of some class of objects are is one problem. The problem of specifying wheh the given object is one and the same as some second object or when two members of the class are one and the same—this is a second problem. But they are problems that are so intimately related that if we have answered the one then we have assured ourselves of an answer to the other.

Also, if we are of a mind to do so, we can give priority to the second problem about the objective conditions under which a theory achieves its theoretical unification. If we do give priority to this problem, then the ultimate presuppositions of the theory will be formulated as the conditions under which any two objects of the theory are one and the same.

Kant's remarks about the first of his test cases has made him the object of considerable abuse by critics who have not always been scrupulous about trying to ascertain his exact meaning. He says that logic entered the sure path of science with Aristotle, that it has taken no step forward since that time, and that gives every appearance of a discipline which is complete. These observations have been widely reported as a statement about Kant's views on the possibility of historical development *within* the science of logic, but in fact they reveal his views about the *limits* of the territory that were staked out for logic at the time of Aristotle. The step which no one has succeeded in taking since Aristotle is a step that has taken possession of a new principality for logicians or that has changed the borders of the original domain. Kant expresses no opinion here about the potential for historical change *within* the domain of logic, but his alleged opinions are usually compared unfavorably with the views of Leibniz and Lambert. Leibniz is given particular credit for anticipating the historical developments that have actually occurred in logic and that have altered the face of modern logic. It is interesting to compare the actual views of the two men.

Leibniz is conventionally credited with two great and useful motives for his work in logic. He wished to develop a "universal characteristic" or a rationalized language which would be adequate for the formulation of all human knowledge. He also wished to be able to respond to any dispute about a point of logic with the reply, "Let us calculate!" That is to say, Leibniz sought to develop algorithms or effective decision procedures for settling questions in logic, procedures that would resemble those of arithmetic and of algebra. Like his friend Lambert, Kant was perfectly well aware of the possibility of development in both directions. He was even capable of using a little persuasive flattery to promote those objectives. For example, in one letter written after the publication of the *Critique* he mentions the "material for an important discovery" which could be accomplished by an able mathematician such as his correspondent; the project is to develop "a type of universal characteristic", following the guidelines of the table of categories proposed in the *Critique*.[26] In addition, there are many passages in Kant's working notes that show how hard and how persistently he tried to think

---

[26] *Gesammelte Schriften*, X, p. 351.

through the implications of his analytic-synthetic distinction for a quasi-algebraic representation of judgments.

In an earlier note Kant had speculated about Leibniz's second objective: "It is of the greatest importance to make a science of reasoning *technical*. The logicians have sought in vain to do this with their syllogistic. . . . Only with respect to magnitudes has the search for algorithms been successful. Shouldn't it also be possible in the critique of pure reason?—not for the extension but for the clarification of knowledge. Through the technical method one can express with the name of every concept its function or, rather, express the functions themselves, both in themselves and in relation to others. (Algebra expresses them only in relation to one another—perhaps this will also be the case with transcendental algorithms.) Only in this way can oversights and mistakes be avoided."[27] This quotation contains some language and some thoughts that will require further exploration, because it bears on the way that Kant conceived the difference between intuitions and concepts on the model of mathematical functions, or expressions composed out of constants and variables. But even without additional elaboration the main thrust of the passage is clear enough. Any fair-minded critic who reads very far in Kant's writings will have to concede that the common opinion about Kant's views on the possibility of development within logic is not in touch with reality. Kant himself faced the question of progress within logic very explicitly when he wrote, "If the question is whether in the sciences of pure reason new discoveries are to be expected, it is clear that in mathematics, logic and pure morals many are possible, . . ."[28]

If Kant's point in the preface does not concern the possibility of progress *within* logic, what then is his point? Without question it is the very same view he was urging upon L.H. Jakob in the same year. The latter has been appointed professor in logic and metaphysics at Halle in 1787; he wrote to Kant seeking advice about the choice of a logic text. Kant may well have had in mind the very passage we are discussing from his new preface when he replied by calling attention to "the necessity noted in the *Critique*, of presenting logic in its purity . . . with omission of all material belonging to metaphysics or to psychology."[29] The common concern which runs through these passages is a concern that we get straight about the borders or the jurisdiction within which the logician exercises his competence. Kant has no concern to block or deny the possibility of progress in the actual exercise of that competence.

[27] *Gesammelte Schriften*, XVIII, p. 34.
[28] *Ibid.*, XVII, p. 360.
[29] *Ibid.*, X, p. 494.

Moreover, we know from our earlier discussion why he thinks that a science such as logic will at any given time present the *appearance* of a science which is complete—why it must always seem to us that the last word has been spoken within the discipline *whether or not* we believe that to be so as a matter of historical fact. The reason, as we have already seen, is that logic is a science which teaches us how we ought to think, not how we do think. Hence it deals with our obligations as rational beings and our actual obligations must always be capable of being made explicit for us—else they would not be our obligations. We can reasonably conjecture that it probably is a result of his early religious education that the thought came to him at all—but whatever its origin his epistemological insight about our obligations was that this is the one thing that we can always claim certainty about.[30] So long as the discussion is confined to what our actual obligations are, and so long as the discussion does not wander off to the unrelated question of what our possible obligations would be under different circumstances than those that provide the occasion for criticism, Kant's point is undoubtedly sound. We can only review, criticize and control our conduct on the basis of the standards that are available to us, and, as a result, our *idea* of that set of standards is the *idea* of a set that is complete. This point is in no way incompatible with an historical opinion about the way sets of standards keep changing. In the sequel, we will see how Kant developed his epistemological insight into a mature and even masterful strategy for putting claims about the possibility of metaphysical representations on the sounder foundation of a criticism.

Kant supposes that Aristotle had the first complete concept of the subject matter of logic, that is, a concept which sufficed to determine the identity of the objects discussed in logic. Kant supposes that something similar occurred in geometry when it dawned upon mathematicians that chapters on the possible thickness of lines or on the colors of triangles do not belong in a book on geometry. The conviction arose that these are simply not the sorts of things that the mathematician is interested in. In both cases, a revolution occurred in men's understanding of what they are investigating. Now there is

---

[30] Theodor Christoph Lilienthal was professor of theology at Konigsberg, "a representative of the old and rigorous orthodoxy," and the pastor who married Kant's parents. When he died, Kant wrote a eulogistic verse that begins: "Was auf das Leben folgt, deckt tiefe Finsterniß; / Was uns zu thun gebührt, des sind wir nur gewiß." *Gesammelte Schriften*, XII, p. 397. The epistemological insight is also revealed in the *Fundamental Principles of the Metaphysics of Morals*, trans. T.K. Abbott (New York, 1949), p. 21: "We do not need science and philosophy to know what we should do to be honest and good, yea, even wise and virtuous. Indeed, we might well have conjectured beforehand that the knowledge of what every man is bound to do, and therefore also to know, would be within the reach of every man, even the commonest. Here we cannot forbear the admiration when we see how great an advantage the practical judgment has over the theoretical in the common understanding of men."

no difficulty in supplying a vague and general description of this moment of the "Copernican revolution" in a particular science. It is the moment when a concern for objects in their full and inexhaustible complexity is replaced by a concern for a specifiable domain of objects—a domain that henceforth will be characteristic for the speciality.

The complications come from the different ways in which this domain of objects can be constituted through our representations of what is in it. We have already seen that for Kant there are *two* types of representation in relation to which conditions might be imposed on a domain of objects. The conditions that affect the identity of objects in the domain might be imagined to affect the way objects are to be conceived and described, or the conditions might be imagined to affect the way objects are cited or are referred to as evidence. Kant believes that in metaphysics and in the disciplines that border on metaphysics both types of conditions exist. He calls the condition on our concepts a *limitation* of our intellectual competence and says that it affects the *scope* of the validity of the judgments within the discipline where the condition exists. He calls the condition on the way objects are referred to a *restriction* on our competence to receive evidence and he says that it affects the *limits* of the validity of the judgments within the given discipline. His idea that the questions about the scope and the limits of possible knowledge must be distinguished has its roots in his views about criticism and we must explore it further at the appropriate time. For the moment, we can continue to use the modern expression *domain of objects*, provided that we hold in mind the fact that we are using it for the sake of convenience to conflate two distinct Kantian ideas. The introduction of limitations and of restrictions can both produce a revolution within a given discipline. However the two processes have different effects and need to be studied separately. We will see that the necessity for this separate treatment is precisely the necessity noted in the *Critique* of keeping logic separate from metaphysics and from psychology.

The effects of limitations on the identity of objects in the domain are easy to illustrate. The reason for this is that these conditions on the way that objects are to be conceived are themselves translatable in concepts of the objects and can be reflected in the actual predicative content of our theory. When the modern logician speaks of a restriction on a domain of objects, he has in mind something comparable to what Kant means by a limitation on the domain and, subject to a very important qualification that is yet to be explored, we know that if a theory has been properly formalized then it is always easy to provide a recipe for the desired translation from a system with restrictions on the domains of the objects to a system that is unrestricted. When the translation has been performed then the presuppositions about the identity of objects in the domain can be formulated as new assumptions within the system that are stated as an ordinary part of the theory about the objects. Quine gives a simple and convincing example of this process which he calls "innocent abstraction". "Thus, consider a theory of bodies compared in point of length. The values of the bound variables [i.e., the objects in the domain of the theory] are physical objects, and the only predicate is 'L', where 'Lxy' means 'x is longer than y'. Now where $-Lxy$&$-Lyx$ [i.e., neither x nor y is longer than the other] anything that can be truly said of x within this theory holds equally for y and vice versa. Hence it is convenient to treat '$-Lxy$&$-Lyx$' as '$x = y$' [i.e., to treat x and y as identical if there are no predicates in our theory by which they can be distinguished.] Such identification amounts to reconstruing the values of our variables as universals, viz. lengths, instead of physical objects."[31]

In the last section we considered the force that identity has in relation to the rules of deductive inference, but now we must ask ourselves what the general principles might be that govern the introduction of assumptions about identity within a theory. At first glance we might think it incontestable that if two things x and y are identical, then every aspect of x (everything, that is, that will serve to differentiate x from something else) is an aspect of y and every aspect of y is an aspect of x. The assumption in question has come to be called "The Principle of Indiscernibility of Identicals". The mate of the principle is called "The Principle of the Identity of Indiscernibles": if every aspect of x is an aspect of y and vice versa, then x and y are identical. Even though the second of the pair has always struck metaphysicians as a bit daring and radical, we might be tempted to take a chance at conjoining the two in order to get a general definition of identity—so that when we assume the identity of two things in our theories, these two principles will spell out for us what the assumption is. However, that solution collides with the changes that Kant singles out as revolutionary in the development of a science. The effects of the collision on each of the two principles gives us a clearer view of the phenomenon to which Kant desires to call our attention.

The revolution that had occurred in deductive logic at the time of Aristotle weakens the force of the first principle. This revolution occurred through a step that is quite similar to Quine's innocent abstraction. When we refer to "every aspect" of a thing we include within the scope of our principle those aspects which are not marked out by any concept in our theory as well as those which are marked out by some concept. The former aspects of things

[31] W.V.O. Quine, "On Universals," *Journal of Symbolic Logic*, XII, p. 75.

will definitely include those which are not marked out by any actual concepts we possess, and they may possibly include some aspects not marked out by any concept at all—whether an actual or a possible concept. These are the aspects of things which do not correspond to any actual or possible predicates in our language. Now it is obvious to everyone how the Principle of Indiscernibility of Identicals is affected by Quine's example in which the only basic predicate by which to mark out the different aspects of things is the single predicate "is longer than". Quine has introduced the concept of identity in such a way that if two objects are identical it no longer follows that they are alike in every aspect but only that they are alike in every aspect for which there is a corresponding distinction in Quine's sample theory. In effect, he has made the identity of objects conform to the conditions under which he can distinguish conceptually between the objects. The fact that his illustrative theory is deliberately kept simple and happens to contain only one fundamental concept only makes more vivid the effects of substituting for the Principle of Indiscernibility of Identicals a principle of the conceptual indistinguishability of identicals.

We have seen that the logician has ample justification for taking such a step. For him the whole force of an identity statement can be exhausted by a specification of alterations that can be made in our ways of conceiving things and, since any other force that such statements can have will not be such as to confer validity on any deductive inference, he can safely ignore it. Essentially the same conclusion can be reached from a different, and a more traditional direction. We might agree to define logic as the science of the necessary and sufficient conditions of the logical possibility of representations (concepts and judgments). On this view a natural (if not entirely satisfactory) definition of the validity of a deductive inference will make it consist in the logical impossibility of a judgment which both affirms the premises and denies the conclusion of the given inference. Now if we follow the older practice and make the concept of logical possibility the central and defining concept in deductive logic, then we will have a natural interest in the two traditional principles which were considered to give the definition of logical possibility. The "Principle of Contradiction" defines the so-called "external possibility" of a judgment (or a concept); it tells us that (external) possibility of a judgment consists in the fact that the given judgment and another judgment which is related to it in a certain way (namely, as contradicting what the first affirms about something) are never both given as true. The same definition can easily be extended to the external possibility of concepts by introducing the idea of what a given concept is true of. The "Principle of Excluded Middle" defines the so-called "internal possibility" of a concept (or judgment); it says that if the concept is an (internally) possible representation of something, either it is true of that thing or false of that thing.

When we make reference to some thing (*ens*, *Ding*) in the statement of such logical principles we assume the reference is to things with a fixed identity or things to which our concept of identity applies. Accordingly, even though the principles as just stated belong to the logical *presuppositions of* all theories about things, we can perfectly well ask how our two principles will look if they are *translated into* the assumptions of a given theory. Not surprisingly, when the principles are formulated in this manner they can be taken to express the defining condition for the concept of logical identity. We have noted this condition to be that something is an aspect of x just in case (or if and only if) it is an aspect of y. But the latter is equivalent to the conjunction of two conditions: The first condition denies that there is an aspect of things that x and that y does not have; the second condition affirms that for every aspect of things either x has it or y does not have it. But on the assumption of the identity of x and y, the first of these is the same as a formulation of the Principle of Contradiction (i.e., It is not the case that there is any aspect of things which x has and does not have), while the second becomes a formulation of the Principle of Excluded Middle. Hence we can say that one of the sources of the great interest that logicians have traditionally had in these principles is that they set out the whole content of the concept of identity when they are formulated as assumptions about the subject matter of a science. This line of analysis not only confirms our previous conclusions about the meaning of identity for logicians but it can also suggest a reason why Kant was so extremely agitated about the dangers of confusing logic and metaphysics.

When we have formulated the logical presuppositions that define the logical possibility of representations as assumptions about things within a given theory, we will be tempted to suppose that these assumptions by themselves determine a domain of objects. We have said, in so many words, that an object which is a "something" (*ens*, *Ding* or *logisches Etwas*), that is, an object which has an identity, is an object to which given concepts and judgments can be related as logically possible representations. We seem to be dealing with the idea of objects that have identity as logical possibilities. By contrast with these objects, an object which is nothing (*non-ens* or *nihil negativum*; *Unding* or *Nichts*), that is, an object which lacks an identity, is an object which is the subject matter of contradictory or impossible representations. Speaking in these terms about something as the subject matter of possible representations and nothing as the subject matter of impossible representations we may seem to be speaking about the subject matter of metaphysics, conceived as the science of being (*ens*) and *non-being* (*non-ens*). Carrying the suggestion a step further, we recall Quine's point that when we do formulate the presuppositions of a theory about the identity of objects in its domain as assumptions in the theory the effect is that of "reconstruing the values of our variables as universals". The language of Kant's day reflects this point by describing the "logical objects" as "logical essences". Kant himself uses these expressions in many places in his writings on logic—even in one place referring to the "logical I" (*logisches Ich*). We can say, therefore, that the identification of logical principles, formulated as assumptions about objects, with the principles of metaphysics amounts to a confusion of these logical essences with real essences or natures. The identification, as we will see, has profound consequences in the metaphysics of pre-Kantian rationalism.

Kant rejects the proposed marriage of logic and metaphysics because he believes that there are not only limitations on the subject matter of metaphysics that reflect conditions of logical possibility in our representations of the subject matter; there are also restrictions on the subject matter of metaphysics. The existence of restrictions reflects conditions on our representations which are not merely logical and are not even merely conditions that have to do with our conceptions and judgments about things. The existence of restrictions is characteristic of all those sciences which, unlike pure formal logic, deal with real possibilities. Thus, logic can at most serve to illustrate one aspect of the revolution that occurs when a science enters its "sure path" and the aspect that it illustrates is not the true Copernican revolution of which Kant speaks. We have agreed that the moment of the revolution is the moment when the identity-conditions of the objects are assumed to be determined by the conditions under which representations of the objects are possible. But we have by no means agreed that the only representations which are possible are possible concepts, or judgments composed entirely from concepts. Logic supplies the necessary and sufficient conditions for the logical possibility of concepts and judgments, but Kant will prove that it supplies only the necessary condition of the real possibility of concepts and judgments. The real possibility of a concept consists in its possession of objective validity, which is the possibility of supplying an object for the concept—an object that is independent of the way in which it is conceived and that can provide its own evidence of the way it is to be conceived. This Kantian distinction between logical and real possibilities is grounded in his distinction between intuitions and concepts. Thus, when we consider the possibility of a revolution in our standpoint concerning the identity of objects, it is not enough for us to consider an "innocent abstraction" in which the conditions of identity of objects are adjusted to our possibilities of distinguishing between objects by descriptive or conceptual means. We also must consider the revolutionary standpoint from which the possibility of the object is determined by the conditions under which there are possible intuitions of objects, or possible references to the object as a source of evidence about how it is to be conceived. These conditions on intuition form the restrictions which are characteristic of mathematics, physics, astronomy, and metaphysics.

The hypothesis that Copernicus formed in astronomy is a particularly striking illustration of the effects of full and all out revolution. First, there was the process described by Quine—a process that contained the fighting to terrain in which Copernicus, as an astronomer, was competent to give battle. When the leading intellectuals in the age of Copernicus were confronted with his hypothesis, they did not all react in fear and ignorance. Many were his superiors in sheer powers of conceptualization, and they were able to point out numerous defects appearing to them to be obvious and to count decisively against the truth of his views. First, the hypothesis conflicted with a number of aspects of the heavenly bodies that were presumed on all sides to be real physical properties. For example, the postulated speed of the earth's rotation would cause it to fly apart. If the earth moves we should feel a wind in our face. Objects thrown up in the sky would not return to their point of origin. Copernicus was not able to reply that these objects were moving along with the earth—among other things there was the established view that elementary bodies cannot partake of two simple motions. Finally, by the best estimate of the distances involved, we should observe a parallactic motion of the fixed stars. This last objection shows that Copernicus not only contained the field of conflict to exclude general physical difficulties; he yielded the terrain of a general astronomy in order to provide a planetary hypothesis. He has conceived his subject matter as the motions of the planets and he limits himself to the task of providing the best account of those motions. This first aspect of the revolutionary achievement of Copernicus looks to be nothing more than the familiar process of departmentalization and specialization of interests. If *these* are characteristics of the modern sciences—even though they be related to conditions for success in science, it might be objected that they furnish a poor model for the metaphysician to emulate. If Kant's Copernican revolution is leading the philosopher down *that* path, the philosopher might prefer not to travel it. As Leibniz, a true metaphysician, observed when contemplating Locke's hypothesis that the understanding of each of us is a blank tablet at birth, these fictions and abstractions are not harmful in themselves but they should never be confused with the real things which vary in infinitely many respects. Before we can estimate the revolutionary potential in metaphysics, however, we must consider the effects of the second aspect of the Copernican revolution.

The scandal which came in time to be associated with the new planetary hypothesis derives from the way in which the new astronomers were prepared to abandon the earth as a fixed and stable point of reference and to experiment with other frames of reference in which the earth moves. In such a mode of investigation everything appears to be in flux—nothing any longer is stable. The reason for this dramatic change is that the significance of all our thoughts about the observable aspects of objects undergoes an alteration, as we change our frame of reference and change our way of referring those thoughts to the objects. Nothing in the primary qualities of an object can be taken any longer to be fixed. If we can, by changing frames of reference, convert an apparently fixed position of the earth into an apparently changing one, we can also change the appearance of the sizes and the appearance of the shapes of things by the appropriate changes in our manner of locating the objects under investigation. Indeed, Copernicus himself had a not wholly rational preference for describing the shape of the paths of motion of the planets as perfectly circular paths, and his willingness to allow the position of the earth to be a changing one was an accommodation to that preference for one description of the paths as opposed to other possible descriptions. There is no clearer or better illustration of Kant's point about the way in which the properties of the things that are investigated by scientists can be determined by the forms of intuition of the object: A change in our system for co-ordinating references to objects alters the projection of the object or its appearance in the co-ordinate system. When we come to study in detail the impact which the Copernican revolution had on Kant's analysis of the conditions affecting the possibility of a knowledge of objects, we will see very clearly how that impact was mediated by some important discoveries by Descartes and other mathematicians. These men discovered a self-conscious and deliberate technique for applying to objects any mathematicized concept of the properties of the objects and applying it in such a way that the effects of the change of co-ordinate system could be made known in advance. Nevertheless, if Copernicus had only a dim grasp of the applied geometry of his own methods, he is a clear example of a scientist for whom the physical appearances of objects are affected by the scientist's own way of representing the objects.

As we study Kant's arguments in the aesthetic we will find additional examples of the manner in which the possibilites of conception and of description can be affected by the form of intuition. We will see that in each case the Copernican revolutionary potential derives from the way in which our manner of fixing the times and places of things can affect the identities of the objects that provide us with the grounds and evidence for our descriptions. It will become clear, particularly in the course of the third chapter, that just as the first aspect of the scientific revolution has its effects on the Principle of the Indiscernibility of Identicals, the second aspect of the revolution and the dramatic, Copernican aspect of the affair occurs through effects on the Principle of Identity of Indiscernibles. That principle, as Kant remarks, is only true for the sciences of pure reason, notably for logic. A critique of the pretensions of pure reason will show us that it does not hold in mathematics, physics or in metaphysics. Thus, we will see that in general it is not true that if two objects are different (or if objects are manifold) then there is some corresponding diversity to be expected in our conceptions of those objects. Since the principle under attack by Kant in the aesthetic is a corollary of the famous, or infamous, Principle of Sufficient Reason, the derivation, implications and final overthrow of that central tenet of rationalism will figure prominently in any complete account of the historical background for the aesthetic.

It is important for those reading the aesthetic to have a clear understanding of how the problem of the possibility of synthetic *a priori* knowledge is related to the possibility of a Copernican revolution in metaphysics. As regards the former, we have seen that from a pure, philosophical standpoint the problem of synthetic, *a priori* knowledge is fully equivalent to the problem of how synthetic or non-deductive forms of inquiry and reasoning are possible: How is abduction, or reasoning which results in new combinations of concepts, possible? How is induction, or reasoning which extends the same concepts to new objects, possible? As regards the latter, we have seen that the revolution by which a science enters its "sure path" is fully equivalent to the problem of the way in which the identities of the objects under investigation can be affected by changes in two principles: What happens if we assume that the necessary condition for the identity of objects of knowledge is limited by the condition under which our conception of objects is possible—by something that affects our competence to formulate descriptions of the things? What happens if we assume that the necessary condition for the diversity or manifold appearance of objects of knowledge is restricted by the forms of our intuition of objects—by something that affects the jurisdiction within which we can summon evidence of the truth or falsity of our descriptions? A little reflection will suggest (though admittedly we cannot now prove) that these two sets of questions are closely related in their bearing on the prospects of successful inquiry in any discipline.

The possibility of a valid abduction depends upon an increase in the deductive strength of some set of beliefs. This process will involve successfully guessing or exercising our imaginations to determine the ways in which it may be fruitful to conceive and describe things in order to gain some deductive unification in those beliefs. Now if the qualitative complexity of the objects of knowledge cannot be assumed to be limited in some manner, we cannot have any reasonable prospect of success in the new combinations of ideas that we try out. Whether or not Kant can defend the particular categories which he proposes as those which introduce an order into our description of things, we need not pause to worry over; it is the deepest problem in the *Critique*. For purposes of comparison with the forms of intuition, we can be content with the bare and abstract statement of the situation as it relates to the categories of the understanding: If the qualitative complexity of the possible objects of knowledge can be shown to be *subject to a limitation* affecting the objective validity of our conceptions of these objects, then we can have a reasonable prospect for success in trying out imaginative combinations of conceptions of objects. If our competence in thinking possible combinations is not unlimited, then there is reason to hope that we may discover the truth about the natures of things.

Of course we know that mathematically inclined readers will be inclined to scoff at such a notion and to suggest instead that the number of different descriptions of a set of objects that are possible *a priori* is always unlimited. "Give me a description of the behavior of objects that you think is true— Boyle's Law will do as our example—and I will give you an unlimited number of forms that the law might have taken!" We should proceed very slowly in our reaction to these mathematically inspired boasts and pretensions. Perhaps the set of alternatives to Boyle's Law tells us nothing about the limitations in our powers to conceive of objects, but merely reflects a feature that Kant was well aware of in the restrictions on our power to take testimony about objects. Should that be the case, then each of the variant forms of the law can be regarded as representing differing appearances of the same reality under suitable adjustments in the arrangement of our system of co-ordinates—our system for applying the mathematical descriptions to the objects of the descriptions. The point is not to decide here and now between Kant and his mathematically sophisticated critic, but only to show in yet another way how the issues of the Kantian analytic are impossible to resolve without an understanding of how they are affected by his aesthetic. And with that observation we come to the comparison of problems that leads directly into the aesthetic.

The metaphysical presuppositions that affect the prospects for success in induction (and, more generally, our prospects for success in any process of finding evidence for our descriptions of things) have a very obvious relationship to our assumptions about the identity of objects. In particular, it is clear that in those forms of induction in which the conclusion is reached on the basis of a sampling the possible diversity of objects from which the sample has been drawn cannot be regarded as a diversity that depends upon differing properties of these objects themselves. Someone who maintains the contrary will find it impossible to explain or even to understand how the number of objects in a sample drawn from an urn can go to infinity even though we can only distinguish a finite number of different balls in the urn on the basis of differences in their properties. What can easily be seen to be a presupposition of induction in these paradigmatic cases is also true for the more complex cases of reasonings from what has been presented in intuition. There is no possibility that induction will work unless there is a possible extension in the number of things we are thinking about without any necessary extension in the number of ways the things can be thought to differ. On the other hand, if one has shown how the number of things under consideration can be enlarged without any necessary alteration in the concepts we are required to have of the things, then one has gone half the way to a proof that induction must be capable of success.

The full problem of accounting for why induction will work and why the sciences that rely upon induction have entered a "sure path" can be illustrated by another of Kant's examples of the Copernican revolution. When Gallileo rolled balls down an inclined plane he was justified in abstracting from their possible differences in color, smell and so on because he had limited his hypothesis to a statement about their primary qualities *and* because the differences between the objects under investigation are differences in spatial and temporal appearances of balls that do not entail any corresponding differences in the properties from which he was abstracting. (The difference in the appearances of the balls is determined by the differences in the times and places the balls are in when we observe the balls and, by the argument of the aesthetic, these differences do not entail any differences at all in the balls *per se*. If there is no difference in the balls *per se* or in what the balls can be conceived to be, then *a fortiori* there is no difference in the properties from which Gallileo is abstracting.)

On the other hand, if the difference in the occurrences of the balls is constituted by differences of the appearances of the balls in time and place, then the physical inquiry has become a study of phenomena that are repeatable and repeatable as many times as one likes. But *if* there is a valid limitation on the ways in which the phenomenon can be conceived to be and *if* the study of the phenomenon is restricted to what can be observed as many times as one likes, *then the inquiry is bound to succeed.* Of course there are several "ifs" in this last statement. The first condition is established by Kant's justification of the categories as containing the limitations on the objective unification or combination of concepts. The details of his argument here are not our main concern, but it is obvious that his argument must depend upon showing that not every logically possible variation in the way in which the phenomena can be conceived or described is a variation or combination that should be attributed any objective significance. If Boyle's Law gives a true description of the relationship between pressure and volume in gases at a constant temperature, then the number of different mathematical forms that this law could take, that are forms that will fit the same body of evidence that suggested Boyle's Law itself, and *that are forms which cannot be regarded as presenting a different appearance of the same relationship* as that described in Boyle's Law, is a number that must be brought down. Just as Copernicus and anti-Copernicus may be describing the same path even though one says it is circular and the other says it has a more complicated shape, so Boyle and anti-Boyle can be allowed to differ in their manner of attributing physical significance to a description without jeopardizing the possibility of success in induction. The demonstration that this is so is not the whole of the justification by any means, but it is an indispensable part and a part to which the aesthetic can be seen to make a contribution. The other "if" in the explanation of why the inductive sciences can enter their sure path to knowledge concerns a means of increasing the number of things which supply us with evidence for our conceptions without jeopardizing the validity of our conceptions. The solution to this problem of the introduction of a manifold into the subject matter of our judgments lies wholly within the scope of the aesthetic.

The failure to distinguish clearly between the two major questions about induction and the corresponding two questions about the possibility of synthetic *a priori* judgments is something that separates a number of recent accounts of knowledge from Kant's account. The root cause is a failure to appreciate the role of the forms of intuition in the Kantian explanation of how synthetic judgments are possible. Many contemporary authors have taken Hume's teaching to heart and they would agree that we can only show why induction can be successful if we can show why things must conform to categories of the understanding and must have the identities of things that fall into certain categories. For example, in the case of things that conform to our concept of substance, we suppose that they are capable of changing in some of their aspects or relationships without any "real" or substantial change of identity. Similarly, in the case of things that we can categorize as possible effects, certain merely apparent changes are clearly to be distinguished from those physically real changes that we must associate with the presence of physical forces that have acted to produce the changes as their effects. Thus, our investigation in physics proceeds under the assumption: "No real changes without a force producing the change or—more generally—without a causal law that describes the change."

But the same authors who appreciate the importance of these categories and principles of the understanding have not always absorbed Kant's point about the presuppositions restricting synthetic knowledge to that which can be given in intuition. The point of the transcendental aesthetic is that we can show why induction will work only if we show how the conceptual unification of knowledge by means of the categories is able to take place for a manifold of objects that are diversified in accordance with the conditions under which it is possible for us to refer to the objects as sources of evidence rather than in accordance with the conditions under which it is possible for us to conceive or to understand the objects. The contrast between the two accounts is expressed in the language of Kant's century when we say that these authors believe that we can show why induction will work by means of an argument that seeks to establish the validity of induction in giving us knowledge of "things-in-themselves". Kant believes rather that we can only establish the validity of synthetic knowledge for "appearances" or for those projections of objects into space and time which conform to the conditions under which the co-ordinated references to things are possible.

There is a well-known anecdote concerning Keynes which will illustrate how far he was from Kant in his thinking about induction and the possibility of knowledge. As we will see later in detail, Kant thought that there was an obvious and an important difference between what can be said about the categories of understanding and the forms of intuition: That which depends for its validity upon what it is possible for humans to conceive is that which depends upon the spontaneous human activity that will occur or can occur in the course of inquiry. But that which depends for its validity upon what it is possible for us to intuit does not similarly depend upon acts that we will perform or even that we can perform. Now there is a treatment of the problem of induction that studies the effects on observed ratios as the sample size goes to infinity, and which seeks to prove on the basis of this study that in the long run the induction must work. The famous jibe by Keynes is that in the long run we will all be dead. This retort has been supposed by some to disparage such arguments and to cast doubt on their relevance to problems about human cognition. The actual or implied suggestion is that the number of possible objects which is the subject matter of mathematical reasoning or of scientific observations is determined in some way by the number of possible acts which humans could actually be imagined to perform. But we have already seen that if the infinitization of a domain of inquiry depended upon what can be enumerated, described individually, conceived, or otherwise differentiated through our spontaneous acts, then no domain would be infinite. Of the objects of such human acts, it is a certainty for each of us and a reasonable assumption for all of us that the number is only finite. But if Keynes intended to attack the arguments about induction by calling into question their consistency with the conditions under which alone human cognition is possible, he has simply confused the two types of conditions which Kantian arguments require us to distinguish.

Suppose, for example, that the argument is designed to show why simple sampling must work. In induction based upon sampling we attempt to reach a conclusion about the probability with which a certain characteristic is to be found in a certain population, where the probability is defined as a limit of the relative frequencies of the appearances of the characteristic in the appearances of objects in the population in the successive samples from the population. If we know that there is such a limit and if we suppose that the sample sizes can go to infinity then we can apply a theorem of mathematics—Bernouilli's theorem—to conclude that of necessity the inductive procedure will work. This is a typical "in-the-long-run" argument and it reflects a very specific instance in recent and contemporary discussions of the possibility of knowledge where the Copernican revolution can be illustrated and its effects assessed. There is little disagreement about the specific deduction from Bernouilli's theorem, the disagreement concerns whether the premises for the deduction can be established in such a way as to provide a general solution to the problem of validity for this class of inductions. The first point to notice, therefore, is that the post-Kantian philosopher will approach these problems in a different spirit than will those who, like Keynes, have retreated to a pre-Kantian point of view. The latter will imagine difficulties based upon the way in which the things, themselves, might be. How do we know that the characteristic is not distributed among the things in such a way that the observed ratios will continue to fluctuate wildly for as long as we continue the sampling, without settling any "true" limit for the population? Even if we suppose that the population is unlimited in size, how do we know that some of the things will not remain hidden and undiscovered by us, so that our samples give only a biased picture of the things themselves? The Kantian answer to such queries is, of course, that the validity of synthetic knowledge can only be established for appearances of things and not for things *per se* and that appearances, by definition, are things that conform to the conditions under which we can refer to them. This is the first point on which the post-Kantian diverges from the pre-Kantian. The second point, and the one which chiefly needs emphasizing for the student of the aesthetic, is that when the post-Kantian turns his attention from the things *per se* to the conditions for the possibility of our knowledge of things, he will expect to deal with *two* sets of conditions and not with one.

In the argument at hand, the first premise is one that brings the number of different possible conceptualizations of the thing down and it reflects the limitations in our understanding of things, rather than any intrinsic limitation in things *per se*. It is a valid presupposition for appearances of objects in the population, though not necessarily for the objects *per se*, that the number of different mathematical descriptions which the appearances in the successive samples could be required to fit is finite. This condition is one that fixes limits for the objects of human knowledge that brings them within the range of the possibilities for the humans who are to conceive these objects. The assumption belongs within the same general class as the assumption made by Keynes when he attempted to account for the possibility of eliminative induction by appealing to a principle of limited variety. There are detailed differences, of course, that reflect differences in the two forms of induction, but the chief philosophical difference is that the Keynesian principle can be interpreted as a dogmatic, metaphysical assumption about the nature of the things *per se* that are the supposed subject matter of inductions. Kant's principles apply only to the appearances.

The presupposition needed to justify the second premise in the argument about induction should provide for the possibility that the samples are drawn from an unlimited reference class. This is the condition that provides for an infinitizing of the subject matter of the induction and which thereby establishes a significance for these references to the "long run". One of Kant's central tasks in the aesthetic, and therefore one of our central tasks in understanding his work, is to show that such a condition can be valid, as a restriction on the objects of empirical cognition. But everyone who reflects for even a moment on the conditions under which the illustrative argument about induction could possibly be a sound argument will realize the necessity of separating the two questions about the possible objects of the induction.

Our pursuit of the historical background of Kant's distinction between intuitions and concepts and of his distinction between the two types of condition on knowledge will carry us back from the eighteenth century to the seventeenth century, and on incidental matters of terminology even back to the thirteenth century. We will discover that Kant inherited strong and subtle arguments from his predecessors and that his employment of these arguments within a transcendental context is decidedly ingenious. But in our pursuit of the historical background to his discussions we can easily lose sight of the fact that what he discusses has a bearing on the treatment of scientific knowledge in our own century. The way in which I have presented in this chapter Kant's goals for transcendental inquiry, his division of the elements of knowledge, and his distinction between the conditions on knowledge has been deliberately aimed at communicating the sense that our problems are continuous with problems developed and discussed by our forefathers. Sometimes, when we make these connections with our past, we will go wrong —as I think many have gone wrong with Kant's analytic–synthetic distinction; but the fact that we will sometimes go wrong does not alter the fact that these connections do exist.

CHAPTER TWO

TRANSCENDENTAL ELEMENTS IN RATIONALISM

I. THE METHOD OF CLEAR AND DISTINCT IDEAS

Kant gives his distinction between intuitions and concepts as a fundamental division within the transcendental doctrine of the elements of knowledge. In any number of passages he contrasts this doctrine with that of the earlier rationalists, who, as he says, admitted only the distinction between clear and distinct ideas, and for whom, therefore, the fundamental divisions are logical rather than transcendental.[1] These earlier distinctions are based upon the assumption that all of our representations are clear or not clear, distinct or not distinct, adequate or not adequate, and complete or not complete.[2] Kant correctly perceived that the acceptance of this dogma has profound consequences for our analysis of knowledge. He also correctly perceived that the acceptance of the dogma will entail the rejection of his own distinction between intuitions and concepts. In order to establish the first of these two points, we need to sketch the outline of an analysis of knowledge that is faithful to the rationalist assumptions about the methodological conditions which our knowledge must satisfy. While the direction of that analysis follows along very familiar lines, the establishment of Kant's second point gives the analysis a somewhat unexpected outcome, or, at least, involves an argument that has been less widely appreciated. We saw in the last chapter that acceptance of Kant's distinction between intuitions and concepts involves a denial of the principle of sufficient reason, and we can assume temporarily that that is so. Accordingly, we will have established the soundness of Kant's second observation if we can produce an argument to show that a version of the

[1] For example, at B61–62.
[2] These distinctions were construed in several different ways within rationalism. On this point cf. M. Serres, *Le Système de Leibniz et les Modèles Mathématiques* (Paris, 1968), p. 119ff. For a general discussion of the methodological differences between Leibniz and Descartes, cf. Y. Belaval, *Leibniz' Critique de Descartes* (Paris, 1960).

principle of sufficient reason is entailed by the formulation of the distinctions that are involved in the Cartesian method of clear and distinct ideas.

Before turning to the details of that analysis of knowledge and to that deduction from its fundamental distinctions, I want to underscore the point that I am interested in this section (and in the next section also) in the establishment of certain logical points whose validity has a bearing upon claims that Kant makes in the aesthetic. Within the rationalist tradition the method of clear and distinct ideas goes back to Descartes and quite possibly there is some historical interest in the fact that a reconstruction of his position shows that he was logically committed to a principle that was accepted as fundamental by Leibniz and his successors. But at the same time it must be stressed that anyone who contemplated only the logical point and who refused to look beyond it to the historical realities would have no understanding of the profound historical difference between the Cartesian methodology and the Leibnizian methodology. For the former, the implication of the principle of sufficient reason is a logical curiosity; for the latter, the assertion of the principle corresponds to a necessity of the system. The differences (though not the logical point of similarity) between the two methodologies have been explored in great detail by Belaval, who calls attention, in particular, to the fact that the problem of the unification of knowledge is handled very differently by these two great rationalists. Leibniz suggests to us that the representations which constitute our knowledge can be connected to one another in conformity to principles of logic and to the principle of sufficient reason. Leibniz also supposes that if our representations can be validly connected to one another by these principles, then it must be possible for different representations to be connected in the same object. The second paragraph of Descartes's first, immature work had expressed a different understanding of how the problem of the unification of knowledge is to be handled. It must be possible for our thoughts to be connected with one another to form one, unified body of scientific knowledge, because each of these thoughts must belong to one thinker with a substantial identity who is, as Descartes tells us, "everywhere the same". Allowing for the incalculable difference between talk of a *de facto* possession of ideas and talk about a *de jure* possession of ideas, we can still say that Kant repeats the first major observation of Descartes's *Regulae* in his own analysis of the possible combination of ideas; Kant's corresponding observation is that my thoughts must be capable of belonging together else they would not all be capable of being mine.

Belaval has pointed out that the Cartesian analysis of the conditions for the possible unification of knowledge led directly to such new and even revolutionary developments as the combination of algebraic and geometrical ideas in his new science of analytic geometry. In later chapters we will return again and again to this Cartesian discovery because of its major importance for the arguments of Kant's aesthetic, but for the moment the point of interest in this development is the one noted by Belaval: The Cartesian analysis of the conditions for a possible unification of knowledge makes it very difficult to see how the ideas that are combined can have an objective validity —the basis or ground of explanation of how they can be connected with one another is in their connection with the subject rather than with the object.

Leibniz invokes his principles of knowledge, including the principle of sufficient reason, to account for the order and the connection in our knowledge. But the Leibnizian solution is inadequate as a solution to the problem of an objective unification of knowledge because, as we have previously seen, Leibniz misconstrued the conditions under which the objects of differing cognitions are one and the same. When Kant turns to these same issues in the *Critique*, he argues in precisely the opposite direction from Leibniz. We saw the beginnings of the Leibnizian analysis of the problem of knowledge in the last chapter, and in this section we will find additional confirmation of Belaval's point about the use to which Leibniz puts the principle of sufficient reason. Leibniz tells us, in effect, that if it is possible to connect our representations with one another in conformity to his methodological principles, then it is possible to account for the way in which different representations can be connected in one and the same object. Kant tells us, by contrast, that only if there are valid principles and concepts which make it possible for different representations to be connected in one and the same object will it be possible to account for how our representations can be connected with one another in a lawful synthesis or combination with one another.

Kant's observation occurs at a point at which he is trying to establish the validity of these principles and concepts that underlie the objectification of our thoughts. He carries the argument back a step further and in a manner reminiscent of Descartes's *Regulae*. It must be possible for my representations to be associated with one another, because otherwise they would not all belong to me as my representations. However, it should be stressed again that Kant's notion of the "association (*Verbindung*) of my ideas" and his notion of the ideas as mine are notions of a logical connection between ideas and of a *de jure* possession of those ideas. The critical turn, which makes a clear demarcation—as we have already seen—between the normative and the factual, is what separates Kant's discussion of the conditions of a personal identity from Descartes's appeal to the thinking substance that is everywhere the same through the processes of thinking different thoughts.

Hume's analysis of the conditions of personal identity is otherwise even closer to Kant's. Hume argues that the identity of the self is ultimately accounted for by the principles of association which bundle the ideas together to constitute the self in its personal identity. Both Hume and Kant agree that we can form no other valid concept of the self that knows. But again, Hume's psychologistic rendering of these principles of association separates his account of the possibility of connection in my ideas from the critical account. Like Leibniz, and unlike Descartes, Kant believes that the principles which determine my logical rights to ideas and which confirm me in the *de jure* possession of ideas are the principles of formal and of transcendental logic. We have already remarked upon his strenuous insistence that it is necessary to keep these principles of the possibility of knowledge distinct from the principles of metaphysics and of psychology. One reason for his insistence upon this point is that his argument for the objective validity of the categories of our understanding depends upon the assumption he shared with Leibniz that there is a type of association of ideas which accounts for the possibility of knowledge and which is neither Descartes's connection of ideas with one another on the basis of their inherence in a common thinking substance, nor Hume's connection of ideas with one another by the workings of the imagination in accordance with the psychological laws of association.

These matters will receive further elaboration as we explore the historical genesis of Kant's opinions, but it should be clear from what has been said that there is something that he borrows from the Cartesian analysis to play off against the Leibnizian analysis of knowledge and that there is something which he borrows from Leibniz to employ against the Cartesian account of the possibility of knowledge. *A fortiori*, we know that there are profound historical differences in the potentialities of the two systems, and even if we cannot yet say with precision what the differences are, we know that they will be important for an understanding of the *Critique*. Nevertheless that acknowledgement of the historical complexities in rationalism to which Belaval and others have called our attention does not detract in the least from the validity of Kant's two logical points about what is involved in the method of clear and distinct ideas. In order to appreciate the truth and the potential significance of Kant's assessment of the rationalist tradition, we should begin with its analysis of knowledge.

The first and the fundamental notion in a Cartesian analysis of knowledge is the notion of a clear idea of something that is before the mind. If we were satisfied with a mere verbal clarification, we could easily furnish a definition of the basic phrase. We could say:

1. D has a clear idea of x if and only if D has a direct and unclouded awareness of x.

But of course the preceding cannot pretend to any very profound analysis of what is involved in having a clear idea. All that it does is to offer us a choice of locutions. There are several other Cartesian locutions which also can be cited as either indistinguishable in their import or virtually indistinguishable. Descartes sometimes, and particularly in his early work, speaks of our intuitions of things. He also speaks of our perception of things by the natural light of reason. These are suggestive, but they are subject to various mis-understandings. For example, no one who reads Descartes carefully will be apt to confuse his use of the word *perception* in these contexts with the modern philosophical use of the term to characterize sensory experiences. It is used to mark out a state of the thinking substance. The same caution needs to be observed with the Cartesian use of the word *intuition*; it does not contrast with *concept* in the manner of Kantian intuitions. The Cartesian intuition is itself an intellectual representation of what a thing is—of a nature.

The other central notion in the Cartesian analysis of knowledge is intro-duced in a definition that will prove to have much weightier implications than our first, merely verbal explanation:

2. D has a distinct idea of x if and only if for every y, if x is y, then D has a clear idea of y.

Among the points to notice about (2) is the fact that, unlike (1), it does propose a serious analysis of the notion that it introduces. Also, unlike the familiar explication of the clear idea in terms of our ability to recognize re-appearances of a thing, this analysis is one that Descartes himself seems to have sponsored. The popular account of clear ideas probably derives from the logic of Port-Royal and is not Cartesian; it wrongly supposes that the object of a clear idea is an appearance (or re-appearance) of a thing, whereas the object of a clear idea for Descartes is a nature or a thing *per se*. But the same consideration, that the object of a distinct idea is a nature, is what makes (2) plausible for Descartes. If I have a distinct grasp on the nature of a thing, then, plausibly, I am aware of what can truly be predicted of that nature, since what can be truly predicted of it is involved in my very conception of it. The other two points to notice about this explanation of distinct ideas are ones to which Descartes himself calls our attention. First, his definition of distinct ideas introduces a redundancy in his famous phrase "clear and dis-tinct idea"; every distinct idea is clear. We may assume therefore that his "and" has the rhetorical force of *sed etiam*: ideas which are not only clear but are also even distinct. The second point which Descartes calls to our attention is that he is committed to a doctrine of simples, and, indeed, his method of clear and distinct ideas could promise us little if he did not embrace that commitment. If it is possible for D to have a distinct idea of x, then the analysis of what x is must terminate at some point and at that point x will have been resolved into a set of y's that are each simple and unanalyzable. We will see that Leibniz and Kant diverge over the implications of that point.

The traditional concept of knowledge has three main ingredients. In Kant's terminology D knows that x is y just in case (a) D judges that x is y; (b) it is true that x is y; and (c) D has objective, rather than merely subjective grounds for his judgment that x is y. It will be recalled from the first chapter that objective grounds for D's judgment that x is y are reasons why it is true that x is y, as contrasted with reasons which merely justify D's judging that x is y. Near the inception of the tradition Aristotle remarked that it is a mark of the man who knows that he can explain to others why what is so is so. Now in general (and without denying that there are a few, uninteresting exceptions), we know that an individual who is merely justified in judging as he does cannot satisfy Aristotle's and the tradition's criterion for knowledge. Such an individual can wriggle off the hook of criticism but he does not possess that type of understanding which the tradition associates with the man who can truly be said to know that x is y. Our paradigm of the former, it will be recalled, is the man who has been told by a reliable witness that x is y and who cannot be blamed if he judges that x is y. He has a justified belief that x is y, and, provided that x is y, there might be a loose and popular sense in which he can be said to know that x is y. But a Cartesian analysis of knowledge, like the Kantian inquiries in the *Critique*, concerns the type of knowledge that satisfies the stringent conditions of having objective support— support which has a bearing on the truth of what is judged. With knowledge something more is at stake than the reputation of the man who speaks. It follows from what has been said that a vital part of any analysis of knowledge will consist in its transcendental explanation of the conditions under which we have what Kant terms "objective grounds" for conceiving and judging as we do. We have interpreted these objective grounds as sufficient grounds for the truth of the given judgment and we expect, therefore, that any analysis of knowledge will state these *sufficient* conditions for truth in our predication. It is not surprising that we discover such a principle in Descartes's discussion of methods. The interesting fact is that he is committed to a version of the principle of sufficient reason which gives the converse of the first principle and which therefore states the *necessary* condition for truth in our predications. The combination of the two principles has an obvious bearing on the rationalist's concept of knowledge because it casts the truth-condition (b) in a new form.

Descartes invoked the notions of clearness and distinctness in his account of the condition under which we have our proper "objective grounds"

(Kant's phrase, not Descartes'). His obvious intent is to insure that D is not merely aware in some general kind of way or in some lazy and partial way, but to insure that what D knows is directly and unambiguously present to him. Provisionally, then, and subject to a further modification, we can say that for a Cartesian "D knows that x is y" will mean (a) D judges that x is y, (b) x *is* y, and (c) D has a clear and distinct idea of x and his judgment that x is y is based upon that clear and distinct awareness of x. The methodological principle by which the Cartesian will satisfy the classical demand that the grounds for judgment must be objective can be formulated in the following way:

3. If having a clear and distinct idea of x entails having a clear idea of y, then x is y.

I will refer to this assumption as the "principle of analytic predication" for the obvious reason that it permits us to predicate truly of x whatever we find to be contained or involved in our idea of x. There is little room to doubt that Descartes himself was committed consciously to this first principle. For example, in commenting upon a proposed proof for the existence of God, he writes, "... that which we clearly understand to belong to the nature of anything can truly be affirmed of that thing. Thus, if to be an animal belongs to the nature of man, it can be asserted that man is an animal." [3]

The fact which establishes the validity of Kant's logical point about the method of clear and distinct ideas is that the converse of (3) can also be established within the context of that method. From the definition of distinct ideas (2), we have: For every y, D has a distinct idea of x if and only if, if x is y, then D has a clear idea of y. (This step is justified by the fact that "y" is not contained in the definiendum.) Hence, we know that if D has a distinct idea of x, then if x is y then D has a clear idea of y. It follows that if D has a distinct idea of x and x is y, then D has a clear idea of y. And thus, if x is y and D has a distinct idea of x, then D has a clear idea of y. Hence, if x is y, then if D has a distinct idea of x then D has a clear idea of y—a conclusion we may phrase as "if x is y, then D's having a distinct idea of x entails D's having a clear idea of y". Suppressing the reference to D as something essential to Descartes's historical method but not to our analysis of its consequences, and taking advantage of the redundancy previously noted, we have established the following:

4. If x is y, then having a clear and distinct idea of x entails having a clear idea of y.

---

[3] *The Philosophical Works of Descartes*, trans. by Haldane and Ross (New York, 1955), Vol. II, p. 45.

The importance of this principle for an analysis of knowledge is self-evident. When (3) and (4) are conjoined they give the necessary and sufficient conditions for its being *true* that x is y. That is, x is y if and only if having a clear and distinct idea of x entails having a clear idea of y. Consequently, we are in a position to eliminate the truth-condition (b) from our provisional analysis of knowledge:

5. D knows that x is y if and only if (a) D judges that x is y, (b) having a clear and distinct idea of x entails having a clear idea of y and (c) D grounds his judgment that x is y on his distinct idea of x.

This analysis has the general consequences that have come to be associated with the later rationalisms of Leibniz and of Wolff. The mark of the later tradition is the way in which it explicitly assumes that everything that we can know at all we can know *a priori* and by means of an analysis of ideas. The result gives the appearance of assimilating connections in nature to the logical structure of knowledge (and, one should add, *vice versa*. Wolff remarks at one point that the discovery of the microscope has proved to be a great aid to the analysis of ideas). The result therefore gives the appearance of reducing all proper and true knowledge to what is now called "analytic" knowledge. Since the analysis is implicated in the method of clear and distinct ideas itself, Kant is correct in his observation about how he relates to rationalism as a whole, even though Belaval is undoubtedly also correct in those observations about the internal strains and diversities within rationalism itself. Furthermore, if Kant is correct in thinking that his distinction between intuitions and concepts is incompatible with the method of clear and distinct ideas, his distinction will collide with the proposed reduction in the truth-conditions of knowledge. But before turning to the description of that collision and to a discussion of how it came about, we must consider a second implication of the Cartesian method. This implication is one that was explicitly drawn by Spinoza and it is one that forms the basis of a very important argument in Kant's aesthetic.

II. SPINOZA'S CONTRIBUTION TO THE AESTHETIC

Lev Shestov once made the perceptive observation that, "The critical philosophy did not overthrow the fundamental ideas of Spinoza; on the contrary, it accepted and assimilated them."[4] The deeper we penetrate into

---

[4] Lev Shestov, *Athens and Jerusalem* (New York, 1966), p. 56.

the arguments of Kant's aesthetic the more we will come to appreciate the profound truth of that remark. The effect of Spinoza on Lessing, by comparison, was superficial and, for all the scandal it caused in Kant's day, it hardly touched the logical substance of the philosophy of Lessing. Spinoza's effect on Kant was less notorious, but it goes to the logical core and substance of his arguments in the aesthetic. A central argument which Kant accepted from Spinoza is a valid argument that Spinoza gives for the fourteenth proposition of the first part of the *Ethics*. Hence, Kant's position in the aesthetic depends upon the validity of the argument for the most provocative and inflammatory aspect of Spinozism—the identification of God with substance. Kant almost certainly had this well-known proposition in mind when he said, disparagingly, "Spinozism is the true consequence of dogmatizing metaphysics."[5] Kant accepted and depended upon the validity of Spinoza's argument, but Shestov is correct in that Kant accepted the argument only after assimilating it to the purposes of his own transcendental inquiry. The final result, as we will see in Chapter Five, amounts to a logical inversion of Spinoza's line of reflection.

In order to establish the logical possibility of this inversion (and in order not to burden the reader with arguments that are moving in different directions at the same time), we need to do two things in this section. We need to show that there is in fact a logically valid argument to Spinoza's metaphysical conclusion. This part of the discussion has a certain independent interest since many critics of Spinoza have suggested that his use of the method of geometry is really only a rhetorical facade enabling him to write his inflammatory opinions in a cool and detached style. For example, Boole, using the *Ethics* as a test case for his newly invented calculus reached a conclusion adverse to Spinoza's power of reasoning; Boole would have done better to draw a conclusion about the limitations of his own calculus. The first part of the analysis in this section, therefore, will serve as a partial rebuttal to Boole, Russell, McKeon, and others in the verdict to be passed on Spinoza's logical acumen. The second and the truly indispensable part of the analysis is to show that there is a valid transcendental deduction of the central premise of Spinoza's argument. This fact is what permits the logical inversion of his argument when it finally emerges in the aesthetic. In the aesthetic, we will see, the argument takes its place as one of several reasons that Kant gives for saying that not all of our representations are concepts—that is to say, not all of our representations are ones that it is logically possible to predicate of many. There we will take up the question of the *soundness* of Kant's reason-

---

[5] *Reflexionen Kants zur Kritik der Reinen Vernunft*, ed. Erdmann (Leipzig, 1884), p. 70.

ing, here we are mainly concerned with the *validity* of the Spinozistic core of the reasoning.

The fourteenth proposition tells us that "Besides God, no substance can be granted or conceived." [6] The proposition is exponible and can be treated as a conjunction of two assertions: It tells us that God is a substance and that nothing other than God is a substance. The first assertion is contained directly within the definition of God (subject to a certain qualification about the implied existence of God that need not delay us). The critical steps in the argument come with the establishment of the second exponent. In order to bring to a clearer view the logical form of this exponent, we must decide whether "is other than God" should be understood as "is not identical to God", where "God" will appear as a singular term. Or whether "is other than God" means "is not identical to something which is the one and only thing which is a god", where "God" does not appear as a singular term—or does not appear as an uneliminable singular term. For reasons which will become apparent in the second part of the discussion, when we turn to the analysis of transcendental elements, the conclusion cannot be interpreted in the first and more natural way. However, it is important to notice that someone who has seen that the critical steps in the argument are valid on one interpretation of the form of the conclusion can easily convince himself that a Spinozistic deduction is valid on the other interpretation. The necessary modifications are trivial and will not affect anything in the first part of the analysis. Since that is so and since the first formulation is neater and less cumbersome, we can formulate the conclusion of Spinoza's deduction as follows:

6. For anything, x, if x is not identical to God, then x is not a substance.

The premises of Spinoza's argument are his definition of the concept of God and his fifth proposition, which affirms that if two substances differ then they differ in their attributes. However, the fifth proposition by itself rests upon that corollary of the principle of sufficient reason which we have already encountered in Chapter One. This latter is our familiar assumption of the identity of indiscernibles:

7. For any things, x and y, if x is not identical to y, then there is a z such that x is z and y is not z.

The definition of God tells us that something is God just in case it is not only a substance, but has all those properties which are essential to sub-

---

[6] *The Chief Works of Benedict de Spinoza*, trans. Elwes (New York, 1951), Vol. II, p. 54.

stance.[7] For the purposes of analyzing Kant's argument, we take this definition as asserting the following:

8. x is identical to God just in case x is a substance and for every y if x is y, then every z is such that if z is a substance then z is (necessarily) also y.

What we wish to show in the first part of the analysis is that (7) and (8) do validly yield (6). We can do this by showing that the conjunction of the first two is not consistent with the denial of the third: Thus, from the denial of (6) we can conclude that some arbitrary individual, which we will call "A" is a substance and so is not identical to God. We know that God is God, so we are able to deduce from (8) that God is a substance and that for any y, if God is y, then every z is such that if z is a substance then z is y. We know from the denial of (6) that z is not identical to God and hence, by (7), we know that there is a z such that God is z and A is not z. We arbitrarily call this "B" and thus God is B but A is not B. Knowing that God is B and using our inference from (8), we can say that every substance is B. Since we have assumed that A is a substance, it follows that A is B. But we have just shown that A is not B. Thus, from the denial of (6) and the conjunction of (7) and (8) we have derived a contradiction. It follows that the deduction of (6) from (7) and (8) is valid. This result completes the first and the easier stage of our analysis.

Evidently Spinoza had good reasons for his conclusion within the *Ethics*, but now we must look beyond that system and those reasons to the transcendental grounds for his reasons. I have already remarked in Chapter One that the principle of the identity of indiscernibles is subject to a transcendental critique, and in the next chapter that criticism will be advanced. For the moment it is the Spinozistic concept of God that should hold our attention. It is quite clearly a concept that has its own special logic, and yet Kant several times noted that our representations of space and time have a similarity to our concept of God. In any event, a transcendental inquiry—one which concerns itself "not so much with the objects of knowledge as with our mode of knowledge of those objects"—would have to concern itself with the question of whether there is any possible justification for a concept such as that which Spinoza introduces through his definition of God. The second stage of the analysis, therefore, will consist in a transcendental deduction of that concept. However, this stage of the analysis is not intended to increase in

---

[7] What I give here is a definition of God based upon His possession of a unitary essence (*Einigheit*—Baumgarten). As I indicate in Chapter Five, section 3, I believe this concept corresponds to one of two closely connected concepts of the positive infinite in early modern philosophy. Of course, if the second stage of my argument in the present chapter is sound, Spinoza was logically committed to such a concept in any event.

any measure the plausibility of Spinoza's conclusions. The argument of this stage does not even appear within Spinoza's system; instead, it is part of a transcendental critique of that system. The purpose of the inquiry is to exhibit the bearing which his methodological commitments have on the shape of his metaphysics. This purpose will be achieved if we can produce a logically valid deduction from those commitments to the following conclusion: If any concept whatsoever is a concept of a substance, then the concept of substance which is introduced through (8) is a valid concept of a substance.

The first step in this stage of the analysis is to collect those methodological assumptions from which such a conclusion might be deduced. We already realize that from the point of view of Kant's intended logical inversion of the argument one prominent candidate to be considered is the principle that:

9. All of our representations are concepts.

We know that by concepts we are to understand representations or terms that it is logically possible to predicate of many. These are representations of a type that can fill the predicate position in different possible judgments. By contrast, singular terms or intuitions (as Kant understands them, not as Descartes understood them) cannot by themselves fill the predicate position, though perhaps they may enter the predicates in various ways. Kant's strategy of inversion in the aesthetic will consist in the proof that, since our representations of space and time have the same logical characteristic as that which makes Spinoza's argument concerning God valid, these representations cannot possibly be predicated of many. Hence they are not concepts and (9) must be false.

Despite the simplicity of Kant's argument once we realize that certain terms like "God", "the world", "space" and "time" have this special logical status, the contrary assumption that all representations are concepts is deeply engrained in rationalist modes of thought. For example, the principle of analytic predication, (3), only makes sense if we tacitly agree to confine it to what can be picked out in general terms. If having a distinct idea of Plato involves having a clear idea of Socrates, still, we cannot truly affirm Socrates of Plato. (The point, of course, is not that the result would be false, but that it is a formulation that makes no sense. I should acknowledge, therefore, that there are logical theories, such as that of Lesniewski, which permit a use of "is" for which the formulation of (3) will make sense in any case. Such a logic is probably better suited to the analysis of rationalist arguments than the standard, modern logics. In such a formulation of (3), the point will be that sometimes the "is" expresses predication but where a singular term is substituted for "y" it must be interpreted in a different way.)

The principle of analytic predication has another interesting consequence. It necessitates a slight revision in the traditional and most basic concept of substance. The most basic sense of substance is the sense in which, as Aristotle says, each philosopher always has asked and will continue to ask, "What is substance?" Even though that basic concept of substance lacks the complexity and the subtlety of Aristotle's own concept of substance and of other special ideas of what substance is, there has always been a technical problem associated with definitions of the basic concept of substance. A brief reference to that technical difficulty will establish the context for Spinoza's modest revision of the traditional formula. Traditionally, the analysis or definition of any concept is supposed to set out the concepts which are contained in the given concept as the concepts which furnish its defining conditions. The technical difficulty is, of course, that concepts such as that of substance are our categories; they are the most general concepts to be found in our classificatory system. Hence, they have no proper internal complexity. Of course, from a logical point of view no concept is entirely without complexity in its parts, but the point about the category is that there is no concept contained within it which is of any use in defining it. The concepts that are contained within the categories as partial concepts are the so-called "transcendentals", which are terms that apply interchangeably to absolutely every thing, and which therefore do not categorize the thing in question. The solution to this technical problem is easy to see. If there is no useful internal complexity to be discovered, we must define by an extrinsic complexity. There are two traditional ways in which that has been done in the case of substance. One solution is based upon a characteristic relation that things in that category have to things in other categories. This first solution is the one that Aristotle adopts when he defines a substance as that which other things can belong to but which cannot itself belong *de facto* to anything else. The other solution is the one that interests us, because it anticipates the transcendental turn taken by Kant. (Kant was well aware of the precedent. He noted that Aristotle's doctrine of the categories is derived from Greek grammar.) The second solution is to consider the external complexity that a thing has by virtue of its relation to our possible representation of it. Conceived in this way, substances are those things whose representations are "subject always, never predicate". But we have just seen that in a framework which includes the principle of analytic predication there are no such representations to be found. Every concept follows from itself and therefore every concept can be predicated of itself. There are no representations whose only legitimate and possible employment is to pick out those ultimate objects of metaphysical reflection and whose lawful employment will not allow them to serve as predicates in judgments. However, it is not difficult to allow for this point within the general context of a transcendental analysis of the concept of substance:

10. Something is a substance if its concept does not follow from the concept of any other thing.

The important point to observe, following out the lines of the second solution, is that this definition is oblique and transcendental—in Kant's sense. It informs us about what it is like to have a possible representation of something that is a substance. The defining condition is the condition which any representation must satisfy in order to be a concept of some substance.

We are in the process of accumulating assumptions which will show that if any concept meets the condition which has just been set out then there must be a concept of a substance such as that which was introduced in (8). The next assumption to be mentioned simply makes explicit the foregoing point about definitions.

11. Any concept which appears as one of the set of defining conditions defining a given concept follows from that concept.

The essential point to notice is that the analysis of concepts is assumed to result in what is called a "definition by abstraction". In this context we will mean by "definable concept" a concept which can be introduced through expressions of the form "Something is . . . if and only if it is   ," or of the form "By" . . . "we mean that which is   ."

A second point to notice about these definitions by abstraction is that each condition may itself be complex and may itself involve relational predicates. This observation should be held in mind as we are weighing the significance of Spinoza's conclusion as the "true consequence of dogmatizing metaphysics." Some observers have held that the determining characteristic of the rationalists's logic is the systematic exclusion of relational predicates. The writings of Bertrand Russell conferred a unique prestige on that opinion, but the characteristic in question apparently has no significance in the matters now under discussion.

A third point and one in the neighborhood of the second is that the traditional forms of definition by abstraction are to be distinguished from the more specialized forms that are called "abstractive definitions". The usual modern view is that this form of definition which has a prominent role to play in Russell's own work on the foundations of mathematics derives ultimately from Leibniz.[8] We have reason to be interested in his employment

---

[8] Hans Reichenbach, "Die Bewegungslehre bei Newton, Leibniz und Huyghens," *Kantstudien* 29, 1934, p. 424. Cited in Reichenbach, *The Elements of Symbolic Logic* (New York, 1947), p. 210.

of abstractive definitions because they appear in his treatment of our spatial and temporal representations and because these are the representations with which Kant's inversion of our present argument will be concerned. Kant's objections to the Leibnizian treatment are not affected by the inclusion or the exclusion of these forms of analysis. These novel forms of definition specify a property (e.g., redness) as something that can be abstracted from a type of relationship that is known as an "equivalence-relationship" (e.g., red-similarity). It is also a fact that Leibniz's exploration of this form of analysis is one of the pieces of evidence that Serres has used in constructing a picture of Leibniz which is absolutely unlike Russell's. If we are to believe Serres, Leibniz had a highly developed and very modern appreciation of the logic of relationships and of structural properties.[9]

With the trivial assumption that our conceptual framework contains at least two basic concepts—which as basic will be logically independent, we can add a corollary to the preceding assumptions:

12. Any concept of a substance is definable.

For assume that A is the concept of a substance and that it is not definable. In this case, we select a second concept, B, which is also primitive and which therefore does not follow from A. The conjunction of A and B will define a concept which is other than A but from which A will follow (by (11)). Hence (by (10)) A is not the concept of a substance. It follows that the denial of our assumption must be true. Even though the deduction of this result is trivial, the result itself has had a fatal attraction for thinkers from Spinoza to Hegel and beyond. (Hegel returns to the Spinozistic standpoint by an argument at the outset of his first major work, which purports to show that our representations of space and time are universal and abstract representations.) If we introduce the metaphysical concept of substance by an analysis that links it to the transcendental possibilities in the representation of a subject matter of representations and if we agree that all representations are concepts, the Spinozistic consequences will be difficult to avoid. We can if we like throw everything into the predicate and leave Nature, or the World, or Space-Time, or God as the only ultimate subject matter. Indeed, if the following argument is sound, we have no choice but to follow Spinoza.

We wish to establish that from the assumptions that have been enumerated this must be true:

13. If there is a concept of a substance, then there must be a concept of substance whose defining conditions are satisfied by every concept of a substance.

[9] Serres, *op. cit.*

In order to establish (13), we assume that C is the concept of a substance. Then we will show that the following is contradictory on that assumption: *Every concept of a substance is such that there is a set of conditions defining it which some concept of a substance does not satisfy.* We know there is a set of conditions, C', which define C. By the assumption we seek to refute, there is a concept of a substance, D, which does not satisfy C'. There must be a set of conditions, D', which define D. Now either every condition in D' is a condition in C' or this is not the case. The former is impossible because D, by hypothesis, does not satisfy C', and hence, there is some condition in D' that is not in C'. The conjunction of that condition with C' will define a concept, E. C will follow from E and hence C cannot be a concept of a substance (by (10)). But the assumption is that C is the concept of a substance. From this contradiction, we conclude that if something is the concept of a substance, then there must be a concept of a substance whose defining condition is satisfied by every concept of a substance. This remarkable concept is what Spinoza introduces as our concept of God. When we have passed from the transcendental conclusion that has just been established to the corresponding definition within his system of rationalist metaphysics we have the first premise of the argument that shows that there is no substance other than God.

Enough has been said to convey our main point. The methodological commitments of the rationalists are not innocuous and they have significant consequences within the *Ethics*. We can compare the situation to what would result if a contemporary metaphysician were to be stung by accusations that his reasonings are sloppy and inexact and were to limit himself to those consequences of his metaphysical assumptions that he can establish within the logical system that Quine has provided in *Mathematical Logic*. Since our metaphysician is a fiction, we will suppose that he conforms to the conventions for this fiction. Accordingly, we must imagine him to be a person who arrives at odd and unusual conclusions about a variety of topics. But in this particular case the oddity of some of those conclusions would reflect an oddity of the logical base rather than the peculiarity of his metaphysical visions. The argument of the next chapter will show that the foregoing comparison to the situation of Spinoza is intended as a serious comparison. Quine introduces the concept of identity into his logic in such a way that individuals are eliminated from his domain of objects. The results frame an instructive comparison to a corresponding feature of rationalist logic.

The great metaphysical significance of Spinoza's argument is that it offers a dramatic solution to the historic controversy about the one and the many. This is a problem that, as Aristotle says, "has been, is and will ever continue to be" the primary concern of metaphysicians. Now the discussion of Spinoza's argument would not be complete without calling attention to an analysis by one of our great contemporary logicians—an analysis that suggests that Spinoza's argument has been known to the tradition since Plato and that it may well have been in Aristotle's mind as he wrote that observation. The analysis by Lesniewski deals with the Platonic doctrine of the "ideal particular". The ideal particular is something that has only every property that is common to all particulars of a given form. What Lesniewski showed is that if the Platonic form is to be an ideal particular then there can be only one thing which has the property which participation in the form is supposed to account for.[10]

This result need not be construed as a reduction to absurdity of the doctrine of forms as ideal particulars. It can be interpreted as showing that the relation of participation is not contained in the relation of diversity. On this hypothesis it is conceivable that Plato's own "Third Man Argument" was intended to show that there is a difficulty in that premise of the argument which asserts that the sensible bed, for example, is not identical to the form Bed—more generally, the premise that there can be many different things which each participate in something that makes each of the different things be what it is. The form Bed can account for what a sensible bed is, or for why it is one thing, namely a bed, which is different from other things which are not beds. But something which is other than the form Bed is necessary to account for what Kant calls the "sensible manifold" or the empirically observed diversity of beds. That which explains why a bed is one thing rather than many things cannot also explain why many things are beds.

When Kant deals with the problem of the many and the one within the context of his transcendental inquiry, he assigns a critical role to the forms of intuition. This leads him to the conclusion that in dealing with the problem it is necessary to mark certain terminological distinctions. If we say that things are many or are manifold (as in, "The appearances of beds are manifold"), we do not mean what we mean when we say that things are different or are not identical (as in "A bed is different from a chair.") Similarly, the unity of an object is not to be confused with the identity of an object. We can illustrate these terminological conventions by considering how they might apply to Plato's non-identity premise in the Third Man Argument—understanding that the main purpose is not to interpret Plato but to illustrate Kant's terminology. We cannot mean that the sensible bed and the form Bed are

[10] The details of this argument will be found in Eugene Luschei, *The Logical Systems of Lesniewski* (Amsterdam, 1962), p. 308-309.

many, or constitute parts of a manifold, because the condition under which things are many is that they can be differently referred to or differently appealed to as evidence in support of some conception or judgment. This condition is that the objects have a different location in space or time. Hence, the form and the sensible particular are not a "many" in this sense—the form does not have a location and its representation conforms only to the conditions for representing things *per se*. We orient ourselves in respect to it by pure thought, rather than by determining where and when it is in its extrinsic relations or relations to other things. On the other hand, we cannot mean that the sensible bed and the form Bed are not identical, because the condition under which things are not identical is that they can be differently conceived— the form has no property that makes it different from the things that participate in it.

The availability of the terminological distinction between unity and identity depends in the transcendental context on a prior distinction between different possibilities of representation in intuitions and concepts. The condition of the possibility of a conceptual representation is such that each representation must be capable of being referred to a many. The condition of the possibility of an intuitive representation is that each representation refers to something that can be uniquely located. On Kant's view, where the possibility of a many is determined by the possibility of our intuitive representations of the many, the character of the manifold is determined in part by our way of achieving references to things. As Kant's Copernican analogy has it, the motions of the observer or, more generally, things that are happening to the observer, are one of the determinants of the succession of appearances in the sensible beds. But on the contrary view and if each representation were a concept, then the manifold to which each representation is to be applied would necessarily be a manifold that is given independently of our capacity to represent it or to appeal to it for evidence. In this case the objects that are represented would be like the Platonic perfect particulars. But if Spinoza's argument is sound, then such representations cannot be concepts because a concept must be capable of being referred to a manifold. Our subsequent development of this line of argument will give further illustration of the ways in which Kant accepted "Spinoza's great logic" and, in accepting it, assimilated it.[11]

---

[11] "Another thing this episode makes clear is that Spinoza's great logic was appreciated only the other day in Kingston, . . ." Wallace Stevens in a letter to Harvey Breit in *Letters* (New York, 1966).

CHAPTER THREE

GENESIS OF A THEORY OF REFERENCE

Kant's discussion of the elements of knowledge in the first *Critique* divides into two parts, a transcendental aesthetic and a transcendental logic. The basis for this division is to be found in his distinction between intuitions and concepts. Of course, Kant does not simply assume and assert that the latter distinction is indispensable for any transcendental inquiry into the possibility of *a priori* knowledge. One of his central objectives in the aesthetic is to prove it against a contrary opinion. This involves proving that our representations of space and time are *a priori* rather than empirical, and that they are intuitions rather than concepts. In the present chapter I will be concerned with the nature of these conclusions and with their historical genesis in the rationalist doctrines of Kant's youth. In Chapter Five I will present and elaborate the arguments with which Kant supports those conclusions in the aesthetic.

One reason for the importance of what is undertaken in this chapter is that Kant never gave a satisfactory public accounting of the character and the motivation of his conclusions in the aesthetic. When he composed the *Critique* he made a deliberate and wholly conscious decision to suppress that kind of information. He did so in the desire to present his position in a proper and "scientific" manner. Kant realized that a work written in the method of the *Critique* makes very few concessions to the reader and he calls attention to the fact that he eliminated examples that would have been a particular aid to the reader. What comes first in the work is always only what is necessary for a proof of the conclusions. In the terminology of his period, his method of presentation is "synthetic" rather than "analytic". This terminology—which should not be confused with Kant's own terminology for classifying cognitions—reflects a long-standing tradition and can still be discerned as a relevant distinction in the way scientific works are constructed. Sometimes, when one reads—let us say—a work on thermodynamics the presentation strives for rigor and for deductive accuracy and completeness. Another work on the same subject may concentrate more on the motivation for the proofs and may strive to explain at every turn what goes on, and why the science has taken the turn in its construction that it has. The *Critique* is the first type of work—by the conscious choice of its author. There is only one exception to this observation about the work. One section of the *Critique* employs a "middle way" between the analytic and the synthetic methods in order to make known in advance the particular content of certain conclusions which are to be established by the synthetic method. The employment of such a middle way had been discussed before Kant and under the same description that he uses—"the discovery of the clue".[1] With this single exception the writing in the *Critique* is uncompromising in its quest for rigor.

Kant was aware that a satisfactory introduction to his critical philosophy will employ an analytic method of presentation in which that which is presented first is not that which is required for the proofs in the science but rather is that which is required for a comprehension and acceptance of the conclusions. After Kant had presented his first *Critique*, he supplied such an introduction in his *Prolegomena to Any Future Metaphysics*. The work has two shortcomings as an account of the transcendental aesthetic. In the first place the *Prolegomena* was evidently conceived more as an introduction to the findings of his transcendental logic than to the conclusions of the *Dissertation* and of the aesthetic. The motivation for the *Critique* is personified in the *Prolegomena* more by Hume than by Leibniz or Wolff, and yet we know that Kant was largely unmoved by Hume at the time that he reached his conclusions in the *Dissertation*. We could of course judge, as Kemp Smith did, that when the results of the *Dissertation* are taken into the first *Critique* the central doctrines of the aesthetic, and, notably, the doctrine of pure *a priori* intuitions become "uncritical" in character. But that solution only removes our difficulty from the *Prolegomena* to the *Critique* itself. The second shortcoming of the *Prolegomena* reflects the fact that in an analytic presentation in which one begins from that which is best known to the reader or to the inquirer the historical context for the presentation can alter the value of the presentation. For Kant's German readers Hume was the exotic and very largely unknown figure whose presence and importance needed to be established in order to account for the motivation of the *Critique*. For our contemporary British and American readers the exotic and very largely unknown figures are the men who fashioned the outlook and the terminology of German scholasticism of the eighteenth century. The serious student of Kant's

---

[1] Johann Lambert, *Neues Organon* (Leipzig, 1764), Vol. I, p. 218; cf. also *Philosophische Schriften* (Hildesheim, 1967), VI, p. 418.

transcendental aesthetic will desire as much information as he can gain about these individuals and their views. As we will discover from our survey of the historical genesis of Kant's theory of the forms of intuition, their tradition, their outlook and their terminology were things that Kant took for granted.

I. SENSIBILITY AND UNDERSTANDING

We have found that a transcendental critique concerns itself with the possibility of knowledge and that the particular kind of knowledge with which it is concerned is objective and scientific. Such knowledge is said to be possible only for a being who is capable of attaining an understanding of what is the case. Now the English phrase "I understand" can be uttered with several different intonations and can thereby communicate several different things. First, if someone is attempting to explain some difficult or technical matter to me, and if I nod and murmur "I understand," I may mean to signify no more than that I have been following his exposition and have managed to mark out and grasp some of the appropriate distinctions. But secondly, if I utter the words in a more emphatic manner, and if I accompany my words with an impatient frown, I may mean to signify that I already have knowledge of that which he is attempting to explain to me. The first *Critique*, the lectures on anthropology, and other materials show that Kant uses a term for understanding that has two senses and that these senses correspond rather closely to those two uses of the English phrase. In the first and the weaker sense the faculty of the understanding is what allows us to grasp or to conceive the differences between things. The understanding—in this first sense—is simply the faculty of concepts. In the second and the stronger sense the understanding is our complete faculty of knowledge; this is a stronger sense because, as we will see, the faculty of knowledge for Kant includes more than a faculty of concepts.

In both explanations of the understanding the concept of a faculty enters in a crucial way. The verbal explanation of what a faculty is is of course easy to provide: Our faculty of understanding as a faculty of knowledge is whatever empowers us to have knowledge or is whatever about us that makes possible our possession of knowledge. However, there is considerable room for controversy about the nature of the doctrine that this verbal explanation conceals. Kant's commentators are divided into two broad groups. Some regard an inquiry into the faculty of knowledge as something that belongs to rational psychology or the metaphysics of the self, and to empirical psychology. Others regard it as something that belongs more properly to a critical philosophy or a discipline that is concerned with our cognitive rights rather than with the facts of cognition. One basic aspect of the issue at dispute is whether one regards the possession of knowledge as one regards the possession of a body and the possession of a tan, or whether one regards the possession of knowledge as one regards the possession of citizenship and the possession of a new automobile. That is, the possession of knowledge is either a matter of fact—as we say that the purple colour belongs *de facto* to Her Majesty's cloak; or the possession of knowledge is a matter of law or right—as we might say that the purple color belongs *de jure* to Her Majesty, even though the queen does not happen in fact to be purple. The same basic issue spills over into our discussion of the possessor of the knowledge. There we have the corresponding distinction between the being and identity of a metaphysical self or an empirical self and the being and identity of something like the forensic person. Thirdly, there is a corresponding distinction between the metaphysical or psychological association of different representations and the lawful or logical association of ideas. And, finally, a whole set of such contrasting distinctions applies to any discussion of the acquisition of knowledge. That is, we can acquire knowledge as we acquire properties, but in the two very different senses of property in which the property is either mine *de facto* or mine *de jure*. In sum, we can say that the discussion of a faculty is the discussion of what is mine and of how it comes to be mine, but having said that, we merely prepare the stage for a debate over what it means to say—in the relevant sense—that something *is* mine.

There is no room for disagreement about the fact that Kant divides the faculty of the understanding into two subordinate faculties, called the sensibility and the understanding. The historical genesis of his theory of the forms of intuition is reflected in this double employment of the term "understanding". In the weaker sense, the faculty of the understanding is whatever empowers us to grasp the differences between things. Since the German word for a difference is, as Kant tells us, a synonym for the word for property (in the *de facto* and metaphysical sense of *property* rather than the *de jure* sense) and since concepts (by a very long tradition) are those representations through which we grasp things or recognize them for what they are, it follows that the faculty of understanding in the weaker sense can be identified as the faculty of concepts. This is one of Kant's ways of defining it. The faculty of sensibility is the other subordinate faculty in the faculty of knowledge. According to one of Kant's definitions of the sensibility it delivers a type of representation through which judgments refer or appeal to one particular object. These representations are called *intuitions* by Kant.

Kant summarizes these matters in his *Logic* when he speaks of the "logical distinction between sensibility and understanding, according to which the latter gives only intuitions, the former only concepts."[2] He goes on to say that, "Both faculties may certainly be considered in another aspect also, and defined in a different manner; namely, the sensibility as the faculty of *receptivity*, the understanding as a faculty of *spontaneity*. But this mode of definition is not logical but *metaphysical*." Each of these two ways of dividing the sensibility from the understanding contains an invitation to misunderstanding, but each of them reflects important truths about the nature of intuitions and of concepts.

The language of the first division might suggest to some that the Kantian distinction between intuitions and concepts was motivated by discoveries that Kant had made in formal logic or by discoveries that Kant at any rate thought he had made. Several things show us that this is not the case. First, there is the fact that when Kant presents us with his list of the forms of judgment he mentions certain ways in which his list differs from that of formal logicians. The latter are justified in their practice of assimilating singular judgments— ones in which there is a reference to particular things—to universal judgments; but, Kant says, the transcendental logician must keep the two forms of judgment distinct. Also there is the fact that Kant confines the subject matter of logic to a consideration of the logical possibility of concepts and does so on the ground that logic is concerned with our possibility of cognition through concepts alone. For example in the *Logic* he writes, ". . . in logic we can only be speaking solely of the logical essence of things. And we can easily have insight into this. It merely requires knowledge of the predicates with respect to which an object is determined through its concept; . . ."[3] Elsewhere he writes in a similar vein, "There are certain propositions which belong in logic but which *through the ambiguity in their expression* are smuggled into metaphysics as belonging to it, and which therefore get taken for synthetic although they are in reality analytic. Among such propositions is the following: The essences of things are immutable. That is, one can change nothing which belongs essentially to its concept without at the same time destroying the force of this concept."[4] These and similar passages make use of a vocabulary in which logical possibilities, logical essences, logical objects, and even logical existence are contrasted with real possibilities, real essences, and so on.[5] However the usefulness of this array of terms comes when we wish to contrast the domain of logical principles with the domain of metaphysics.

---

[2] *Introduction to Logic*, trans. Abbott (London, 1885), p. 26–27.
[3] *Gesammelte Schriften*, IX, p. 61.
[4] *Ibid.*, VIII, p. 236.
[5] *Vorlesungen über die Metaphysik* (Erfurt, 1821), p. 281; *Gesammelte Schriften*, XVII, p. 500, p. 522; XVIII, pp. 102–3.

Where we are merely concerned to demarcate the area of formal logic as Kantians conceive it, we can do so without invoking these unfamiliar notions.

The ultimate and final concern of formal logicians is with the deductive relationships between propositions and with those aspects of propositions that make a difference in their deductive-relationships. If we include the formal or logical principles for the definition of terms among the principles of formal logic, and if we construe differences in meaning as corresponding to possible differences in the entailment relationships between propositions, then we can say that the formal logician is concerned with all those differences between propositions which reflect differences in meaning—to the extent, at least, that those differences in meaning affect the entailment-relationships between propositions. Since the basic differences in meaning are conveyed by the predicates in propositions, we might carry the logical analysis of deductions a step beyond propositions and say that the basic elements whose relationships are studied in formal logic are the terms which convey meaning in propositions. Kant undoubtedly expresses a sense of this possibility when he says—as he does on several occasions—that it comes to virtually the same thing whether we define the understanding as the faculty judgments or whether, having defined concepts as predicates in logically possible judgments, we define the faculty as the faculty of concepts.[6] Kant's explanation of why there is no important difference in the two definitions repeats—in his own terminology—what has just been said about the subject matter of formal logic. Kant tells us that the results of both definitions are the same because in either case the understanding is being explained as a faculty of rules. Now a rule, taken most generally, is something that prescribes conduct or behavior, and conduct includes a large number of different things. However it is clear that the conduct which Kant principally must have in mind here is the conduct of thought—that is, when he speaks of rules here he has in mind the same sort of conduct that he has in mind in those other passages in which he tells us that formal logic teaches us about how we ought to think, not how we do think. The rules which the understanding supplies to us as the faculty of concepts or of judgments are the rules that determine how we are entitled to think or how we are to be permitted to think about some subject matter. Since, as we have just seen, the things that determine the (logically permissible) course of a deduction can be viewed indifferently as propositions having an internal complexity or form and as the elements of the proposition that constitute its distinctive form, either concepts or propositions can be regarded as the rules to which the principles of logic apply. The important point to

---

[6] *Vorlesungen über die Metaphysik*, p. 157; cf. also *Gesammelte Schriften*, XVI, p. 40.

notice in all of this is Kant's judgment about what logic can ignore and can abstract from in its treatment of propositions. Logic abstracts from differences in reference as such. That is to say, if it were possible for us to imagine a case of two propositions that differed in what each referred to but where that difference could never possibly be reflected in any difference of a predicative kind between the two propositions, the formal logician could safely ignore such a hypothetical difference since the hypothesis of such a difference could not affect his judgment about the validity of any deduction. If we extend the area of concern of formal logic to a certain type of modal logic that deals with differences between logical and real possibilities that are similar to those explored in Kant's transcendental logic, the point would need qualification. Later I will supply that necessary qualification, but the main picture in logic shows that Kant is right in his opinion: Formal logic does not know and does not need to recognize his distinction between concepts and intuitions, or between that which gives propositions their meaning and that which gives propositions their referential content.

Since the point in question has an important bearing on the way in which Kant chooses to organize the arguments of his *Critique*—putting some in an aesthetic and some in a transcendental logic, the matter is worth reviewing on its merits. In the last chapter I made reference to a modern system of formal logic that has several instructive things to teach us. Quine's *Mathematical Logic* shows that in the development of a deductive system which is adequate to handle the most complicated reasonings of mathematicians a special category of singular terms is a luxury rather than a necessity. Quine demonstrates this feature of his system by the unusual form which he gives for his definition of identity. He makes the identity of any two things, x and y, consist in the fact that anything is an x just in the case that it is a y. Since the definition is presented in such a form that it applies regardless of the type of (non-logical) term that replaces "x" and "y", it holds in the case in which these are replaced by representations of particular individuals. This is true despite the fact that the syntax of the defining propositions would seem to demand that everything replacing "x" be a class-term. An obvious point about classes is that their being, and hence their conditions of identity, consists in the being or the non-being of something else—namely, of the members of the class, if any. The point which corresponds to this, as a point about class-terms is that they fill predicate positions and thereby represent things only indirectly and by means of other terms through which they can be predicated. Intuitions, as Kant conceives them, are not *just* singular terms—there is a story to be told about intuitions that relates to the forms of intuition and which may or may not be a story to be told about every singular term. But intuitions *are* singular terms: They are representations through which other representations can be referred to their objects, and they are not representations which by themselves can fill the predicate position. Now in Quine's system there are no such terms and, as a result, the corresponding "proper" individuals or non-classes are viewed as things that can be dispensed with entirely. As Quine points out, "What was regarded as a non-class becomes reconstrued as a special sort of class, viz., a class having itself as sole member. If we think of the matter in this way, we must of course abandon the term 'non-class' in favor of a more neutral designation—say 'individual'. Everything comes now to be thought of as a class, but individuals are distinguished from other classes by the peculiar circumstance of being their sole members."[7]

Having set out this peculiar circumstance for us, Quine goes on to make the significant and, for our purposes, interesting assertion that, "From a formal standpoint, actually, there is no need of assuming that there is any such x [any individual] at all." This belief of Quine's is reflected in Kant's distinction between the aesthetic and the logic. Is the belief sound? Undoubtedly, the first and best evidence on the issue must come from those who are competent to speak about systems of formal logic. The weight of informed opinion seems to favor Quine's position and a number of distinguished logicians, like Church and Fraenkel, have echoed his judgment.[8] Hao Wang illustrates this consensus when he tells us that "so far as mathematics and mathematical logic is concerned, it is possible to get along without non-classes."[9] At the appropriate points in our later discussion we will see how Kantian ideas from the aesthetic can be applied in ways that disturb this orthodoxy, not only in regard to mathematics but also in regard to mathematical logic; but we must recognize the fact that many formal logicians are willing to dispense with individuals altogether. Another point worth considering is that Quine's system is not as radical in the treatment of individuals as it might appear to be. It only makes explicit a feature shared by other, more ordinary, systems of logic—including both type-theories and set-theories. The system of formal logic in *Principia Mathematica*, for example, has a category of terms which are not terms of predication because they are terms of a lowest type. But it has many times been remarked that nothing affecting the validity of any argument that can be analyzed in this system would be altered if we interpret those terms as standing for properties or classes rather than for individuals. If

[7] W.V.O. Quine, *Mathematical Logic* (Cambridge, 1957), p. 135.
[8] A. Fraenkel, *Abstract Set Theory* (Amsterdam, 1953), p. 16. A. Church, *Journal of Symbolic Logic*, IV, p. 176.
[9] Hao Wang, *Journal of Symbolic Logic*, XV, p. 109.

Kant's doctrine of the forms of intuition is sound then we can expect many paradoxes when such a system is applied to the analysis of synthetic knowledge or to the analysis of the forms of judgments that enter as premises and conclusions in synthetic reasoning. The fact that these systems of deductive logic have this feature can be expected, for example, to lead to apparent paradoxes of inductive reasoning. But it remains a fact that the systems do have this feature and that formal logicians are generally easy in their own minds about the tenuous status of non-classes in their type-theoretic systems. The history of set-theory in the present century suggests a similar point of view there. Fraenkel and Bar-Hillel call our attention to the fact that Zermelo's first formulation of his theory of sets was intended to include a category of terms that stand for individuals. That is, he wished us to regard two of these terms as equivalent and inter-substitutive only on the condition that the terms denote or refer to the same things.[10] In Kant's special terminology, this condition amounted to a restriction on reference rather than a categoreal limitation and, as such, it has no effect on the deductive power of the system or its putative freedom from contradiction. At any rate, most later formulations of set theory have not preserved this feature of Zermelo's original system. One noteworthy exception is the system presented by Bourbaki.[11] Kant's distinction between the aspects of a mathematical proposition through which it appeals to the evidence in its own branch of mathematics and the aspects of a mathematical proposition through which it achieves a deductive unification with other propositions is reflected in the philosophy of this group of mathematicians, and has caused individual members of the Bourbaki group to polemicize against the view that the subject matter of set theory provides a foundational branch of mathematics to which everything else can be reduced. Thus, for example, though there may be correspondences between the structures studied in geometry and in some other branch of mathematics and though these correspondences are reflected in the fact that the establishment of a result in geometry may involve a reference to the way in which the parallel result was deduced within its own domain, still there can be no talk of a reduction of the geometrical theorem to the principles of the other branch. The notion of a geometrical proof—as contrasted with the notion of a geometrical deduction—involves the idea of an appeal to evidence that is specifically geometrical. These polemics have a Kantian edge and they appeal to distinctions in the analysis of mathematical knowledge which are not

---

[10] A. Fraenkel and Y. Bar-Hillel, *Foundations of Set Theory* (Amsterdam, 1958), p. 29ff.

[11] N. Bourbaki (pseud.), *Journal of Symbolic Logic*, XIV, p. 1ff.

preserved in the ordinary systems for the formalization of mathematical propositions and for the study of their deductive relationships.

Among the various logical systems that share the relevant characteristic of Quine's system the most important example for our purposes is the system of Leibniz. We have seen that Quine's system gets it characteristic from the fact that he employs a principle of extensionality—a principle we can all agree upon as a definition of identity for classes—as a general definition of identity. Now Leibniz accepted a principle of identity of indiscernibles and this is, as Marcus has noted, a principle which has effects on identity which are comparable to the principle of extensionality. If we use either to define identity, we have taken a first step in the direction of what Quine himself calls "innocent abstraction" or the substitution of abstractions such as classes and properties for individuals in our interpretation of the subject matter of propositions. Now it used to be said that Leibniz would have accepted a definition of identity via identity of indiscernibles and, if this were true and if we accept Marcus's claim about the effects of the principle—a claim to which we will return, then the point about Leibniz's system would obviously follow. Recently the serious students of Leibniz have cast doubt on the role of the principle in his understanding of identity, so we cannot argue the point through a direct comparison between his system and Quine's system. What we *do* know about Leibniz's views, however, is that he experimented repeatedly with the reduction of inclusion to identity. Thus, he takes "*A* is identical to *B*" to be equivalent to "*A* is *B* and *B* is *A*" as a step in his analysis of "*A* is *B*".[12] But for the effects in which we are interested it is immaterial which relationship is taken to be primitive. If we define inclusion via identity, then "*A* is identical to *B*" will yield "*A* is a subclass of *B*"—either directly or through the relation of inclusion to containment. This in turn means that Leibniz's logic cannot admit a category of terms that are proper singular terms. *A fortiori* Leibniz's logic does not recognize Kantian intuitions. Kauppi arrives at essentially the same conclusion in her study of Leibniz, though her conclusion is founded on a more profound study of his writings and is supported by a different kind of consideration from the one just adduced.[13]

If we assume that Kantian intuitions are a type of singular term—an assumption that will be argued for in the next chapter—and if we assume further that formal logic does not need to recognize this category of terms in order to establish the validity of any form of deductive inference, we can

---

[12] L. Couturat, *La Logique de Leibniz* (Paris, 1901), p. 345.
[13] R. Kauppi, *Über die Leibnizsche Logik* (Helsinki, 1960).

explain why Kant's doctrine of the elements of knowledge divides the constructive parts of the first *Critique* in the way that it does. The transcendental logic is quite obviously written on the model of the traditional texts in formal logic. It deals with the possibility of concepts, judgments and inferences as these are elements of an *a priori* knowledge. The other main branch of the discussion of the elements of knowledge is transcendental aesthetic—a branch that has no analogue in the traditional logic texts because it deals with terms that do not have any direct role in determining the purely formal conditions for the logical association or combination of concepts. As the contemporary Leibnizians prefer to phrase it, formal logic deals with logical truths or truths that obtain in every possible world. Kant's organization of the *Critique* is itself an indication that he does not dispute that general point of view about logic. When he includes his aesthetic in the *Critique*, he does so on the evident ground that a transcendental inquiry or inquiry into the real possibility of knowledge must deal with the cognitive value of our representations as representations of things in this world. One branch of this inquiry is necessarily devoted to the conditions under which it is possible for concepts and judgments to be referred to things in this world as the things that provide evidence for their representations. This inquiry will reveal to Kant that these conditions—the conditions for the possibility of intuitions of objects—are that the objects can be located in time or in space and time. His arguments in the aesthetic remain to be considered, but the arguments that were analyzed in the last chapter bring us this far: If it is true that the formal logician is not expected to deal with the question of how a Leibnizian monad or a substance whose essential capacity is to represent things can orient itself in the world as a thinking thing—how it is possible that some of its thoughts are referred to one thing as their ground and some of its thoughts are referred to another thing as their ground, it is also true that by taking the logician's doctrine of the elements of inferences as our doctrine of the elements of knowledge we open the door to Spinozism or the view that in the final analysis it is *not* in fact possible for some of our thoughts to be referred to one thing and some of our thoughts to be referred to a different thing. Instead of providing an explanation of how our thoughts can be ordered to different worldly objects, a true philosophical understanding will reveal the paradox that all our thoughts are ordered to one thing, God or Nature, as the one substantial reality. The American logician Peirce expressed essentially the same idea at a later stage in the history of logic in the course of a discussion of the problem of providing criteria to determine what parts of a proposition should be regarded as parts of the predicate as the logician gives his analysis of the proposition. Peirce remarks that from the logical point of view we can, if we like, throw the whole of the non-logical content of each proposition into the predicate of the propositions, leaving the ultimate subject matter of each proposition as the same thing, namely the world.

Kant's transcendental doctrine of elements shows that he is not prepared to accept passively the metaphysical consequences of the formal logician's analysis of knowledge. His dissertation of 1770 already disputes the Spinozistic implication. That work anticipates a central doctrine of the aesthetic when it sets out the presumption that our representation of this world should permit the possibility of a co-ordination of a multiplicity of different substances. If this possibility is excluded by the rationalist's presuppositions about the elements of knowledge, the proper conclusion to draw is not that Spinoza's logic is *per se* defective, but rather that when we are conducting a transcendental inquiry into the possibility of representing things in this world rather than a formal logical inquiry into the possibility of representing things in general (or "things in logically possible worlds") our transcendental logic must be prefaced by a transcendental aesthetic. Our theory of how explanation and understanding are possible must include and presuppose a theory of reference.

The foregoing remarks about the structure of Kant's transcendental inquiry have been premised on the assumption that the first *Critique* is organized around the first of Kant's two ways of distinguishing the sensibility from the understanding. It will be recalled that the first way turns on the distinction between two kinds of representation which differ in their relations to their objects. Kant mentions a second way of distinguishing between sensibility and understanding; this way is metaphysical, he says, and involves the distinction between receptivity and spontaneity. A long line of Kant-scholars in Germany have stressed the importance of this way of viewing our faculty of knowledge.[14] Some have even decided that the ultimate presuppositions on which the arguments of the first *Critique* rest are drawn from a radical metaphysics of the self or a "proto-ontology". One of Martin Heidegger's earlier works was devoted to Kant and to the problem of metaphysics, and the interest in Heidegger's views has undoubtedly done much to popularize the metaphysical interpretation of the *Critique* that had previously been sponsored by Wundt, Heimsoeth and other responsible students of the work. On Heidegger's view the possibility of metaphysics or of the "understanding of being" depends upon the possibility of an understanding of the

---

[14] F. Paulsen, *Kants Verhältnis zur Metaphysik* (Berlin, 1900); M. Wundt, *Kant als Metaphysiker* (Berlin, 1924); H. Heimsoeth, *Studien zur Philosophie Immanuel Kants* (Köln, 1956); and G. Martin, *Kant's Metaphysics and Theory of Science* (Manchester, 1955).

being of the self. He calls our attention to a passage from the *Critique* which says, in part, "there are two stems of human knowledge, namely, *sensibility* and *understanding*, which perhaps spring from a common, but to us unknown, root." (A15) Heidegger comments on the passage as follows: "The fundamental constitution of the essence of man, "rooted" in the transcendental imagination, is the "unknown" of which Kant must have had an intimation when he spoke of the "root unknown to us"; for the unknown is not that of which we know absolutely nothing but that of which the knowledge makes us uneasy."[15] The source of this uneasiness is alleged to be an analysis of the constitution of our human subjectivity which points to a faculty of sensibility as a constitutive part of the essence of reason. "What is to happen to the honorable tradition according to which, in the long history of metaphysics, *ratio* and the *logos* have laid claim to the central role? Can the primacy of logic disappear? Can the architectonic of the laying of the foundation of metaphysics, i.e., its division into transcendental aesthetic and logic, be preserved if the theme of the latter is basically the transcendental imagination?... By his radial interrogation, Kant brought the "possibility" of metaphysics before this abyss. He saw the unknown; he had to draw back."[16]

Heidegger is justified in supposing that his own interpretation of transcendental inquiry makes the organization of the *Critique* an inappropriate vehicle for Kant's ideas. It also raises in an acute way the question of whether Kant can give a non-circular argument to carry him from pure logic with its table of the forms of unity in judgment, via the transcendental investigation of our *a priori* concepts and intuitions, and to the metaphysical first principles of any scientific knowledge. This latter question goes to the issue of the form and the possible validity of Kant's transcendental arguments and thereby goes beyond the issue of the mere organization of his writings on the subject. The transcendental arguments have indeed sometimes been characterized as inherently either circular or question-begging. Kant himself acknowledges that his transcendental deduction will appear to many to offer only one hypothesis among many that could be entertained. That is, he could be construed as taking the metaphysical foundations of empirical science for granted, as offering us an argument to show that these statements are implied by a second group of statements which he labels the "transcendental conditions" of the first group, and as concluding that these transcendental conditions must obtain. Schematically his argument would have the form:

---

[15] M. Heidegger, *Kant and the Problem of Metaphysics*, trans. Churchill (Bloomington, 1962), p. 167.
[16] *Ibid.*, p. 173.

"If A, then B, but B. Therefore, A."[17] This form of argument may be valid, but only as a very weak form of argument establishing no more than that A is a plausible guess under the circumstances described by the minor premise.

It is difficult to know who to credit with the first observation that this is the true form of Kant's arguments, but certainly the idea was present in a work on the transcendental method that was published by Max Scheler near the turn of the century. Scheler's reading of Kant is interesting for a second reason. He raises the issue of the relationship between the transcendental method and the methods of psychologism. If our analysis of the transcendental conditions of empirical knowledge is not to be left entirely unsupported and if our analysis cannot locate the ultimate grounds where Heidegger suggests they are hidden—namely in a radical metaphysics of the self, then perhaps these grounds are furnished by a rational or empirical psychology of the self. Indeed many readers of the *Critique* must have suspected that Kant's ground-plan is dictated by a set of psychological assumptions about our faculty of knowledge—and by a rather crude faculty-psychology at that.

We know that the history of Kant-scholarship has been plagued by the dispute between the two rival interpretations of Kant's basic distinctions and fundamental principles: One view is that they are the descriptive concepts and principles of metaphysics or of empirical psychology. The other view is that they are the evaluative and normative principles of a science of criticism. On the second view, Kant's idea of criticism is similar to the idea of criticism that was prevalent in the law in his day. Criticism in the law is the science that is concerned with establishing the validity of various types of legal instruments—wills, acts of the legislature, and so on—whose validity can be contested and which are therefore subject to probate or proof. Critical principles in a transcendental inquiry can also be compared to principles of formal logic, which, on Kant's view, teach us how we ought to think rather than giving a description of how we do think. Critical principles are similar in that they provide the basis for an evaluation of our rights and responsibilities as cognitive agents. The chief rivals to such an interpretation hold that the basic distinctions and fundamental premises of Kant's discussion in the *Critique* provide either a metaphysical or an empirical description of our nature as cognitive agents. Amidst this clash of authorities—where our reason must decide—Scheler's analysis proposes a very proper and very instructive issue: Which line of interpretation can provide a coherent account of the logical

[17] Max Scheler, *Die Transzendentale und die Psychologische Methode* (Jena, 1900). More recently this line of criticism has been pursued by Ledger Wood in "The Transcendental Method," in *The Heritage of Kant*, ed. D. Bowers and R.W. Bretall (Princeton, 1939).

structure of Kant's argument in the *Critique*? How does it avoid circularity or the begging of questions? Why is it *supposed* to work? What did Kant imagine that he stood to gain by regressing from metaphysics and from the empirical sciences to a consideration of their transcendental conditions? These are legitimate problems, but we have seen that for Heidegger there are no answers to these questions to be found in the *Critique*. Kant's inquiry brought the primacy of logic into question and, though Heidegger does not explicitly say this, we can suppose that for him the organization of the work around the divisions of traditional logic texts is an empty shell. Furthermore, we know that Heidegger's own reflections after the appearance of the work on Kant brought him increasingly to doubt the legitimacy of the type of question we have raised about the logical structure of the *Critique*. By contrast, the tradition which interprets Kant's basic divisions and fundamental premises as normative or evaluative has an answer to these problems which is plausible in itself and which corresponds to views that we know that Kant held about the nature of such principles and about their logical relationships with other principles.

Transcendental inquiry is a sluiceway through which fish can pass down to the rivers of metaphysics and on to the broad seas of empirical science. If the critical interpretation is correct, this sluiceway is an extraordinary contrivance —constructed in such a way that there can be no question about the identity of the fish that enter in the proper direction and constructed, also, in such a way that no fish can make their way back up it to produce exotic spawn in the headwaters of the critical philosophy. The logical principles which permit the passage downstream are clear enough. First, and in general, if we know what ought to be the case, we have the foundation for a valid inference to what can be the case in our conduct. We know that Kant has a profound sense of the general importance of this principle, because we know his anxiety about the possibilities of applying it in a *modus tollens* argument to challenge our statement of obligations. For example, I might argue that if I ought to tell the truth, then it must be possible for me to tell the truth, but, since I am under a psychological compulsion in all my acts and I am not free to tell the truth or not tell the truth, it follows that I do not have an obligation to tell the truth. The pains which Kant took to destroy the minor premise of this argument are notorious. We also know that Kant was prepared to apply the general principle to our conduct as beings who represent things to ourselves: We know that he regards the principles of formal logic as normative and we know that he derives from formal logic conclusions about the logical pos- sibility of representations. The second stage in the argument down was treated in the first chapter, and we noted the ample precedents in eighteenth century mathematics and metaphysics for an argument from the conditions of the possibility of our representations of objects to the conditions of the possibility of the objects of our representations. But how do we respond to Scheler's charges about the circularity or the question-begging character of the arguments in transcendental philosophy?

The fundamental insight which governs Kant's strategy is evidently his realization that the concepts and principles which are to be applied in the review, the criticism and the control of conduct cannot themselves be justified by or undercut by an appeal to descriptive or factual principles—whether they are principles of empirical psychology or principles of a metaphysics of the self. On this reading of the situation, Kant protects himself against a substantial threat to his position when he writes of "the necessity noted in the *Critique* of presenting logic in its purity ... with omission of all material belonging to metaphysics or to psychology." There is no doubt at all that for Kant formal logic is itself a normative and properly critical discipline which has more in common in the character of its principles with the principles of ethics and with the principles of the philosophical foundations of jurisprudence. Since we know also that his transcendental philosophy borrows certain concepts and principles from formal logic, we know that it retains this distinctively critical character in some of its parts—for example, it will have the character of formal logic in the critical foundations that it supplies for the possibility of analytic knowledge *a priori*. The contentious assumption is that it retains that critical spirit in the other parts and, particularly, that it retains that critical spirit in the aesthetic where there is an assumption about the possibility of knowledge which is not shared with formal logic. If we make the assumption that the aesthetic does engage in a criticism of the validity of the representations, then we can conclude from what we know about Kant's views on the peculiar status and dignity of normative principles, that his results are immune from revision on the basis of any empirical claim or discovery.

The basic norms of personal conduct and the principles that determine our rights and responsibilities cannot have an empirical support or refutation. The possibility of appealing to experience to discredit Kant's first principles is blocked by his analysis of the concept of a critical principle. Any such principle is something that it must be possible to apply to the criticism and the control of what is actually observed to occur in conduct. If these critical principles were conceived to have the status of empirically descriptive principles, then they would be shaped, determined or selected on the basis of what experience teaches us about our own conduct or that of others. But in this case the principle loses its peculiar dignity and status and comes instead to record what is the case. If I am considering a true principle of criticism and if the situation to which the principle addresses itself does not obtain—for example, if I as cognitive agent find myself with a conclusion that I have no right to, then my obligation is to bring the situation into line with the principle rather than to bring the principle into line with my delinquent practice.

When we compare the foundations of a transcendental inquiry into the possibility of knowledge with the first principles of ethics, the comparison naturally suggests that Kant's well-known concern about the possibility of an ethical relativism may be matched by a concern about the possibility of a relativism in the critical foundations of the possibility of knowledge. One main concern of his strategy in both areas will be to construct a set of principles that are immune from empirical review and that, accordingly, will escape from the relativism and ethno-centricity of principles that reflect the empirically observed differences between men at different times and in different cultures. At the very least, we can be sure that Kant had entertained the possibility of relativism in the foundations of transcendental criticism since we know that one of his most illustrious students had attacked him from that direction—just as we know that Fichte had come at his position from the side of a metaphysics of the self. Hereder's *MetaCritique to the Critique of Pure Reason* has a form of cultural relativism lying very close to the surface of the argument. What Herder explicitly declares is that we should examine the forms of language in order to determine the categories of the understanding, instead of seeking these concepts in the forms of judgment that are suggested by pure, formal logic. The manner in which Herder invokes this idea leads to a very obvious question about the implications of the cultural and historical differences in symbolic forms. Herder has of course been a main inspiration for those later thinkers who have accepted relativism in the critical foundations of knowledge.

As long as these linguistic, anthropological or psychological inquiries remain at the level of the facts about our representations and as long as they do not pretend to inform us about what it is that is possible in our representations, Kant has a straight-forward rebuttal of Herder's proposal. If I assign to someone the right to a concept or principle on the basis of a transcendental inquiry, the assignment cannot be overturned successfully by evidence which shows or tends to show that in fact he does not possess the concept. The case is analogous to the situation in formal logic, where a principle that determines how a person ought to think cannot be refuted by evidence concerning how he does think. Again, the crucial point about this aspect of Kant's strategy of argument is that a principle which is critical is one which functions and must function as an independent variable in relation to our varying practice. Our practice is what ought to be altered and controlled to bring it in to conformity with our critical principles. The essence of debauchery consists in the tendency to let our principles be shaped by our natural habits and desires. The essence of intellectual free-bootery consists in the tendency to let our view of the ideas we have a right to maintain be determined by the natural tendency of our minds to think certain thoughts. Such at any rate seems to have been Kant's view of the matter, and it must be admitted that the difference in status between critical and factual principles forms a very effective sluice-gate or barrier against inferences that would seek to run up the stream of Kant's transcendental arguments.

The foundations of a properly critical philosophy can support any number of romantic tenements inhabited by individuals who glory in the idiosyncracies of human thought. The more serious challenge to Kant's foundations comes from those philosophers who are prepared to follow Fichte and Heidegger and to insist on the necessity of an underlying metaphysics of the self. What becomes of the primacy of logic, asks Heidegger, if inquiry into our essence as cognitive agents should call into question the very fundamental distinction between our faculties of sensibility and understanding? The assumption behind his question is that the principles which will determine the possibilities of representation and, in particular, the possibilities of synthetic *a priori* representation are those metaphysical principles which describe the constitution of the self and which establish the conditions for the metaphysical identity of the self. The dialectical seriousness of this objection when compared with Herder's objection derives from the logical point that a "cannot" of metaphysics will appear to be sufficient to overthrow a "should" of criticism. Since Heidegger intimates that his line of analysis of the problem of knowledge follows Kant's own deepest insights into the nature of the thinking self, our first consideration must be to show that this is not so and that the ultimate subject matter of Kant's critical philosophy is not the ultimate subject matter of any possible metaphysics. Our second consideration will then be to show that Kant can start his fish down the sluiceway without calling upon metaphysics and without calling upon assumptions that are as strong and as uncertain as those provided by a metaphysics of the self. An understanding of these two points should clarify Kant's general strategy in dealing with objections of the form that Heidegger sponsors.

Philosophers have inherited two master-concepts with which to organize their thinking about the ultimate subject matter of thought and discourse. The two ideas are very different and come to us from different historical periods. The first idea derives from Greek scientific and philosophical thought. It is the familiar idea that what we are talking about or thinking about *in the last analysis* in science and philosophy is always a substance. Substances are the ultimate objects of discourse, when the discourse is factual and descriptive. The second grand idea comes to us from Roman legal thought. It is the idea that what we are talking about or thinking about *in the last analysis* in law and morality is always a forensic person. A person (in the tradition of Roman law) is the ultimate object of discourse, when the discourse is critical and prescriptive. While these ideas have some important similarities, they have equally important differences. We have just seen one important similarity. Both persons and substances are alike in that they can be defined by their relationship to a type of discourse or thought. One obvious difference in this respect is in the type of discourse that picks out each as its subject matter. The more important difference about this relationship is in a fact which Kant exploits very skillfully in his transcendental deduction of the categories. A substance is presumed to have a being that is independent of all thought or discourse about it. The ultimate substances are metaphysical realities. The forensic concept of a person began to pull apart from the scientific concept of substance precisely at the point when it was realized that the being and the identity of the things subject to the acts of a court can be determined by judicial decrees and by legislative acts. There are many types of legal person which have absolutely no being independent of judicial decrees or other acts of incorporation. The whole and entire story about who these persons are and what they are capable of doing is disclosed by a study of those valid principles that govern the conduct of these persons.

Substances and persons are alike in that they each admit of a second form of definition whereby they are defined by their possible relationships to other things, rather than by their relationships to discourse or to thought. A substance can be explained as something to which other things can belong *de facto* but which cannot itself belong to any other thing. A person can be explained as that which other things can belong to *de jure* or by right but which cannot itself belong to another. There is again the very obvious difference in the relationships that define substances and persons. The one is metaphysical; the other is juridical. The difference is reflected in other contrasts between persons and substances. Each is one thing in which a multitude of properties are combined or associated. But the status and the nature of the association of the properties are entirely different in the two cases. Where thoughts, or other properties, are combined together in a substance *de facto* the principles or laws of association (*Verbindung*) are principles that are factual and that describe the manner of the association. Furthermore, the basis for the association, conceived metaphysically, is the identity of the underlying substance. The ideas, or other properties, are associated with one another by virtue of their relationship to one and the same thing. But where thoughts, or other things that can belong as a matter of right, are combined together in one forensic person, the basic principle of the association is not a factual principle. Moreover, as we have just seen, the association (*Verbindung*) of the things that belong together by right and in conformity to that principle is what determines and constitutes the identity of the forensic person. In understanding the shape of Kant's ultimate premises (on the critical interpretation of his argument), one cannot stress too much this difference in the ultimate premises of metaphysical and critical arguments. In the metaphysical arguments the ultimate premises refer to those substances which are invoked or presupposed as the sources of unity in the subject matter. In the critical arguments the ultimate premises cannot refer to persons, because the possibility of a person itself depends upon and is constituted by the possibility of some assemblage or association of elements *de jure*. In the latter case there is no other possible explanation of the identity of the person other than that which is given by an account of the possibility of the synthesis or association of those things which form a valid association. It is particularly difficult for those who have been raised in the traditions of Anglo-American common law to perceive the vast difference between substances and persons in the other legal tradition. Of course, when one is considering an association as a legal person, one has the sense of obvious conceptual differences, but then it is easy to suppose that the human beings who have formed that association are the ultimate bearers of the legal rights and responsibilities and that these human beings are after all substances. The conceptual point needs to be illustrated for human beings who are persons and who are also substances: The conditions of identity of the two are radically different in the Roman law tradition. For example, we might consider some man who has lived a blameless existence and has acquired a legal right to a good name, free from reproach. The man dies, is cremated, and his ashes are scattered—or whatever else is necessary for an admission that there has been a substantial change and that nothing any longer retains the identity that the man had as a substance. Metaphysically and scientifically speaking, the man no longer exists. Nevertheless if another person should happen to defame the deceased, the courts in the Roman tradition acknowledge that the man still retains and bears the right that he earned while alive, and the courts will act to protect him in that right. In our English tradition with its robust Aristotelian common sense the matter will be handled differently. The good name of the deceased is treated like a disposable asset. It passes to the heirs of the deceased who acquire the right to protect the good name of the man along with their rights to his other goods. In the Roman tradition this right to a good reputation is held to be so intimately tied up with the identity of the person who acquired it that it cannot be alienated from that person. In order to preserve and protect the right, the law confers a kind of personal immortality on the individual. Such examples illustrate the very important point that a substantial identity is neither a necessary nor a sufficient condition for a personal identity.

The first and most primitive concept of a person in the tradition of the Roman law is said to be the concept of that which has the capacity to act and to be acted upon within a legal forum.[18] This brings us to the issue of whether, when Kant assumes capacities of the cognitive agent to act and to be acted upon, he is assuming a natural capacity like the capacity to balance cups of tea on one's nose or whether he is assuming something like the capacity of a corporation to use and to be used. When Kant carries his analysis of the faculty of the understanding back to an assumption about the identity of the knowing self and to the conditions which make possible that identity is he discussing the identity of a metaphysical and substantial self? If we think the answer is affirmative, we are placing Kant in the tradition of Descartes. In the second paragraph of his first work Descartes had proposed a subjective, rather than an objective, solution to the possibility of the association or combination of our thoughts into a unified whole. He announced that the unification of our cognitions must be possible because the self which possesses these cognitions is always and everywhere the same. He thereby understood the self to be a substantial thing and he made the basis of his explanation of the possible association of thoughts derive from a metaphysical principle according to which a substantial unity can underlie and make possible a combination of different accidents in the substance.

There are a number of different indications that Kant does not intend the Cartesian solution. He begins his discussion of the way in which representations are combined in the cognitive self by giving us a patient explanation that he will be concerned with our rights of possession of certain concepts, rather than with the facts of possession. Also, when he choses a term for the fundamental act of the cognitive self, he employs a word that is customarily applied to the valid acts of a legislator (*Aktus*), rather than to acts in the psychological or metaphysical sense. He reminds us that the one concept which cannot be derived from experience is the idea of association (*Verbindung*) in our representations. Now this particular term has both a legal and a factual employment, but what Kant says about it does not square with his usual view about

---

[18] The text gives the common view. Some have argued that the concept can be traced to Aristotle or the earlier Stoics; cf. J.W. Jones, *Law and the Legal Theory of the Greeks* (Oxford, 1956), p. 153.

metaphysical concepts. His position is not that these concepts cannot be derived from experience; his position rather is that metaphysical concepts cannot be justified as objectively valid on the basis of an appeal to experience. (As a factual concept, the concept of an association in our ideas had actually been suggested to Hume by the Newtonian concept of a gravitational attraction that causes material bodies to combine themselves into physical systems in the manner described by the law of gravitation.) A final indication that Kant does not intend a descriptive account of the association of our ideas is that when Kant reaches the ultimate premises in the proof of the objective validity of the concepts of the understanding he treats the identity of the self as something that must itself be accounted for. In order to see the significance of that fact, we must recall the position of his assumption in the overall argument. Kant's argument has two sides. On the one hand, if he can establish that there must be a possible association of my various representations and if he can assume from the transcendental aesthetic that some of my representations present a manifold in intuition, then he can argue that the association is possible only if the representations are connected with one another by being connected in objects. Then the pure concepts of the understanding can be justified as my concepts of objects in general and, thus, as concepts that must be employed to give objective unification to my representations. This side of the argument does not concern us directly. The other side of the argument does, for here Kant must show that the association of my various representations *must* be possible.

Kant's argument runs directly contrary to the metaphysical account that had been offered by Descartes. Kant argues that the association of my representations with one another in accordance with valid principles must be possible because otherwise we cannot account for my consciousness of my self as the same through the various acts of representation. This part of this side of the argument merely underscores the obvious point about the identity of any legal person: The possibility of an identity in a legal person is determined and explained by the possibility of a valid association of the various rights to act and to be acted upon. When these legal possessions have been combined in accordance with some general principle or principles for such combinations, then the alleged possessor of these rights assumes a legal identity, and otherwise it lacks such an identity. The further aspects of this side of the argument are what reveal the genius of Kant's critical strategy. Why must there be a possible consciousness of myself as one and the same through the various acts of thought? Kant says that an "I think" must be capable of accompanying each of my representations, because otherwise the representations would not be mine. If we assume that he means a possession *de jure* rather than a possession *de facto*, then we can easily understand why Kant feels that he has reached an area of ultimate epistemic certainty.

Kant's basic epistemological insight is that our obligations are the only things about which we can reach final certainty. An obligation is something that applies to me as my obligation only if it is possible for me to become conscious of that obligation. The reason for this is that I must be capable of modifying my conduct on the basis of my recognition of my obligation, and I cannot do so unless, by taking heed of what my obligations are, I can become aware of what my obligations are. From the epistemological point of view normative or critical principles apply to me in a way that is entirely different from the way in which factual or descriptive principles apply to me. It is possible for the latter to apply to me as a psychological or metaphysical self, even though I am unable to detect the fact by taking heed of my situation. If Kant's basic intuition concerning the status of the moral law was the keystone of his transcendental strategy, his ultimate starting point in the deduction of the concepts of the understanding can be read as the corresponding point about the domain of my rights and responsibilities as a cognitive agent. Where an idea can be mine in the sense that I have a derived or an original right of possession, and where an idea of mine is an idea for which one can legitimately request a proof of objective validity in cognition, it must be possible for me to become conscious of the idea as something in respect to which I do have these rights and these responsibilities. Otherwise, the claim that I have the rights or the responsibilities would not make sense. This is the line of reasoning which will insure that all the fish that are admitted down the sluiceway of the transcendental argument are fish that have been properly tagged in the argument.

If the principles that determine the objective validity of concepts are truly critical principles, then the possibility of a synthesis or association of concepts *a priori* will be a possibility that resembles the possibility of a deductive inference. That is, the sense of "possible" here is roughly the sense of "That is permitted" or "That is in conformity to the applicable norms." The use of the word in that sense had ample precedents in Kant's day. For example, one of the important uses that Leibniz had made of the concept of possibility conveys the idea of that which is morally permissible.[19] Thus, the possible being of a synthetic connection of ideas will have the status of connections of

---

[19] Letter to Bourguet (March 22, 1714), *Philosophischen Schriften*, ed. Gerhardt (Berlin, 1875), Vol. III, p. 568; and Letter to Bernouilli (July 25, 1699), *Gesammelte Werke*, Vol. III, p. 597—cited in A. Heinekamp, *Das Problem des Guten bei Leibniz* (Bonn, 1969).

ideas in general as formal logic characterizes those connections. Possible being, unity and goodness are concepts to which formal logic gives precisely the same extension in the discussion of judgments, that is, in the discussion of the connection of representations as it is permitted by the principles of formal logic. Thus, that which brings the representations together in the judgment and gives the judgment its integral being is the form of the judgment. And from the logical point of view, it is the form of the judgment which also makes the judgment be a good or a well-formed judgment rather than a defective or ill-formed judgment. If the possibility of synthetic connection is a similar kind of possibility, governed by critical principles rather than descriptive principles, then the conclusions about that possibility will not be metaphysical conclusions and will not necessarily presuppose any metaphysical views about the self.

If we agree that the transcendental inquiry does not carry us back to any metaphysical assumptions about the self, what are we then to make of the faculties of sensibility and of understanding? Each faculty marks out an area of our possessions as cognitive agents; indeed, Kant's concept of a faculty (*Vermögen*) can itself be regarded as a concept of our goods or possessions. The one faculty marks out that which is mine by virtue of how I can act and the other marks out that which I have a right to by virtue of how I can be acted upon. Now the concepts of spontaneity and of receptivity which enter the picture at this juncture in the argument are concepts which had long been employed within the context of normative theorizing. For example, Crusius provides a typical illustration in his *Instruction on how to live rationally* where the concept of human spontaneity is introduced early in the development of his practical philosophy.[20] The only novelty in Kant's discussion consists in the way in which he associates those concepts of our spontaneity and receptivity as juridical beings with the concepts of our understanding and our sensibility. Thus, when we define pure intuitions in a way that makes clear the basis of our right to these representations, we regard ourselves as passive or receptive. We have a right to these representations in our status as beings that can have rights to the possession of representations conferred upon them. The basis for the right is what can be given to us or what we can borrow. When we define pure concepts in a way that makes clear the basis of our right to these representations, we regard ourselves as active. We have a right to these representations by virtue of what we can do ourselves in cognition, and our rights are those that are classified as rights of "original possession". The

---

[20] Christian Crusius, *Anweisung vernunftig zu Leben* (Leipzig, 1744; reprinted Hildesheim, 1969), pp. 45–46.

only novelty in Kant's application of these notions of what we can do and what we can receive is his special application of them within the critical analysis of cognition; their application and discussion within practical philosophy in general had long been anticipated.

It is important to realize that when one talks in the practical or legal spheres about something which acts or is acted upon, the relevant criterion to employ in determining whether the thing has acted or has been acted upon is whether there is any change in the nature or the status of the rights and the responsibilities of the persons involved in the transaction. This question is not, and should never be confused with, a question about actual causal interactions between the things that are involved. For example, if I allege that you have affected me in my possession of some bit of property, I may have a valid legal point *even though you can show that there is no causal chain that connects any action of yours with any actual effect in me*. Nothing has to "happen to" me in any factual or descriptive sense, in order for your action to affect me in my legal possessions. This point about the way in which legal possessions enter into relationships of affecting and being affected that are quite different from the actual causal links between things is, of course, something that is already implied by saying that persons are not substances. In due course we will see that this point has great significance for Kant's discussion of the validity of intuitions, where our rights are the rights of possible recipients of valid representations. But in order to appreciate the beauty of Kant's transcendental strategy it is necessary to observe how the same point applies to our faculty of spontaneity.

What does it mean to say that I am conscious of myself as a pure agent in thought, or as a being that thinks through a faculty of spontaneity? Here we confront a special instance of what, for Kant, is one of the fundamental problems of a pure practical philosophy. The criticism of actions as my actions is possible only where there is the justified presumption of my spontaneity as an agent. My spontaneity is of course my positive freedom as a practical agent and it is easy to illustrate the interest of criticism in the question of whether I can be presumed to be free. The situation can be fairly compared to those cases in the law when the same issue arises in the criticism and probate of some representation for the purpose of determining that it is a valid representation. For example, a last will and testament may be subjected to criticism to determine if it does indeed represent the will of the deceased. In such a case the critics of the will have an obvious interest in the question of coercion. By the same token, if one were launching an attack on the possibility of wills in general, as they are conceived to be in the law, one would have an obvious interest in showing that no alleged testament can exist without reflecting coercive influences that invalidate it as a proper and binding will. Does the defence of the possibility of all such representations require a metaphysical explanation of why I am free, or even a metaphysical description of how I am free? Kant's answer is that it does not. In considering all the various things that can belong to me in my status as a spontaneous being, Kant argues that an objective reason why these do belong to me is not necessary. It is sufficient if we can produce a subjective justification or a reason why we are justified in conceiving of ourselves in the given way. In regard to practical principles it is true that I would not be justified in accepting a principle as one that governs my conduct unless I were justified in believing that I am able to act in conformity with the given principle. However it does not at all follow that I must be able to produce objective reasons that explain how or why I am able to act on the principle. Thus a normative principle can characterize my obligations even though I lack any physical, psychological, or metaphysical insight into the question of how it is that a being like myself *is* able to act in conformity to the principle. The same situation confronts us in the discussion of the rights that we can possess as persons. Metaphysical discussions of the thinking substance trade in objective justification of the content of what is alleged or judged to be the case, but in the critical foundations of metaphysics we can make do with subjective reasons for presuming or judging about the status of our representations. If we keep in mind the legal origins of Kant's idea of philosophical criticism, the justice of this distinction will be obvious to us.

Consider a typical case of criticism in the courts—an application of the general study of the validity of legal representations. A court, for example, may be hearing a challenge to the validity of some will or testament. It will surely accept as evidence of the validity of the document evidence that justifies a presumption that the will was not coerced and *such a presumption is nothing but a subjective reason* for believing that the will is a spontaneous representation of the intentions of the deceased. When we introduced the distinction between objective and subjective reasons in the first chapter, we gave the testimony of trustworthy witnesses as our example of something that is a reason for believing but not (in the majority of cases) a reason for what is believed. Yet the mere fact that a will has been properly signed and witnessed helps to create a presumption in favour of the validity of the will. There is a further, instructive point of comparison between legal criticism of wills and the philosophical criticism of pure concepts of the understanding. A will is more than the expression of the intentions of some person; it purports to assign rights to some beneficiary. In order for that assignment to be a valid act, the things that are assigned have to belong among the goods and chattels (*bewegliches Vermögen*) or the real estate (*unbewegliches Vermögen*) of the person making the assignment. Now in the case of an ordinary will the signature of the testator only creates a presumption that he was aware of the goods that he was assigning, but it does not create a presumption that the goods were his to assign. In the case of the faculty (*Vermögen*) of the pure understanding, it can be argued that the case is different. In the court of pure reason, where we are concerned with the rights to that which originates within the understanding itself, the fact that the understanding is conscious of something that it alleges as its own creates a legal presumption that it *is* its own. The appropriate model here is not the model of the person framing a will. It is Kant's preferred comparison of the understanding to a sovereign legislative body. The situation with the pure understanding might be compared to those acts in which a sovereign legislature delegates certain powers to some subordinate creature, such as a town or a city. If the question were to arise as to whether those powers are within the competence of the legislature to assign, the fact that they are recognized as such in some given act of the legislature will create a presumption that these powers are among the goods (*Vermögen*) of the sovereign body. The modern reader who has difficulty with that understanding of the matter, or indeed with any discussion that passes from the case of private testaments to the case of public acts creating subordinate bodies within some jurisdiction should recall that in Kant's legal tradition the discussion of jurisdiction is treated as a special case in the general discussion of the rights in property.

Heidegger and others have given us a fair sense of the way in which Kant's transcendental foundations become entirely problematic when his distinction between sensibility and understanding is conceived as the subject of a psychological or a metaphysical analysis. By contrast, the critical interpretation of his foundations suggests that he had a brilliant strategy for closing off philosophical debate. To summarize the main points that have just been made about that strategy, we know that his argument ultimately gets back to the question about the possible identity of a being that combines a faculty of sensibility and a faculty of understanding. If the latter are understood to be constituted of those valid representations that we possess in our status as possible recipients and through our competence as spontaneous agents, then the identity of the self can only be constituted and explained by the possibility of associating such representations together with one another—hence we are led to the necessity of an objective deduction of the categories, since representations of the sensibility and the understanding can only be validly combined by principles that go beyond the critical principles of formal logic and that obligate us to combine the representations with one another by combining them in objects. The metaphysical interpretation of the two faculties presents us with representations which are ours *de facto* and hence it will be the metaphysical understanding of the identity of the self that will provide the only ultimate understanding of how the faculties can be the faculties of one being. Heidegger correctly points out that Kant provides no clue as to what such an understanding would reveal. If it is asked how the critical interpretation can exempt Kant from the necessity of providing some insight into the nature of the self to which the possibility of knowledge is ascribed, the reply will be that in a critical analysis of the rights or responsibilities of a person a subjective justification is sufficient to establish the validity of the representation of those rights as belonging to the person—if we know that a person represents something as belonging to himself, we need a justification of the validity of his representation but we do not need an explanation of how it is possible for him to have that consciousness of what is his. If it is asked how the critical interpretation can explain the possibility of a complete listing of our categorial obligations or of the principles that make possible the valid association of concepts and intuitions, the answer is that these principles can be applied to the criticism of our efforts to gain knowledge only if it is possible for them to be made known to us. On each of these points the critical strategy contrasts favorably with a metaphysical strategy. The attempt to import metaphysical foundations into criticism destroys the virtues of Kant's arguments. The attempt to improve his results in that manner destroys those results.

II. HISTORICAL MOTIVES FOR KANT'S DISTINCTION

We know that for philosophers in Kant's tradition all of our representations are concepts and we know that Kant eventually came to write "Not all" beside Meier's statement of this view. What brings Kant to his dissenting conclusion? The arguments in the *Critique* for the existence of an intuitive component in our knowledge are good arguments but they are not very helpful for someone who is attempting to gain a comprehension of the distinction or of Kant's motives in introducing the distinction. Perhaps the most striking evidence of this general conclusion is the fact that Kant omitted any reference to the problems surrounding the principle of the identity of indiscernibles and yet anyone who has grasped that principle and who has grasped the nature of Kant's objections to the principle will be led by natural steps to reflect that perhaps not all of our representations are general concepts.

The principle of the identity of indiscernibles admits of several different formulations. A metaphysical formulation of the principle tells us that two things are identical if all the properties of each are (or must be) properties of the other. This is equivalent to the judgment that two things are distinct only if there is a property of the one which is not a property of the other. Another formulation of the principle (or, it might be argued, the formulation of a different but related principle) is at least in part transcendental. It tells us that two things are identical if every possible concept of each is a concept of the other. In the pre-Kantian tradition concepts are representations through which we can discriminate between things or become conscious of the differences between things. If we agree to understand the term *difference* as Kant explains it—namely, as a synonym for *property*, the two formulations of the principle are virtually interchangeable, but they do continue to point us in different directions when we come to inquire into the truth of such a principle. The one invites us to think about the way the world might be—and we will be encouraged to look for models of the world that are counterexamples to the principle. The transcendental version invites us to think about the way our conceptual or representational framework might be.

We know that each version can be conjoined to a complementary principle that tells us about the consequences of assuming that two things are identical. Thus the principle of indiscernibility of identicals tells us that if two things are identical then every property of each is (or must be) a property of the other. The conjunction of the two has often been proposed as our definition of identity. Such definitions have an effect comparable to the definition of identity in *Mathematical Logic* which was mentioned in the last section. Identity of indiscernibles is by no means equivalent to the principle of extensionality—the principle that defines the identity of classes on the basis of their common membership, but nevertheless, as Marcus notes, instances of the former may "be interpreted as extensionality principles in that they equate identity with the slightly weaker relation of indiscernibility which requires that to be distinct means to be discernibly distinct."[21] If we employ the principle to state the conditions under which any two things whatsoever are identical, then we commit ourselves to a special understanding of the nature of our metaphysical elements. Very roughly, our view will be that all things, including proper individuals, are more like classes than we might otherwise have had reason to suspect. But by the same token an argument has been developed that runs in the other direction. If we are contemplating the transcendental version of the principle and if we are presented with convincing examples of possible metaphysical elements that do not satisfy it, then we will be inclined to withdraw the presumption that every possible representa-

---

[21] Ruth Barcan Marcus, "Extensionality," in *Mind* Vol. 69 (Jan. 1960).

tion is a concept. If it is indeed an historical fact that this second line of reflection was an important motive in Kant's introduction of the theory of intuitions, the development of his views parallels the discussion of the principle of identity of indiscernibles in our own century.

Whitehead and Russell made use of the principle to define the identity-relations for various types of things in *Principia Mathematica*.[22] Their definitions of identity drew sharp criticism from Wittgenstein, from Ramsey, from Waisman, and from others.[23] There were also many who defended the *Principia* on this point, and among the defenders Grelling was one of the first to point out the difference between the metaphysical and the logical or transcendental aspects of the problem.[24] In the course of the attack the principle had been criticized on the grounds that it is metaphysically false. Grelling replied by noting that within the *Principia*, since the principle appears as a mere definition of terms, the question of its metaphysical truth or falsity is not entirely appropriate. His intention seems to have been to shift the terms of the discussion to a consideration of what the effects of the adoption of the principle will be within one's conceptual or linguistic framework. An example of the way in which he imagined that subsequent discussion would be conducted might be provided a version of set theory that was proposed by von Neumann. For technical reasons that probably had very little to do with any feelings that von Neumann had about an appropriate set of metaphysical commitments he introduced a special category of terms which were intended to stand for non-elements. Confronted with the proposal to define identity in this system by means of the suggested principle, he would point to the effects on that category of terms and would urge as his reasons against the proposal his position and non-metaphysical reasons for devising the system as he had done. If Grelling imagined that future commentary on the principle would be conducted in this positivistic and non-metaphysical spirit, he was bound to be disappointed. What that commentary *does* reveal is an increased sensitivity to the inter-relationships between metaphysical and logical or transcendental aspects of the discussion.

It has already been pointed out that Zermelo's first version of a set theory for mathematics and the more recent system of Bourbaki contain categories of terms that can be substituted one for another only on the condition that the terms refer to the same individuals. In these systems as in the first *Critique*

[22] A.N. Whitehead and B. Russell, *Principia Mathematica* (Cambridge, 1957), I, p. 168.
[23] L. Wittgenstein, *Tractatus-Logico-Philosophicus* (London, 1955) 5.5302; F.P. Ramsey, *The Foundations of Mathematics* (Patterson, 1960) p. 30ff.; and F. Waisman, "Über den Bergriff der Identität" in *Erkenntnis*, VI (1936), p. 56ff.
[24] Kurt Grelling, "Identitas Indiscernibilium," *Erkenntnis*, VI (1936), p. 252ff.

being one and the same thing is supposed to have a different force from any extensionalized version of *being identical to*. It is interesting, therefore, that such a category of terms has been suggested, if it is not conclusively proved, by metaphysical objections to the principle of identity of indiscernibles. Black, Bergmann, Wilson, Ayer, O'Connor, Rescher and Pears are among those who have discussed the issues related to it.[25] The arguments by and between these seven thinkers were summarized for us by Charles Baylis.[26] This summary of recent agreements provides a useful reference point for a discussion of Kant's historical situation:

Despite the varied authors and approaches the articles of this group build up to a considerable measure of agreement: 1. the principle of the identity of indiscernibles is philosophically uninteresting unless it is taken as necessary. 2. Two reasonably correct statements of the principle are as follows: (a) If two objects are numerically different there is at least one property possessed by one of them that is not possessed by the other. (b) There cannot be mere numerical difference without qualitative difference (i.e., difference in some quality, property, or relation). 3. Unless certain relational properties, e.g., *identity* and *difference*, are excluded by a suitable restriction the principle becomes trivially true. 4. A suitable restriction is provided by the requirement that nothing is to count as a property unless it can be specified in general descriptive terms without the use of any reference to individuals. 5. If this qualification is put in, it seems to be possible to conceive of consistent universes in which the principle is contingently false, e.g., (a) a radially symmetric universe, (b) a universe entirely composed of an infinite series of qualitatively identical sounds. 6. In such universes it is impossible to distinguish the qualitatively identical things in purely predicative terms. 7. The above principle, namely (6), is itself trivial. 8. Even in a universe such as the one described in (5), it would be possible to distinguish qualitatively identical items by non-descriptive individual reference expressions such as "This" and "That".

My purpose in citing the apparent agreement on these eight points is not to provide evidence for the necessity of a distinction between terms that refer to individuals and terms that are predicated of individuals. My purpose is to show that there is a philosophically plausible account that can be given of the genesis of this distinction in Kant's writings. Having that objective in mind, we will wish to assure ourselves that the first four of the eight points correspond to features of the historical setting within which Kant encountered the

---

[25] Max Black, "The Identity of Indiscernibles," *Mind*, 61 (1952), p. 153; Gustav Bergman, "The Identity of Indiscernibles and the Formalist Definition of 'Identity'," *Mind*, 62 (1953), p. 75; Neal Wilson, "The Identity of Indiscernibles and the Symmetrical Universe," *Mind*, 62 (1953), p. 506; D.J. O'Connor, "The Identity of Indiscernibles," *Analysis*, 14, no. 5 (1954), p. 103; Nicholas Rescher, "The Identity of Indiscernibles: A Reinterpretation," *Journal of Philosophy*, 52 (1955), p. 152; David Pears, "The Identity of Indiscernibles," *Mind*, 64 (1955), p. 522.

[26] Charles Baylis, *Journal of Symbolic Logic*, XXI, p. 86.

principle in question. We will need to remind ourselves that the fifth point corresponds to Kant's early counter-examples to the principle. And finally, we will wish to be certain that the last three points correspond to the moral that Kant was prepared to draw concerning the principle. When we have these assurances, we can claim to have identified a plausible motive for Kant's distinction between intuitions and concepts.

The first and second points are both indicated by Kant's declaration that "Leibniz's Principle is that *numerica diversitas* must also be *specifica diversitas*."[27] What this shows us is, first, that whether or not Leibniz actually affirmed the principle under discussion in Baylis's summary, Kant believed that he did. The latter rather than the former is surely the relevant consideration in discussing the genesis of Kant's thought. Secondly, Kant's formulation of the principle shows that he regarded the principle as an expression of what is, or is alleged to be, necessary. The restrictions which are mentioned in Baylis's third and fourth points are guaranteed by the datum with which we began. That is, we know that in the rationalist's logic every representation is said to be a concept. What is more to the point is the fact that Kant was perfectly clear in his own mind about the significance of this feature of their logic for a discussion of the principle. Thus, he writes in the *Fortschritte* (discussing developments in philosophy since the time of Leibniz and Wolff): "*With mere concepts of the understanding* to think of two things apart from one another which are completely the same in respect to all internal qualifications (of quantity and quality) is a contradiction; it is always one and the same thing thought twice (numerically one)."[28] The emphasis that he put on the given restriction almost certainly guaranteed that objections to the principle would direct his attention to the possibility of other kinds of representation, and we will see that that is how he interprets the situation.

Baylis mentions objections to the principle which are philosophically more sophisticated than those that were advanced by Kant. However, the two sets of counter-examples are surely related in a family way. Kant offered his famous illustrations of the so-called "incongruous counterparts". For example, I notice that although my left hand and my right hand, considered by themselves, are numerically distinct, there is not any property that the one has and the other does not have (or at any rate could not have). Why are they distinct? Even more naively, one might be brought to wonder what it is about my right hand and my left glove that prevents the one from fitting into the other. Each of us makes the discovery of the difference as a small child,

---

[27] *Gesammelte Schriften*, XVIII, p. 381.
[28] *Ibid.*, XX, p. 280.

though not all of us will have asked for an explanation of the possibility of the difference. Kant brought this discovery forward as an early objection to Leibniz's principle.

The existence of these counter-examples evidently brought Kant to ask how it is possible for me to be presented with the two things and to know that they are different even though I cannot conceptualize the one as something which is different from the other. On the assumption that all my representations are concepts, the answer would appear to be that I cannot be presented with the two things. Hence, in order for Kant to preserve the force of his counter-examples, he had to break with the assumption about my representations. There is clear historical evidence that Kant made precisely this connection between the falsity of Leibniz's principle and his own distinction between intuitions and concepts. The outcome of his reflection, therefore, corresponded to Baylis's eighth point. Kant says explicitly that the plausibility of Leibniz's principle derives from the fact that ". . . he admitted only a discrimination through concepts and did not wish to recognize any specifically different kind of representation, . . ."[29]

There is some evidence that Kant would also have accepted Baylis's sixth and seventh points. In a note on Leibniz's principle, Kant wrote: "Internal difference is no requirement for the concept of different things; on the contrary [it is] difference of place. It is thus no requirement for appearance; therefore, the principle is false, though true for reason; that is, I can through reason only concede different things where the internal qualifications are different."[30] There are certain aspects of this passage that must remain undiscussed and unexplained at this point in our discussion: in particular, how does difference of place come into Kant's deliberations and what does he mean here by *appearance*? Still what is clear about the passage is that it suggests that Leibniz's principle is true, so long as it is protected by the necessary qualifications about the mode of representation that is in question in the principle.

In summary it is fair to say that there is a line of reflection that could carry a competent modern philosopher from the discussion of Leibniz's principle to the formulation of a distinction between two types of representation. Also it is fair to conclude that Kant believed that his own intellectual development had taken precisely that course. He says as much in looking back over the developments since Wolff. We can extend our knowledge of motives behind Kant's distinction between intuitions and concepts, but we are not likely to strengthen in any substantial degree our confidence about one of his motives.

[29] *Ibid.*, XX, p. 282.
[30] *Ibid.*, XVIII, p. 156.

Before we turn to other factors that played a role in the formulation of Kant's distinction, we should review certain consequences of the distinction that are bound up in an intimate way with the principle of identity. The first consequence is associated with Marcus's observation about how the indiscernibility principle, and others like it, "equate identity with the slightly weaker relation of indiscernibility which requires that to be distinct means to be discernibly distinct." Now we know in the first place that Kant made a distinction between being distinct and being discernibly distinct. As he writes in an early essay: "... it is quite a different thing to *distinguish* things from one another and to cognize the distinction of things."[31] But the value of Marcus's observation comes from the fact that it will lead us to predict that in rejecting Leibniz's principle Kant was forced to recognize a distinction between different senses in which we can say that things are identical. This point has great historical interest for the reason that prior to Kant (and within his immediate tradition) there is no consistent distinction to be discovered between the use of the term for identity (*Identität*) and the use of the term for unity or oneness (*Einheit*). Also prior to Kant (and within his immediate tradition) there is no consistent distinction between saying that things are identical (*identisch*) and saying that things are one and the same (*einerlei*). Yet all who read far enough into Kant's *Critique* will come upon his distinction between identity and unity in an object (or in the self). The evident ground for his distinction is our familiar fact that things can be two or can be manifold without necessarily being discernibly different or nonidentical. If our claim about the direction of Kant's thinking in the discussion of the indiscernibility principle is sound, we should expect that Kant will explain the difference in the types of identity transcendentally or by reference to the possibility of representation. Again, the historical facts support the conjecture. By way of explaining the two relationships Kant says, "With identity I compare two subjects that have the same predicate; with unity I compare two predicates or concepts, which have one subject."[32] If we are to get the point of this explanation, we must bear in mind that in Kant's tradition the term "subject" usually refers to the subject matter of the act of judgment or of comparison. As Baumgarten says, the subject is the "materia circa quam" or subject matter. Thus the subject of a judgment is not a term or a subject-concept; the subject of a judgment is the object that the judgment is about. Accordingly, when Kant equates identity with the condition that

---

[31] *Introduction to Logic*, p. 93.
[32] *Gesammelte Schriften*, XVIII, p. 34. By contrast, Baumgarten uses *identical* (*identitas*) and *the same* (*eadem*) interchangeably; cf. *Gesammelte Schriften*, XVII, p. 36 and p. 83ff.

the two subjects have the same predicate or concept, he is simply equating identity with indiscernibility. The novel idea of unity is an idea that allows that two different concepts can be unified or brought together in an object which is the same object for each of the different ideas. But precisely the same idea is one that allows for objects which are *not* numerically the same to be the objects of conceptions which are precisely the same. As we saw in the first chapter when discussing Hume's problems and the problems concerning induction, this new idea of diversity or of a numerical manifold has an important role to play in the Kantian analysis of the possibility of knowledge. If we had to change our conceptions whenever we changed the references in our judgments, it is evident that induction would be ruled out as impossible.

As we consider the consequences of Kant's scepticism about unrestricted applications of the principle of indiscernibility, we must also bear in mind that it implies a scepticism about the principle of sufficient reason. Because of the assumed relationship between the two principles, the distinction between intuitions and concepts that plays a role in his objections to the first principle is a distinction that we should expect to find related to his objections to the second principle. In order to come to a proper understanding of these connections, we must begin by exploring some of the complexities in the traditional formulations of the principle and in the terminology that came to surround the principle. This terminology carries a significant burden in Kant's aesthetic.

The vulgar or popular formulation of the principle simply tells us that nothing is without its reason. But when this assertion is interpreted in one way it is (or gives the appearance of being) a metaphysical principle, and when it is interpreted in another way it is a logical or transcendental thesis. Each of these lines of interpretation will give rise to a further refinement of the principle. For example when the principle is interpreted in the first way the scope of the principle includes all the possible *objects* of knowledge. On this interpretation we face the choice of construing the term "reason" as meaning something different from the term "cause", or of following the more common practice among the rationalists and of construing the two terms to mean the same thing. As Couturat remarked, ". . . for Leibniz as for the Cartesians the relation of cause to effect is identical, at bottom, to the logical relation of principle to consequence." [33]

The existence of these several ways of interpreting the principle reflects a long and standing tradition concerning the use of the term "reason". Since this tradition has an important bearing on the distinctions of the aesthetic, we should remark some of its main features. The linguistic practice of Saint

---

[33] *La Logique de Leibniz*, p. 222.

Thomas provides a convenient illustration of some interesting features of the tradition. First, he uses the same word to mean the concept or the conceptual definition of a thing and to mean the essential nature of a thing. The latter is not a concept; it is what is grasped or intended through a concept of a thing. But the assumption is that if we do know a thing through its concept or definition, we know the thing in its essential nature. The second and more important linguistic point is that knowledge of a thing through its concept or definition is traditionally called "knowledge of the thing *per se*". Such knowledge was always contrasted with knowledge of the thing *per accidens*. The latter, by contrast, involves the use of terms which are not suited to appear in the definition of the thing and which are said not to form part of our concept of what the thing is. The most important example of such terms—for the purposes of understanding the aesthetic, at any rate—is the example of terms which involve locating the thing in time or in space. Since things can change their "time when" and their "place where" without ceasing to be what they are, these are said not to belong to the thing *per se*. Now this ancient terminology was still alive and well in Kant's day among the so-called "German scholastics", who had translated the terminology into German as a part of their general project to bring the Latin distinctions into their native language. The *ens per se* became the *Ding an sich* and the latter has subsequently been translated into English from Kant's German as the *thing in itself*. This translation has become too firmly entrenched to be remedied, but that does not prevent us from noticing that the job of translation was not a well-considered one. The source of the difficulty is that the scholastics also bequeathed to Kant and to us the concept of a thing in itself (*ens in se*). There are some important and well-known arguments in scholastic literature which turn on the demonstration that there is only a popular and inexact equivalence of the two notions. An example is the argument of Saint Thomas designed to refute the suggestion that since God is known as an *ens per se* (e.g., God cannot be represented through a place where or time when) the same concept of substance which applies to creatures must apply to God. None of this would matter very much if the same distinctions had not been carried into Kant's century in the arguments concerning the nature of space and time. From the arguments about whether or not space, for example, is "absolute" the distinctions pass over into the aesthetic where, as we will see, they continue to play a role in the argument. However, the point to be emphasized at the moment—and it can hardly be given sufficient emphasis—is that the concept of the "thing in itself" was not originated by Kant. It is the concept of that which is known through its *ratio* or concept. When Kant denies that we know things in themselves or things *per se*, what he says is entailed by his doctrine that our knowledge is never purely conceptual—and it is entailed not by some new or strange sense which he gives to the phrase *Ding an sich* but by the plain sense in which it had always been understood in the discussions of the principle of sufficient reason among Kant's immediate predecessors.

The intimate association of the concept of a reason, of the principle of sufficient reason, and of the doctrine that all of our representations are concepts is a pronounced and remarkable feature of the philosophical landscape within which the *Critique* appeared. One can appreciate the connection by noting Wolff's discussion of the reason (*Grund*) in his *Vernünftigen Gedanken*. He explains that a reason for something is "that through which one can understand why something is . . ." [34] His subsequent comments make an explicit connection between having reasons and possessing concepts of things. "For as long as a thing has a reason why it is, one can know it, that is, one can conceive it." [35] And again, "Whatever is not conceivable, does not allow of being explained intelligibly."

The same connection between concepts and reasons is evident in the writings of Baumgarten, Gottsched and Lambert. Each of them associates our ability to produce a reason for anything with our ability to give a sound demonstration of any true proposition. Gottsched remarks that "Since anything which is true must have a reason why it is true rather than false, it follows that anything which is true can be demonstrated; that is, it can be justified through the indication of a reason that it must be true. Now since each truth is a proposition and since each proposition taken together with its reason yields an argument which could be expressed in a syllogism, it follows that one could prove any truth at all with formal syllogisms." [36] The first of the syllogistic figures was considered to give the form of argument required for the production of reasons. As Lambert points out, the middle term in such first figure syllogisms is, or purports to be, the reason for the predication contained in the conclusion. [37] This middle term always appears as a term of predication and thus we know that it must be a concept (predicable of many) rather than an intuition. Unless the middle term were general it could not be distributed and the syllogism would not be valid.

The ultimate reason for the truth of the conclusion was discovered in a complete conceptualization of the subject matter of the conclusion. When we

---

[34] Christian Wolff, *Vernünftigen Gedanken von Gott, der Welt, und der Seele des Menschen* (Frankfurt, 1736), p. 15.
[35] *Ibid.*, p. 36.
[36] Johann Gottsched, *Erste Gründe der Vernunftlehre* (Leipzig, 1766), p. 56.
[37] *Neues Organon*, I, p. 156.

can provide a definition of the subject term that has that complete concept as its *definiendum*, we are able to provide a demonstration for every truth about the given subject matter. Accordingly we can say that one formulation of the principle of sufficient reason holds that every true proposition can be known *a priori* or through a demonstration of its truth. Baumgarten gives an example of this interpretation of the sense of the principle when he tells us that an immediate corollary of the principle is that everything which can be known *a posteriori* can also be known *a priori*.[38]

With the principle of sufficient reason interpreted in this spirit Kant's scepticism about the identity of indiscernibles will obviously translate into a scepticism about our capacity to give reasons for everything. Whether or not this is judged to be possible will depend upon whether or not the conditions which determine the existence and the uniqueness of the objects of our representations are entirely conceptual and are entirely to be given through the definition of the subject-term. These issues parallel the doubts that Lambert had expressed earlier about the basis for our assumptions about the existence of the objects of mathematical definitions. Lambert, it will be recalled, had challenged Wolff's views on this subject. The idea that every proposition can be demonstrated from definitions he countered by the observation that in mathematics the typical forms of definition themselves require justification— the definitions assume the existence and uniqueness of the things in which they connect or unite concepts. Perhaps Lambert did not associate this criticism of Wolff with the falsity of the principle that all our representations are concepts. But Kant certainly makes the connection.

It comes out, for example, through a careful reading of Kant's discussion of the ontological argument. This form of argument purports to prove from a definition of God that God exists. In the course of his rebuttal of the proposed proof Kant explains what he would have hoped might settle the issue were it not for the fact that his opponents are victims of a certain illusion. (B626) They do not recognize the difference between our representation of the existence of objects and those representations that are real predicates. Our real predicates are concepts of things which can appear as part of our specifications of what the things are. Our representation of the existence of things occurs as we position or locate the things as the objects of our concepts and judgments. Hence what is at the base of Kant's objection—and what makes it difficult, as he sees, for him to present an objection that his opponents must concede—is the fact that his opponents have not anticipated his own distinction between intuitions and concepts. The illusion which

---

[38] *Gesammelte Schriften*, XVII, p. 27.

prevents them from seeing that there is a distinction between logical and real predicates (and which, by implication, prevents them from accepting this distinction as the basis for a decisive objection to the ontological argument) is the illusion that the purely formal conditions of the possibility of representation are the only conditions of the possibility of representation. With this mention of a certain illusion Kant makes reference to those earlier passages in which he had set the task for a transcendental dialectic by giving his general characterization of transcendental illusion: it is the belief that I can extend my knowledge of objects by inferences that are drawn in conformity with the principles of formal logic alone. (B86) The reader who wishes to understand his later comment about how his opponents are victims of an illusion must be prepared to refer back to those earlier passages in which Kant characterizes transcendental illusion and in which he presents the forms of intuition as conditions under which alone the objects of knowledge can assume a position *as* objects of knowledge.

A second point in Kant's treatment of the ontological argument also looks back to the definitions and arguments that have gone before. Kant tells us that he is only prepared to grant to his opponents the logical possibility of the concept of God. In a footnote he remarks that the logical possibility of a concept only guarantees that the object of the concept is not a *nihil negativum*. This expression is quite clearly intended to convey some reasonably precise or technical concept. If we turn back to the section in which Kant had explained it, we discover that here too his analysis of the ontological argument ultimately comes to rest on his distinction between intuitions and concepts. Kant distinguishes a *nihil negativum* or object of a logically impossible concept from an *ens rationis* or "object of a concept to which no intuition can be found to correspond". What Kant is telling us in the body of his text, therefore, is that, in granting the logical possibility of the concept of God, he withholds the right to insist on a proof of the real possibility of the object. Now the proof of this real possibility will involve us in showing that God conforms to the conditions under which God can be located by us as an object of intuition. Since the latter involve the location or the locatability of the object in space or time, Kant has good reason to suppose that God is not within the domain of our possible knowledge.

Kant's treatment of the ontological argument has been cited as a typical case of his treatment of transcendental illusion in our representations of the self, the world, and God. Kant begins from a supposed proof of some metaphysical proposition, or set of propositions. If the proof were sound, it would illustrate the application of a principle of sufficient reason; and if the principle were sound, it would lead us to admit the possibility of some extension of our knowledge through a principle governing only our concepts of things. In each discussion Kant exposes the illusion as the supposition that a knowledge through pure concepts alone is possible—knowledge that moves beyond the boundaries set by the forms of intuition. As a consequence if one agrees that Kant's scepticism about the possibility of proofs in rational psychology, cosmology and theology is related to his doubts about the principle of sufficient reason, one must also agree that it is related to his doubts about the principle that all of our representations are concepts. The historical significance of this point is considerable, because the evidence suggests that the doubts which finally were crystallized in the final sections of the *Critique* belonged to the earlier stages in the motivation of the work.

III. FROM "TRACTARIAN" TO CRITICAL VIEWS ABOUT REPRESENTATION

When Kant abandoned the view that all representations are concepts in favor of the view that some of our representations are intuitions, he evidently changed his mind about the possible relations between representations and objects. His earliest views are contained in a lengthy fragment which the editors of the Academy edition of his writings date to about 1756. The passage attracts our attention because it expresses Kant's first (or second) thoughts and can be compared with his later, critical views. The passage has an additional interest for readers today. Kant's thoughts show a clear resemblance to what Wittgenstein appeared to wish to convey in his *Tractatus Logico-Philosophicus*. The term which Kant employs for the relationship between representation and object is *refers*—a term that he later employed to define intuitions. But his earlier characterization of the relationship that he has in mind betrays no hint of his later doctrine of the forms of reference:

A representation is an internal determination of the mind, insofar as the mind is referred by that representation to certain other things. (It) is that determination of the mind which refers to other things. I say that it *refers* if its constitution is in conformity with that of external things, or if it conforms to external things.[39]

The evident redundancy in this passage is due to the fact that Kant repeats his thought in two languages, Latin and German. The fact that there are these miniature versions of a Rosetta stone to be found throughout Kant's writings will be a great aid when we turn to more purely terminological issues in the next chapter. Still the doctrine which begins the passage we are concerned

[39] *Ibid.*, XVI, p. 76–77.

with has no great philosophical novelty and no particular similarity with Wittgenstein's earlier views. But notice the way in which Kant goes on to analyze this relation of conformation, which he has invoked to define representations. In the immediately following paragraph Kant considers an explanation of that relationship according to which the representation "has precisely that similarity to the represented thing which a painting has to the depicted object." Kant rejects that account. He makes it very clear that one cannot say that the representation is a kind of mental image or copy of the thing in which parts of the representation have properties that match properties of the parts of what it represent. He continues:

What is it, then, in the representation which corresponds with the representation? The representation, because it derives its nature from the represented thing, corresponds with it in that it is composed out of its partial concepts in the same way that the whole of the represented object is composed out of its parts. Thus, for example, one can say: the notes [i.e., the signs in the musical score] of a piece of music are a representation of the harmonic connection of the sounds. Not as if a note were similar to a sound but because the notes are in the same connection with one another as the sounds themselves.

This explanation of how representations are related to what they represent should be compared with Wittgenstein's better known discussion of the possibility of linguistic representation:

At first glance the proposition—say as it stands printed on paper—does not seem to be a picture of the reality of which it treats. But nor does the musical score appear at first sight to be a picture of a musical piece; . . . The gramophone record, the musical thought, the score, the waves of sound, all stand to one another in that pictorial internal relation, which holds between language and the world. To all of them the logical structure is the same.

There can be differing explanations of the origin of this thought in the *Tractatus* and these need not concern us. But Kant clearly owed his idea to his Leibnizian presuppositions about representations. As Couturat and many others have remarked, the idea that the logical structure of representations is the same as the structure of the world was a commonplace among the Leibnizians. The most vigorous of the recent presentations of that theme occurs in the study by Michel Serres. He even goes so far as to suggest that the idea of this structural correspondence is the leading and dominant idea, not only in Leibniz's analysis of the nature of representations, but, indeed, in

Leibniz's entire monadology.[40] He pursues the idea of structural correspondences through a number of different parts of the Leibnizian corpus.

Kant's later and more critical views about representation take a different
tack. Kant's basic assumption in the *Critique* is that the concept of representation is a generic concept and that our representations perform a large variety
of different jobs. For example, before launching his discussion of the division
of the genus, representation, Kant has reminded us that Plato's idea of a
republic does not have a direct role in cognition, because nothing is to be
found in reality that in any way corresponds to the idea. Nevertheless, says
Kant, we do ourselves a great disservice if we simply reject the idea altogether, without acknowledging the great practical importance of the idea, the
significance that the idea has in stimulating us to bring about the conditions
in which the idea would find some corresponding reality. Also, Kant calls
our attention to other ideas which do have a role in cognition but which serve
only a regulative function—such ideas also do not correspond in their
structure to the structure of reality.

A second, but related, observation by Kant is that it is incorrect to assign
a particular classification to a representation without regard to the context
in which the representation is functioning and without regard to the particular
job to which our analysis is directing attention. Thus, for example, we are
concerned in this chapter with the genesis of Kant's distinction between
intuitions and concepts, and we have discussed this distinction at times as
though it could be applied in some absolute way and without regard to the
role of the particular representation in a particular cognition. Kant de-
nounces this suggestion: "Cognition through concepts is called *discursive*,
that in intuition is called *intuitive*; in fact, both of them, bound together with
one another, are required for knowledge, which is, however, named by the
one that in each case I am principally attending to as the determining ground
of the knowledge."[41]

From what has been said one can detect a dim but real analogy between the
way in which Kant's maturing views reflected an increased sensitivity to the
different roles assumed by our representations and the growth in Wittgenstein's awareness of the many different things we can do with words. Supposing that Kant's thinking did develop in such a way, we would be mistaken to
search for a single key to his changing views on the possibility of representation. Having acknowledged this complexity to the problem of his motivation,
we can locate one sure and powerful influence on his thinking about the

---

[40] Michel Serres, *Le Système de Leibniz et les Modèles Mathématiques* (Paris, 1968), I,
p. 58 and passim.
[41] *Gesammelte Schriften*, XX, p. 266.

difference between intuitions and concepts. The influence comes from mathematics and mathematical representation. This influence is easy to overlook because the *Critique* omitted the actual examples of cognition which would have fleshed out his account. As we read the *Critique* today, our tendency is to fill in the missing examples with knowledge that is expressed in the natural language—for example, "The sun is the cause of the warming of the rock." It should be remembered however that Kant was the son of Leibniz and Newton, that his interest is particularly in scientific cognition in the *Critique*, and that he believed that there is only as much science in a given discipline as there is of mathematics in it. For these reasons an empirical equation—a proposition formulated in the language of mathematics—will sometimes give the more pertinent illustration of Kant's particular point. How does this bear on the genesis of Kant's distinction between intuitions and concepts?

Our point of departure for the answer to this question takes us back to the way in which the mathematicians had conceived the distinction between constants and variables in the days just before the *Critique*. Euler was a mathematician with an almost unbelievable productivity at the frontiers of mathematics, but he also wrote several of the more influential and better known introductions for the general reader. In his work we find that the comparison between general or discursive concepts and mathematical variables had already been made well before the writings of Kant. For example, his *Introductio in Analysin Infinitorum* gives the following explanation of constant and variable quantities: "A constant quantity is a fixed quantity that always preserves the same worth."[42] And, "A variable quantity is an undetermined or universal quantity, which comprehends in itself every determinate value whatsoever." The way in which the critical phrases in these explanations tie the notions to the terminology and distinctions of the traditional analysis of judgments in logic is something that not all of Euler's readers could have been expected to know. But he continues in a way that makes the connection explicit: "Just as, that is to say, from ideas of individuals ideas of species and genera are formed, so the variable quantity is the genus, under which any determinate quantity is contained."

There are a number of points that suggest that Kant had the same comparison in mind as he formulated his distinction of intuitions and concepts. For one thing he talks about the combination of intuitions and concepts in judgments in the same terminology that Euler goes on to employ in talking about the combination of constants and variables in equations. The historic term for the mode or the form of the combination of these expressions in

---

[42] Leonhard Euler, *Opera Omnia*, Series I, Vol. 8 (Berlin, 1912), p. 17.

mathematics is the term *function*. Euler explains functions as follows: "A function of a variable quantity is an analytic expression howsoever combined from that variable quantity and numbers or constant quantities." The modern reader must walk with caution over this ground, because we are accustomed to a different use of the concept—one in which a function is a mode or form of dependency of one thing or one set of things on another thing or set of things. The American logician Church, who regards the mathematical concept of a function as one of the primary ideas imported into modern logic, has called our attention to this important shift in the history of the term. Originally, "function" was used to pick out forms of mathematical expression— that is, it had a use comparable to the use of "form" in traditional logic. Church tells us that "the major generalization" by which our modern and more abstract notion of function was achieved should be attributed to Dirichlet in 1837, or about a half century after the term was used in the *Critique*. Dirichlet, we are told, was the first to succeed in "freeing the idea of a function from its former dependence on a mathematical expression."[43]

When Kant turns his attention in the *Critique* to the forms of judgment by which the combination of representations in an object is possible, he titles his inquiry a study "Of the Logical Function of the Understanding in Judgments". We have every reason to suppose that he had the mathematician's sense of the term in his mind. First, there is no ambiguity about the history of the term or about its general significance. Leibniz is credited with the introduction of the term in a paper of 1692.[44] It had subsequently been used by others in very much the same sense that we have encountered in Euler. For example, Bernouilli wrote, "We here denote by *function* of a variable quantity a quantity composed in some way or other of this variable quantity and constants."[45] The mode or the way in which the composition out of constants and variables occurs gives us the form of the mathematical thought. If we suppose that Kant associated intuitions and concepts with these mathematical constants and variables, it was only to be expected that when the inquiry turned to the forms of thought in understanding he spoke of "logical functions".

There are many passages in Kant's notes and papers which reveal the influence of this mathematical precedent in the discussion of expressions. Kant tries again and again to give a mathematical expression to non-mathematical propositions, such as "A body is extended", using the constants and the variables of mathematical equations—that is, "a"s and "b"s, and "x"s

[43] Alonzo Church, *Introduction to Mathematical Logic* (Princeton, 1956), p. 23.
[44] *Acta Eruditorium* (Leipzig, 1692); reprinted in *Mathematische Schriften*, Abteilung 2, Vol. I, p. 266.
[45] J. Bernouilli, *Opera Omnia* (Lausanne, Geneva, 1742), II, p. 241.

and "y"s. We have already encountered one of the motives behind these efforts: He realized that it was a matter of "the greatest importance" that we should attempt to "make a science of reasoning technical". "Through the technical method," he reminds himself, and he is undoubtedly recalling the work of Holland and Lambert,[46] "one can express with the name of every concept its function, or, rather, express the functions themselves, both in themselves and in relation to others. (Algebra expresses them only in relation to one another—perhaps this will be the case with transcendental algorithms.)" An equation which expresses a function in itself is presumably one which has the general form of $x = fy$, or—to select an expression of a function in arithmetic—"Twelve is equal to the sum of seven and five". When Kant says that algebra gives us only functions expressed in relation to one another, he probably has in mind the pure equations of algebra which give rise to the definition or inter-definability of functions. An example would be $x - y = x + (-y)$. The other possibility is that he has in mind a related use of the term "*function*", by which the whole expression, $z = x^2 + 3x + 2$, would be called a function.[47] At any rate, one apparent motive for considering the representations of thought on the model of algebraic equations is clearly to facilitate the techniques of calculation and reasoning.

This motive is closely related to Kant's feelings about the importance of mathematics in empirical science. Newton's mathematical formulations of his physical theory provide the obvious model for Kant here. It was this feature of Newton's work which had allowed—or had appeared in the eighteenth century to allow—those extraordinarily impressive calculations of quantitatively exact predictions which did so much to establish the supremacy of Newton's natural philosophy.[48] Today we realize that there was a certain amount of fudging in those deductions, but if the spirit of quantitative exactness was partially a sham, we cannot suppose that Kant was aware of that fact or that, being aware of it, he would necessarily have had a different opinion about the importance of mathematics in scientific reasoning.

There is no doubt that the development of algebra and, later, of analysis facilitated the calculations in all of the branches of science that could be made technical through the employment of these algorithmic techniques. At the same time, it must be remembered that the growth of algebra gave rise to a

---

[46] The reference to Holland is explicit in Kant's next note: *Gesammelte Schriften*, XVIII, p. 35. Lambert gives a longer list of authors contributing to the *mathesis universalis* for ontology in his *Schriften*, III, p. xx; we can suppose that Kant at least saw that.

[47] The particular illustration is from Johann Lambert, *Opera Mathematica* (Zurich, 1946), I, p. 251.

[48] R.S. Westfall, "Newton and the Fudge-Factor," *Science*, 179, p. 751 (Feb. 23, 1973).

problem within mathematics itself and within the disciplines that borrowed the language of mathematics. In order to appreciate the mathematical antecedents of Kant's doctrine of the forms of intuition, we must recall what the problem was and how it was solved. The problem arises from the fact that the long chains of algebraic reasoning came to involve the sheer manipulation of representations and from the fact, too, that in the course of the development of mathematical techniques for handling these calculations representations were admitted into algebra and analysis for the purpose of facilitating the reasoning. The result was that algebra came to contain expressions that the mathematicians were not sure that they knew how to interpret. Similarly, the resources of algebra were of no use to physicists until they learned a way to determine the possible physical significance of algebraic equations and the solutions to algebraic equations.

If Leibniz was the great exponent of the search for algorithms and for wholly new calculi, Descartes was the father of attempts to make mathematical concepts intuitive and of attempts to explain the possibility of attributing physical significance to empirical equations.[49] In this sense Descartes is the obvious father of Kant's doctrine of the forms of intuition. Descartes's major proposal was an analytic geometry in which the value of the numerical expressions is assured by means of an interpretation which identifies those values with parts of space, or to what can be given a position in space or time. When we take this way of dealing with the problem of interpreting our empirical representations as the model for a logical reconstruction of the interpretation of all empirical representations—and not merely those that are expressed in actual empirical equations, the result either will be, or will be comparable to, what Carnap calls a "C-language" in his *Logical Syntax of Language*. Three or four features of such a Cartesian system of representations are particularly important for an understanding of Kant's distinction between intuitions and concepts. First, and most obviously, there is the distinction between the terms which are employed to fix the references of the descriptions and the terms which are employed to give the descriptions. There is, in other words, a distinction built into the C-language between the way in which the object is picked out or located as the object which will verify or falsify the description and the way in which the object thus picked out or located is described or characterized. It is this aspect of the C-language which is family-related to Kant's distinction between intuitions and concepts.

Secondly, the terms of predication or description in such a system of representation can be connected with one another by being referred to the

---

[49] Y. Belaval in the very instructive and useful work *Leibniz' Critique de Descartes* (Paris, 1960) gives an extended discussion of this contrast between the two rationalists.

same position. This occurs when they are assigned to the same terms of reference. The terms of reference are co-ordinated with one another by virtue of the fact that the objects of reference are located as parts of a common spatial or temporal manifold. This possibility of a systematic coordination of the references is the distinguishing feature of a Cartesian approach to the problem of giving physical significance to empirical laws that express the fact that one physical quantity or set of quantities is a function of or depends upon other physical quantities. We will discover that when Kant first turns to a consideration of his doctrine that the representation of a multiplicity of things in one world involves the representation of space and time as forms of intuition he borrows the language as well as the concept of the act of co-ordination.

A third very important point to recall about the Cartesian method of co-ordinating mathematical descriptions is that our way of achieving reference to objects not only has to be distinguished from our way of describing them, but even has to be assigned a logical priority over the way in which the objects are described. To take a concrete example, we know that we cannot look at an empirical equation that describes for us the shape of some object and know that we are dealing, for example, with the equation of an object with a circular shape. First, and before we can construe the physical significance of the equation, we have to know how the references have been taken in assigning the interpretation to the equation. As we will see when we turn to Kant's positive arguments in the aesthetic, this fact that Descartes brings to the algebraic expression a representation of a space which is not contained in the expression, but is a presupposition of its having a physical significance, is a central fact for Kant's transcendental inquiry into the possibility of empirical knowledge. A fourth point that we know about the Cartesian co-ordination of descriptions—or perhaps the point should count as a second way of looking at the point that has just been made—is that when we change our system of co-ordinates we must alter the mathematical description of the object to conform to the change in the system of reference. For example, one mathematically permissible change in the system of references will require us to construe the mathematical description of an orange as the representation of a two-dimensional figure—as a figure in the family of ellipses, for example.

The truth of this fact has been brought home to everyone who has ever studied elementary geometry and who has encountered some of the very different ways of mapping the earth. By a suitable choice of his scheme of projection and by a suitable choice of his center of reference the cartographer who lives in Basel can offer us a map of the world in which Switzerland appears as one of the larger nations. There is some empirical evidence to suggest that such a map will correspond more closely to the map that the unlettered citizens of Basel will draw of their world,[50] but that fact by itself has no great interest for the student of the aesthetic—after all these maps are representations of *models of* the world and Kant's analysis is concerned with our knowledge of the things *in* the world. The relevance of these elementary examples of an employment of a Cartesian system of co-ordinates for giving physical significance to a representation of the places on the earth's surface comes from an historical accident. The accident was that the man with whom Kant had originally planned to collaborate in the writing of his *Critique* had made a special study of the mathematical aspects of the basic problem of cartography. Lambert was the first mathematician to put the choice between different cartographic projections of the earth on a sound analytic footing, so that the cartographer who could tell the mathematician which aspects of the description of the earth are to be preserved in the projection of it could (hopefully) be told by the mathematician whether the requirements could be met and, if so, which projection would come closest to preserving the desired characteristics.[51] The fact that Kant had these applications of the Cartesian method in mind as he discussed the forms of intuition is strongly suggested by the two terms that he uses for the objects of intuition, as well as by the points which he makes about these objects.

The undetermined object of an empirical intuition is called an *appearance* (*Erscheinung*). (B20) The individual object of a pure intuition is called an *image* (*Bild*). (B140) These two terms, and particularly the first, were the terms that were habitually employed by mathematicians in Kant's day to describe the results of a mathematical projection—whether it resulted in a representation of objects in the real world or whether it resulted in a representation of objects in a model of the real world. In either case the projection represents its object by means of a method of referring to the parts of an extensional manifold. Among the mathematicians the results of any such projection were called appearances, but Kant is very evidently using the term in a more restricted way. When he calls something an appearance he wishes to call attention to the fact that it is something that has been located or referred to as an object of knowledge, he wishes to call attention to the fact that our way of locating it as an object of intuition makes its position as a possible object of thought or description be something that is only fixed relative to a presupposition about the form of intuition or the system of reference, and, finally, he wishes to call attention to the fact that appearances—

[50] Cf. *Images and Environment*, ed. R.M. Downs and D. Stea (Chicago, 1973).
[51] Johann Lambert, *Notes and Comments on the Composition of Terrestial and Celestial Maps*, trans. by W.R. Tobler from the edition of 1772 (Ann Arbor, 1972).

unlike other things that might be imagined as possible objects of knowledge—must come within the limits of empirical description or description
based upon observations of things. We have seen how each of these points
was related to the others in the thoughts of Copernicus and of Descartes as
they analyzed the conditions under which we could come to a better understanding of the earth and of its planetary orbit. Every system for empirical
description—every system of reference that realizes the preceding three
points—will make the relative position of the object, its relative shape, its
relative size, and so on, depend upon the way in which its position is fixed in
relation to possible observers. The naive and pre-Copernican view takes this
obvious point to mean that the center of the system of reference should be
fixed by the position of human beings, or other possible observers, in the
universe. The more critical and post-Copernican discovery is that the choice
of the form of intuition is what determines the physical significance of the
descriptions of the objects and that the form of intuition must be studied in
terms of this role that it has as a presupposition for the possibility of empirical
description. The objects are the things that are located or given position by the
forms of intuition, as a condition of the possibility of a mathematical description and understanding of those objects. The obvious and very practical
significance of this insight is that sometimes the observer is not regarded as
having a fixed position at all—let alone having a fixed position in reference to
which the positions of everything else are to be determined. Sometimes the
observer must be set in motion. This idea that the observer must be set in
motion within space and time is of course the specific idea by which Copernicus and Descartes realized that they could preserve the mathematical description of paths of the planets as circular paths. However, it must be understood
that for Kant's analysis of the conditions of the possibility of empirical
description the discussion of the Copernican revolution and the way it sets
the observer in motion is only a dramatization of the conceptual issue. The
central point is that the form of intuition can no longer be regarded as something that is determined by considerations that reflect the spontaneity of the
observer—his ability to move around in space, to look at things from different
angles, and to think of things in accordance with concepts of his own devising.
Instead, the discussion of the forms of intuition is a discussion of the way in
which the objects can be given a position in space and time as a condition of
the very possibility that they can be described and explained. The forms of
intuition represent the possibility that we can locate ourselves, as observers,
in relation to a world of objects; and, as such, the forms of intuition reflect
the mere receptivity of the observer in regard to the conditions under which
the objects can be given. The alternative view—the view that was swept away

by Copernicus—would regard the empirical objects as things that can be located and described as objects in space and in time in accordance with conditions that have their origin or their explanation in us, the observers of the things. But this view is entirely mistaken and the conditions under which the objects are located as objects of empirical descriptions do not reflect something that depends upon us as observers or that is within our control as observers. What can we, as observers, control? We can control our actual positions, we can control the sensory content that we choose to attend to, and we have great freedom in the aspects of things that we choose to attend to. But none of this determines the location of the objects of empirical description, when these are considered to be appearances in the post-Copernican and post-Cartesian sense. What else is there about us, as observers, that might be supposed to be reflected in the position of empirical objects *as appearances*? One thinks here of the usual assortment of factors that are not within our control, but that might be held to be relevant in determining the apparent position of objects—our optical equipment, the way our brains process the signals received from the sensors, the peculiarities of human psychology that are responsible for the qualities of our sensations. But none of this is any more relevant to the location of the appearance than the factors that *are* within our control. The point to keep in mind as the legacy of Copernicus and Descartes is that the position of an appearance is determined by a presupposition about the way the objects are given, rather than by something that happens for one reason or other to be true about us as observers. The presupposition that determines the way the object must be located is the form of intuition, which is a co-ordination of the appearances in their relationships with one another. Given that these appearances have been oriented in relationship to each other, and given too that these appearances have been categorized by us as the appearances of empirical objects (something that demands more than the representation of the appearances in conformity with the form of intuition), *then we can orient ourselves as empirical objects in relationship to this world of empirical objects*. The upshot of this analysis is the revolutionary idea that the location of appearances in the world of objects does not depend upon any truth about ourselves, even though we can and do spontaneously change our positions in relation to the appearances.

Unless Kant is able to make out a distinction between the empirical descriptions that apply to the observer (or that apply to the objects observed—descriptions that may include a specification of the positions of each) and a system or form of reference to objects which is not itself subject to empirical description because it is the presupposition of the empirical significance of all such description, then everything that has just been said will be bound to appear paradoxical or even contradictory. The just measure of his success will be provided by the arguments of the aesthetic, but what is important now is to realize the source and the nature of the concept of appearance which Kant carries into the *Critique*. His concept is a philosophical generalization of the mathematical concept of appearance that appears in the aftermath of the Cartesian discoveries. An appearance is the undetermined object of an empirical intuition and, as such, it must conform to the form of intuition or the condition under which it can have a location in space or time as a possible object of knowledge. This is the generic concept of appearance—the Cartesian or mathematical concept of appearance as something given in conformity to a scheme of reference that is employed in order to make possible an algebraic or analytic representation of objects. This general concept of appearance must be carefully distinguished from a much more special and particular concept of a *mere* appearance or of an appearance *to us* of something. If an appearance is something picked out and described in accordance with the form of intuition, an appearance to us is not only picked out in conformity to a form of intuition but is also picked out in conformity to the condition that as our actual position changes the description of the appearance must also change. As I walk about a house and as I refer my descriptions to what I see, my descriptions must obviously change. These merely perspectival changes in appearances—that is the Copernican idea—must obviously be distinguished from a change in the appearances of the house that is due to the rotation of the house before my eyes. In the first case, nothing but the appearance of the house is changing, while in the second case, the house is changing in its appearance. The philosophical generalization which philosophers had achieved in the concept of appearance after Copernicus and Descartes is one that permits the concept to be employed in both of these cases and not merely in the case in which the appearance to the observer is changing. To repeat, the appearances of empirical objects are oriented in relationship to one another in conformity to a form of intuition, and only thereby can we be oriented as observers in relationship to those objects. The question after Copernicus is no longer "Where are the objects of the solar system or the universe in relation to us?" but rather "Where are we in this system of planets and this system of galaxies?"

Unless we bear in mind that for Kant the concept of appearance becomes a more generic notion that includes the notion of an appearance to some actual observer, we will be victims of a very common misconception about what Kant has in mind. The source of the misconception is Kant's repeated explanation that he calls the object of a representation an appearance when he wishes to call attention to its dependency upon our way of being affected by objects and to stress that it is not a thing in itself. Many readers have assumed that Kant has in mind a causal theory of perception in defining appearances and that according to such a theory an appearance is the effect in us of an unknown or even unknowable cause. But this causal account is precisely the wrong theory to have in mind to get at the basic sense of appearance in Kant. The full set of considerations that show it to be wrong will not be available until we have had the opportunity to study his use of the terms "affected" and "thing in itself", but we can already appreciate that the explanation must be on the wrong track. If appearances were understood to be the effects in us of causes that are not themselves the direct objects of empirical knowledge, then changes in the appearances would of course imply changes in these unknown causes. But of course there is not any such correspondence. The sequences in the changes of appearances is the same whether I am walking around the house or the house is rotating in front of me. In both cases the correct description to be referred to the object is dependent upon the way in which reference to the object is achieved, but what marks the first sequence out as a merely apparent change is the fact that it results from something that we do and in our way of relating to the object. Nothing at all is happening by way of change in the house or in things *per se* and, accordingly, there is no reason to posit any changes in an unknown cause of the appearances as we account for the change in the appearances.

The concept of a relationship which is the kind of relationship in which we are affected in our knowledge implies either changes in the objects which determine changes in what can be known about the objects or changes in the form of our relationship to the objects which must be reflected in changes in the value of what is known about the objects. Evidence to show that the latter is possible—that an idea of a causal connection between the appearance and some unknown object that is its cause is not involved in Kant's idea of the way objects affect us, will be presented in the next chapter. There is one peripheral but related point of terminology that should be mentioned now, because it conceivably is related to the mathematical origins of the Kantian terminology. Kant calls a representation which is subject to an alteration that reflects the changes in the way in which we are affected by objects *affected*; he contrasts these with representations that are called *pure*. His language appears to correspond to a very old tradition in algebra according to which equations and other mathematical expressions are pure or affected. They are pure if there are no particular constants as coefficients in the expressions.[52] If they are affected, they contain a set of those particular values to be given

[52] David E. Smith, *History of Mathematics* (New York, 1958), II, p. 449–450.

empirical significance when the expression is interpreted in a co-ordinate system. These particular values can change in the several ways that we have been discussing.

The contrast between pure and affected representations reminds us that appearances can be the subject of *a priori* conceptualization according to Kant. This doctrine will be either puzzling or flatly unintelligible unless we bear in mind that an appearance is a thing whose description presupposes a form of intuition and whose description will vary in conformity to variations in our way of referring descriptions to their objects. When Kant turns to the way in which non-empirical concepts can be provided with the objects of a pure and non-empirical intuition, he introduces a second term to describe these referential projections of objects. He speaks of the pure image which is the object of a single intuition and of the schema which is the procedure whereby a given *a priori* concept can receive its objects. One point to notice is that this second term, like the term appearance, comes out of the mathematical tradition in which Cartesian co-ordinates are employed in the representation of the things in the world. Lambert's analytic results concerning cartographic projections were extended by Kärsten in a well-known paper that had appeared in the *Proceedings* of the Bavarian Academy. His regular term for these projections or appearances of objects is *Bild* or *image*. The image of an object such as the earth is that object as it is represented to be in some co-ordinate system of reference.[53] The term *co-ordinate* had been invented by Leibniz to express one of the basic concepts in the Cartesian treatment of algebraic equations.[54] Consequently, unless we wish to credit Kant with an independent act of invention we can suppose that he is using the term in the same or in a related sense when he uses it to describe the form of things in space and time when the world is considered in relation to our possible representations of it.[55] What we are representing to ourselves, he tells us, cannot be a world unless it contains a plurality of substances whose being with one another is co-ordinated.

The genius of Leibniz originated more than a few isolated terms or concepts. His own study of what an idea is anticipated Kant's analysis of the forms of intuition and proceeded under the inspiration of mathematical models. When Leibniz discusses the way in which an idea corresponds to that of which it is a representation, he offers us the analogies of the relationship of

[53] W.J.G. Kärsten, "Theorie von der Projectionen der Kugel zum astronomischen und geographischen Gebrauch," *Abhandlungen der Churfürstlich-Bayerischen Akadamie der Wissenschaften* (Munich, 1768), Volume 5.
[54] Gottfried Wilhelm Leibniz, *Mathematische Schriften*, Abth. 2, Vol. I, p. 266. Cf. Smith, *History of Mathematics*, II, p. 324.
[55] *Gesammelte Schriften*, II, p. 389.

a solid to its plane projection (i.e., to the appearance of the solid in the plane) and the relation of the set of numbers to the set of numerical signs. In a passage which anticipates both Kant's earliest analysis of representations and his later ideas about the form of intuition Leibniz explains that one thing expresses another (in his sense) when there is a fixed and ordered relation between that which can be said of the one and of the other. It is in this way, he says, that the projection of an object from a perspective expresses the geometrical properties of the object which is projected.[56] There are many passages in which Leibniz carries this idea back into his analysis of perception and of empirical knowledge. But the more characteristic passages carry the idea forward into metaphysics where he discusses our nature as beings which represent things to ourselves. For example, he relates the difference between our nature and God's nature to the difference between our perspectives which are always at a finite distance from the object and God's perspective which he locates at Desaurges' point at infinity. In the appearances of the objects from the latter perspective—appearance being used here in its mathematical sense—everything is projected to the same plane and nothing is left obscured behind something else. A second illustration is his treatment of the different philosophies of history which were apparently suggested to him by the different linear mappings of the historical record. Serres has shown the immense suggestiveness of the underlying mathematical model in Leibniz's discussion of the concept of representation in these and other instances. At the same time, we must recall our earlier results on Leibniz's views concerning the transcendental doctrine of elements. These results prove that, if Leibniz anticipated Kant by bringing the mathematical concept of an appearance into the discussion of cognitive representations, Kant was nevertheless first in working out the implications of this model for the elements of knowledge. Kant is the one who gives the careful defence of the view that there is an intuitive element in knowledge, and that this element presupposes space and time as forms that make possible the co-ordination of references to objects. Still, there cannot be any doubt that if Kant was inspired by the example of co-ordinate languages in mathematics in giving his account of how are ideas are referred to their objects and in giving his account of the objects themselves, Leibniz had earlier been inspired by the same example.

---

[56] Letter to Arnauld, *Philosophische Schriften* (Berlin, 1875), II, p. 111; quoted in Serres, *Le Système de Leibniz*, I, p. 145.

CHAPTER FOUR

TERMINOLOGY IN THE AESTHETIC

> Wortgrübelei! wird man sagen. Wer mit Wort-
> grübelei sein Nachdenken nicht anfängt, der
> kommt, wenig gesagt nie damit zu Ende.—*Lessing*

There is no denying that a difficult terminology has hampered efforts to understand the transcendental aesthetic. We can cite the reaction of Thomas De Quincey as an obvious illustration. He was one of the first in England to read the *Critique* and Kant's obscurity had not yet become celebrated. *Life and Manners* records an impression of the aesthetic in a passage of splendid indignation. De Quincey refers to those two "cabalistical phrases," "intuitions" and "forms, a priori," and he complains, "Kant repeats these words— as a charm before which all darkness flies; and he supposes continually the case of a man denying his explanations or demanding proofs of them, never once the sole imaginable case—viz., of all men demanding an explanation of these explanations. Deny them! Combat them! How should a man deny, why should he combat, what might, for anything to the contrary appearing, contain a promissory note at two months after date for 100 guineas? No; it will cost a little preliminary work before *such* explanations will much avail any scheme of philosophy, either for the *pro* or con."

De Quincey directs our attention to a problem which has to do in part with the specific meaning of specific terms. This aspect of the problem is the easiest to face. It can be solved by a statement of what those terms mean, together with evidence to show that they do mean what they are said to mean. There is another aspect of the problem which is more difficult to deal with and which relates to an idea about Kant's language that has been very widely held. The idea is that Kant used words in some arcane and highly idiosyncratic way. The most extreme form of the idea is that his philosophical terminology has a Kantian source and a Kantian sense, so that only a person who had studied the terms in the context of Kant's own writings can hope to understand what his terms mean. If this idea were sound it would have a direct and obvious bearing on the line to be taken in interpreting his works. It would also have a bearing—less obvious but no less real—on certain issues of substance to which his philosophy speaks. His own terminological practice would conflict with his views on the status of logical principles in general and of rules of definition in particular.

I. THE ETHICS OF TERMINOLOGY

Many distinguished students of the *Critique* have rejected out of hand any suggestion that the meaning of Kant's terms is arbitrary and is determined by Kant's own individual will or decision. They assume that for the most part his terminology belonged to his philosophical community and they look as a matter of course to the works of that community for enlightenment about what the terms mean. This assumption would hardly be worth remarking, if it were not for the larger number of commentators who assume the opposite and who deny to Kant the conscience of a German scholastic.

Kemp Smith appropriated De Quincey's idea as part of what has come to be known as the patch-work interpretation of the *Critique*. The *Critique* was stitched together like an old-fashioned quilt that makes use of discarded bits of cloth coming from various periods in the life of the quilt-maker. The dating of sentences and paragraphs depends upon alleged discrepancies in what Kant writes. Among the major discrepancies are those that reflect Kant's fumbling efforts to shape a new terminology. Thus, after Kemp Smith has told us that ". . . Kant flatly contradicts himself in almost every chapter", he goes on to add that ". . . there is hardly a technical term which is not employed by him in a variety of different and conflicting senses."[1] The conclusion which Kemp Smith draws from these real or imagined discrepancies is that Kant frequently did not believe what he wrote in the *Critique* at the time that he wrote the *Critique*. His attempt to sustain the conclusion raises some rather interesting issues in the logic of the history of philosophy.

First, the reasoning by which the patches in the patch-work are defined is not a form of reasoning which anyone should subscribe to uncritically. As an example of the difficulties it presents, there is Kemp Smith's willingness to reason from the logical inconsistency of two propositions to the fact that Kant did not believe both propositions at the time of their assertion, or apparent assertion, by him. It is hard to credit that Kemp Smith or any other

[1] Norman Kemp Smith, *A Commentary to Kant's 'Critique of Pure Reason'* (New York, 1950), p. xx.

philosopher would recommend evidence about a person's beliefs as a proper basis for a proof of the consistency of a set of propositions—let us say, for a set of axioms in transfinite arithmetic. Yet when he represents the first as a sound demonstration, he says the same about the second. There are other and more sober grounds for objecting to the procedures of Kemp Smith, but the central point to be noticed here is that his leading idea about Kant's terminology is inconsistent with any patch-work interpretation of the *Critique*.

In order to see that the two simply cannot be combined, let us suppose that we have accepted the principle that the meaning of Kant's terms is determined by Kant's own individual decisions as these are to be discovered in his literary practice. On this basis we will never be able to establish that Kant ever contradicted himself. The obvious reason is that we will be able to make an unlimited number of distinctions between the meanings of words in different contexts. In point of fact, this possibility is not merely something conjured up in the fevered imagination of Kemp Smith's opponents. The logic of their own principle brought the patch-work theorists to precisely that result. The plain evidence is there in the earlier volumes of *Kant-Studien* which were written under the inspiration of Vaihinger and Adickes—men whose work inspired Kemp Smith as well. There, for example, we can discover a book-length study which distinguishes, or purports to distinguish, dozens of different meanings which Kant assigned to the word *Bewußtsein* in the *Critique*. But if we accept that terminological principle, Kant is protected against every charge of inconsistency. "When threatened by a contradiction, draw a distinction!" The existence of such a procedure—and who among us will care to deny that there are philosophers who have acted on such a maxim to save themselves or to save their favorite ancestors—indicates that there is an internal strain in the patch-work program. Anyone committed to the program will join with the rest of us in denouncing the idea that the meaning of Kant's terms is a function of Kant's own decisions and conventions.

Among those who have rejected the patch-work approach, there are many who retain the terminological principle. For example, Paton has been an influential critic of the patch-work theory but he retains essentially the same idea about Kant's language. At the outset of his study of the *Critique* Paton declared an intention to "expound [Kant's] doctrine in his own terminology." An extreme form of the same idea is evidently behind Paton's belief that a commentator "cannot be asked to meet all possible criticisms or to expound his author in the terms of current philosophical terminology."[2] It seems fair to say that Paton not only accepts the idea that Kant's terminology belonged

---

[2] H.J. Paton, *Kant's Metaphysics of Experience* (London, 1936), I, p. 17.

—either in fact or by right—to Kant, but also adds the idea that it is very different from any terminology that belongs to us. On these assumptions we will be hard put to separate the task of understanding the *Critique* from the task of learning to make appropriate moves with a rather special Kantian jargon. Many students of the *Critique* over the years must have shared the impression of De Quincey that Kant uses strange words in an arbitrary and idiosyncratic way. Instead of seeking to combat that impression, Paton would have us elevate it to the status of an hermeneutical principle. If that is to be the principle, we should be clear about some of the logical and historical limitations of the principle.

In the first place it is simply naive to hope that any standard interpretation of a theory can be fixed by treating its terms in the suggested manner. If we have mapped out all the deductive, logical connections within the theory so that, whenever you make a remark using the vocabulary of the theory, I am able to supply the appropriate response—pointing out some consequence of your remark if I agree and wish to elaborate it, or replying with a relevant counter if I disagree with your remark—what then? You and I may possess entirely different understandings of the theory; indeed the number of different interpretations available to each of us need not even be finite. The fact is that two philosophers can each agree to all the moves which the other makes within a Kantian terminology and yet have entirely different conceptions of what is at issue. In order to see that the point does not concern some remote or out of the way possibility, we should recall that famous encounter between Ernst Cassirer and Martin Heidegger in which the discussion took off from the latter's interpretation of Kant. Although no one can say for sure what was actually said on that occasion, there are several transcriptions that have circulated widely for many years. They give an instructive picture of how such matters can proceed. At the outset and while the discussion was conducted in the language of the *Critique* Cassirer expressed amazement at Heidegger's unwillingness to call himself a neo-Kantian. By the close of the session and after each had lapsed into his own philosophical dialect, the two no longer even seemed to be in communication. This encounter not only illustrates a logical point about interpretations but also illustrates a truth familiar to historians. If we assume that our author has imposed his own will on his vocabulary and thus begin by depriving ourselves of any source of extrinsic evidence about his meanings, we are very apt to end by imposing our own will upon his text. Every sensible and fair-minded reader of *Kant and the Problem of Metaphysics* will have the suspicion that Heidegger embraced such a fate with enthusiasm. If the same thought does not arise so easily when we read the work of Paton, the explanation may be less with his terminological principle than with the firm resolution he has added to stick to the terminology of the *Critique* in expounding Kant.

We should also be clear about the incompatibility between Paton's approach and the views that have been attributed to Kant in earlier chapters. Kant's logic is a normative logic and his logical principles, including the principles of definition, are critical principles. That is, they make it possible for us to review, to criticize, and to control our individual idiosyncracies of conduct. If Kant's linguistic practice conformed to his standards in these matters, it not only reflected that general point of view but it also reflected his special distaste for intellectual free-bootery or for unfettered private enterprise in matters of terminology. Those are the standards of our times and should not be read into the behavior of Kant. He looked back to earlier traditions and, in truth, he made a conscious and determined effort to be a good "German scholastic". That is, he regarded philosophical terminology as the common property of a school of philosophers rather than as the private property of some individual. He treated himself as one who is bound by the existing conventions in respect to terminology except in those rare and special cases in which the necessity for a new term has become obvious. It should be noted that there are only a very small number of cases in which Kant claimed for himself the honor of proposing terminology for a distinction that had been won through his own efforts. In these attitudes Kant was a school philosopher. Kant regarded himself as having a special obligation as a member of those generations who were pioneering in the production of scientific works in German. That is, he felt an obligation to use the vernacular in such a way as to preserve and to transmit the spiritual capital which had been accumulated by the Latin authors. Kant's texts and, most especially, his working notes show that he took this obligation very seriously. When he wishes to fix the sense of a term in his notes and publications he nearly always appends in parentheses the Latin equivalent. Sometimes in his marginal notes on the works of other philosophers we find him correcting their translations from the Latin. Sometimes in his own work he enters a special plea to justify some incidental terminological decision. Who is there today who would attack him for his decision to use "pure" rather than "absolute" to describe a certain class of *a priori* judgments or would care why he reserved the latter term for a more appropriate employment? Anyone who is willing to assert that Kant fixed the meanings of his words in accordance with the real or the perceived necessities of his own thought is a poor observer of Kant's practice and a poor recorder of Kant's declared intentions.[3]

---

[3] *Gesammelte Schriften*, VI, p. 206.

The precedents for Kant's use of a term are often to be found in other branches of study. It must be remembered that Kant had professional responsibilities in several different branches of science and learning over a long period of time. Also it must be remembered that the transition to the vernacular was a problem in these other fields as well. The central fact however is that these precedents do exist and can be exhibited. Any detailed treatment of terminological issues is bound to seem to some to be a mere quibbling with words. But the words of Lessing that headed this chapter can justly be applied to the aesthetic: A discussion that does not begin with this quibbling about words can continue forever without getting anything said.

II. INTUITIONS AS SINGULAR CONCEPTS

A word which has caused as much confusion as any in the discussions of the aesthetic is the word *Anschauung* or *intuition*. The chief points which I wish to explain and to defend about this term are these three: First, intuitions are elements or constituents of our knowledge and the knowledge of which they are elements is propositional knowledge. The second major point is that intuitions belong to the same genus as (general) concepts and, if we wish to be specific in the designation of intuitions, we can call them singular concepts. Intuitions differ from general concepts in that each intuition is a representa- ion of a thing which is one and is present and in that each general concept (*Begriff*) is a possible representation of many things which may or may not exist. The third point is that the fundamental definition of *intuition* in the *Critique* makes use of the relationship that intuitions have to their objects and that this relation is that of reference. Hence, we can also say that intuitions are referring terms and that general concepts are terms of possible predica- tion. For the sake of completeness I add a fourth point to this list. There is a derivative and secondary sense in which a representation is what gets repre- sented (in an act of representation—in the primary sense) and an intuition is what is intuited (in an intuition—again, in the primary sense). These second- ary senses may play a certain role in the later parts of the *Critique*, but they have no importance in the arguments of the aesthetic to which we will be turning our attention.

Each of my three main terminological points would be disputed by some good and sensible commentators. For example, H.J. Paton tries to clarify the nature of intuitions in the following way: "It must be sufficient to say at present that the phenomenal object (such as a chair or table) is directly and immediately given to intuition. Whatever be the part played by thinking, when we feel the hardness and see the color of a chair, our minds are in an immediate relation to the chair, and the chair is so far immediately present to our minds."[4] The evident thrust of these remarks is to associate intuitions with the kind of direct sensory awareness of which seeing and feeling are paradigms. This interpretation is similar to one which Kemp Smith proposed; he wrote, "*Anschauung* etymologically applies only to visual sensations. Kant extends it to cover sensations of all the senses."[5] We will see directly that Kemp Smith's etymological point is extraordinarily misleading and that his conclusion is flatly false. Because he accepted that conclusion as true, he was prepared to defend the remarkable verdict that "the most flagrant example of Kant's failure to live up to his own Critical principles is to be found in his doctrine of pure intuition."

There is abundant evidence showing that Kant used *Anschauung* to describe an element in knowledge. For instance he writes in the *Fortschritte* that "As far as man is concerned . . . all knowledge of things is composed of concept and intuition. Each of the two is, to be sure, representation, but is not yet knowledge. To represent something through *concepts*, that is, in the universal, is called *thinking*, and the capacity for thinking is called the understanding. The immediate representation of the individual is intuition. Knowledge through concepts is called *discursive*, that in *intuition* is called intuitive; in fact, both of the two, bound together with one another, are required for knowledge, which is named by the one which in each given case I am principally concentrating on as the determining ground of the knowledge."[6] This passage shows very conclusively that intuitions and concepts can be parts of the same thing. It would be easy to assume from this fact that, since concepts are undoubtedly parts of judgments or propositions, intuitions can be also. In truth common practice of his day as well as Kant's own discussion of the term,[7] would support a translation of *Erkenntnis* by *judgment* rather than by *knowledge*. But the term was unfortunately not fixed to one sense. In particular, it was also used to cover what we would now call sense-experience. Consequently the passage does not rule out the suggestion that intuitions are the constituents of a direct sensory awareness. What it does show us is that, if Kant conceived intuitions as elements that are involved in seeing or hearing, he must have held that concepts also are elements in seeing or hearing.

The conclusion that Kant had propositional knowledge in mind as he discussed *Erkenntnis* is supported by a later passage from the same work.

---

[4] *Kant's Metaphysics of Experience*, p. 97–98.
[5] *A Commentary to Kant's 'Critique of Pure Reason'*, p. 79.
[6] *Gesammelte Schriften*, XX, p. 325.
[7] For example, at *Gesammelte Schriften*, XI, p. 315–316.

Kant tells us that "Knowledge is a judgment, from which a concept issues that has objective reality. . . . One of the two species of representation taken by itself, does not constitute knowledge, and if there should be synthetic cognitions *a priori*, then there must be *a priori* intuitions as well as *a priori* concepts."[8] There is no doubt that cognitions, as these are to be understood here, are judgments composed of intuitions and concepts. There is also no doubt that Kant's critical account of the possibility of synthetic *a priori* knowledge intends to assign a role to *a priori* intuitions. Now it may be true, as Kemp Smith will argue, that the doctrine is not a judicious one for Kant to defend, but the mere fact that he could express the doctrine at all tells us something about what he means by the term *Anschauung*. The two facts that cognitions containing intuitions are judgments and that some intuitions are not empirical serve to rule out *sense-experience* or direct *sensory awareness* as terminological equivalents for Kant's term *Erkenntnis*.

It is true that Kant does argue that all of our experiences (*Erfahrungen*) contain intuitions as parts or elements. What we are to make of this fact obviously depends upon how we construe his term for experience. The evidence on this question shows pretty conclusively that when Kant speaks of our experiences he has in mind our empirical judgments.[9] Hence the fact that intuitions are elements in experiences tends to support rather than to undercut the notion that they are elements in a propositional knowledge. For example, he writes, "All experiences (*Erfahrungen*) are nothing but synthetic judgments."[10] Later in the same work we read, "The objects of the senses provide us with occasions to make judgments. These judgments, so far as they are true, are experiences."[11] Similarly in another passage Kant explains that "the judgment which expresses empirical knowledge is experience."[12] These examples can be multiplied many times to show that when Kant discusses what he calls an experience (*Erfahrung*) what he has in mind is an empirical judgment.

Since Kant uses the word *Erfahrung* for a form of propositional knowledge, where the judgment is based upon objects of the senses, our English word *experience* is probably not well suited to convey his meaning to contemporary philosophers—or to those for whom an experience is something that an empirical judgment can be based on. Scientists employ the word

---

[8] *Ibid.*, XX, p. 266.
[9] It should be pointed out that the term *Erfahrung* is also used in the singular to describe the totality of our empirical judgments. The words *Nature* and *natures* are used in a corresponding way by Kant. A nature is the real essence of some empirical object, while Nature is the organized whole of these real objects.
[10] *Vorlesungen über die Metaphysik* (Erfurt, 1821), p. 26.
[11] *Ibid.*, p. 147.
[12] *Gesammelte Schriften*, XVIII, p. 318.

"observation" in a manner that ranges usefully between the act of noting or of recording what has been seen, heard, or otherwise made an object of some personal inspection and the judgments or the remarks that record the results of the act of observing. It thus preserves some continuity with pre-Kantian philosophical terminology. For example, Couturat summarizes Leibniz's usages in this fashion: "Tant qu'elle n'est pas demontrée, la loi empiriquement induite s'appelle simplement une 'observation' ou 'expérience', sans doute parce qu'elle ne fait que traduire ou résumer les phénomènes et qu'elle n'a pas d'autre portée."[13] We will see that Kant's more immediate predecessors preserved the same tradition in the way they used the German *Erfahrung*. Sadly, we are many generations too late for such reflections to have a practical bearing on the linguistic habits of those who discuss Kant in English.

My first major point about intuitions is that they are elements in a form of judgment. Someone who accepts the evidence for this point but who also defends Paton's understanding of intuitions will surely reply that the point merely reflects the outcome of Kant's argument in the *Critique*—an outcome according to which there is a judgmental element in our sense-experiences of seeing and hearing. Such a reply and such an analysis of the matter are seriously flawed. For one thing there is a conflict with Kant's own advice about the best way to present the critical philosophy to students in lectures. He suggested to Beck, "I begin by defining experience by *empirical knowledge*. Knowledge, however, is the representation, through concepts, of a *given* object as an object."[14] There has to be a reasonable presumption in favor of the view that Kant is referring to an analytic exposition designed for beginners, rather than a synthetic exposition designed to present the material in the perfected form of a scientific treatise. In the first type of presentation one begins with what is common knowledge or is knowledge that can be presumed to be shared by speaker and hearer. It is, of course, conceivable that Kant was recommending the other method for use in the classroom, but it is highly unlikely. The fact that the definition in question does reflect common knowledge rather than the outcome of a Kantian analysis is confirmed by the evidence that Kant's contemporaries and predecessors used the word *Erfahrung* in the same manner as that indicated in the definition.

A substantial objection to the view that Paton and Kemp Smith have of intuitions is that it makes the doctrine of an *a priori* intuition a mystery. Yet there is no doubt that Kant not only held the view before and while he wrote the *Critique*, but even developed and extended the doctrine. Thus, when he

---

[13] L. Couturat, *La Logique de Leibniz* (Paris, 1901), p. 264.
[14] *Gesammelte Schriften*, XI, p. 315.

discusses "the intuition of myself through synthetic *a priori* propositions"[15] he clearly is not talking about a direct relation to the self in seeing or hearing, or in other forms of direct sensory awareness. There is a particularly striking example of the way in which the doctrine of *a priori* intuitions was undergoing development and change in the *Opus Postumum*. It can be mentioned here, even though an appreciation of the drift of Kant's thought will necessarily anticipate my second point that an intuition is a singular concept or a representation of one object. All readers of the *Critique* and many who have only been exposed to transcendental philosophy through Coleridge or Emerson will be familiar with the Kantian concept of the idea (*Idee*). When Kant divides the genus of representations, he separates intuitions from concepts and then he introduces ideas, as follows: "The pure concept, in so far as it has its origins in the understanding alone (not in the pure image of sensibility), is called a *notion*. A concept formed from notions and transcending the possibility of experience is an *idea* or concept of reason." (A320) Quite clearly, Kantian ideas are so far from our experiences that they have nothing at all to do with Paton's "immediate relation to the chair" which we are in when we see the chair or feel its hardness. Yet in Kant's last unfinished work he realized that some of these ideas of pure reason must, by one of his definitions of intuition, be classified as intuitions: "Ideas are not concepts, but on the contrary, pure intuitions, for there is only *one* such object."[16] Kant's line of reflection is perfectly transparent for anyone who does not insist on explaining intuitions by the relations in sense-experience. Discursive representations are ones that can hold for every object (*für alle Objecte*) but we can only have intuitive representations of a totality of objects (*des All der Objecte*),[17] and for this reason ideas such as the idea of Nature (conceived as the systematic totality of all real objects) must be regarded as intuitions. It goes without saying that the point I seek to make with these passages is not doctrinal but terminological. The terminological point is that from first to last Kant used the word *Anschauung* in contexts where there can be no question of a reference to immediate sensory awareness.

The very first occurrence of the word in the *Critique* provides additional evidence against the view that would connect the term with sense-experiences. In the preface to the first edition, Kant writes, "As regards *clearness*, the reader has a right to demand, in the first place, a *discursive* (logical) clearness, and secondly, an *intuitive* (aesthetic) clearness through intuitions, that is, through examples and other concrete illustrations." (Axviii) The most

[15] *Ibid.*, XXXII, p. 67; cf. p. 97.
[16] *Opus Postumum*, ed. Buchenau (Berlin, 1936), I, p. 78–79.
[17] *Gesammelte Schriften*, XXII, p. 67.

natural and sensible reading of this passage is that Kant has in mind two types of clarification which can be illustrated as follows: "All causal judgments (for example, the judgment that the sun warms the rock) exhibit a synthetic connection of concepts (that is, the judgment involves a concept whose application to the subject matter of the judgment is justified by being connected in the object and through a real relation to our ground or basis for the judgment.)" In the foregoing example, the "that is" precedes—or is intended to precede—a logical or discursive clarification of Kant's idea of a synthetic connection. The "for example" precedes an intuitive clarification of his idea of a causal judgment that occurs when we are able to refer to something that will serve as evidence that there are causal judgments. It is barely conceivable that Kant was using the word *intuition* in the way in which Paton and Kemp Smith suggest that he used it. If so, then Kant is saying that the reader has a right to expect pictures or some other such source of sensations. The only obvious candidates for a picture-book *Critique* are the algebraic and geometrical representations of judgments which are to be found in the Kantian *Nachlass* or working notes. An obvious difficulty with this reading is that Kant goes on to remark that intuitions were contained in the first draft of the *Critique* but were removed to compress the size of the work. There is no credible evidence that there ever was an illustrated or picturebook version of the *Critique*. Consequently, it is safer to suppose that Kant removed some perfectly commonplace elements of philosophical prose than to suppose that he removed anything very sensational.

Kemp Smith believed that Kantian intuitions are sensations of the various senses because he believed that this usage is a natural extension of the original sense of the word *Anschauung* and that "*Anschauung* etymologically applies only to visual sensations." There is no more than a grain of truth in this argument from etymology. While the word *Anschauung* does not itself have the history that Kemp Smith ascribes to it, it does derive from a root that applies to vision. In fairness to Kemp Smith we should note that Kant also calls attention to the fact that "The word *Anschauung* (*intuitus*) contains the suggestion of seeing." However that point is very far from establishing that Kantian intuitions are "sensations of the various senses", nor does it rule out their definition as elements in judgments. Indeed Kant goes on in his next sentence, following the one that has just been quoted about intuitions, to remark that the word *Begriff* (*conceptus*) contains the suggestion of grasping the objects of touch.[18] Yet there is no doubt at all that concepts are elements

---

[18] *Ibid.*, XXII, p. 97.

in possible judgments; in point of fact, Kant says there is only a difference
in emphasis between the phrases "our concept of a thing" and "our judgment
about a thing".[19] As for the word *Anschauung* the entry in Kluge reveals that
it was introduced by the German mystics who used it, not in relation to
sensory awareness, but in connection with a type of spiritual apprehension.
But the point in any case is moot, since Kant was quite evidently translating
the Latin term *intuitus*, as any number of passages in his published and un-
published writings will show. The Latin term also was a term of art—Day and
Boehner locate its origin in the school of Duns Scotus.[20] By way of explaining
the term, Boehner tells us, "This first, immediate cognition is called by
Ockham, following Duns Scotus, *intuitive cognition*. It is the basis for a self-
evident existential statement, viz. that the thing which is experienced exists,
is present, has such and such a condition, etc. It is to be noted that the existential judgment is an operation of the intellect alone, and that the intuitive
cognition which is at the basis of it, even if it concerns an object of sense, is
an intellectual intuitive cognition or a primarily intellectual awareness of an
object."[21] Without any doubt Kant's *doctrine* of intuition is different from
the doctrine of the Franciscan master, but I will argue that Kant's *definition*
does not differ in any essential from the definition that was proposed by
Duns. Whether we can agree that they are identical will depend upon how
much of the Scotistic doctrine we are prepared to unpack directly from his
definition and how much we attribute to his other, independent assumptions
about our knowledge.

Duns held that there are two basic types of human cognition which do not
necessarily differ in their objects but which do differ in the so-called "ratio
formalis", by virtue of which the intellect cognizes the object.[22]

Intellectio est duplex, una quiditativa, quae abstahit ab existentia, alia quae
dicitur visio, quae est existentis ut existens.[23]

Thus in the case of abstractive cognition that which makes the object be an
object for the intellect is something quiditative or essential. Now we have
already seen that Kant agrees that the "logical object" of an abstract or
general concept (*Begriff*) is a "logical essence". In the case of the intuitive

---

[19] *Vorlesungen über die Metaphysik*, p. 157; cf. also *Gesammelte Schriften*, XVI, p. 40.
[20] Sebastian Day, *Intuitive Cognition: A Key to the Significance of the Later Scholastics*
(St. Bonaventure, N.Y., 1947).
[21] Ockham, *Philosophical Writings*, ed. and trans. P. Boehner (London, 1957), p. xxiv.
[22] Yolanthe Zielinska, "A Neo-Scotist Theory of Perception in Twentieth-Century
Philosophy," in *De Doctrina Ionnis Duns Scoti*, IV (Rome, 1968), p. 660.
[23] *In Meta* VII q. 15 n. 4 (Ed. Vives VII, p. 436); cited in Zielinska, op. cit., p. 660.

cognition that which makes the object be an object for the intellect is the actual presence of the object or the present existence of the object: "Cognitio autem intuitiva est objecti ut objectum est praesens in exsistentia actuali."[24] So far Kant and Scotus are in perfect harmony.

The differences begin to mount when we introduce the Scotistic conviction that intuitive cognition is also cognition of the separate existence of the object (*per se existens*) rather than cognition of the object in its relations to others.[25] But at this point we must make a special effort to distinguish carefully between what Duns Scotus built into his definition of intuition and what he is able to derive because of his other assumptions about cognition. We have already encountered the distinction between the *thing-in-itself* or *ens per se*, or *secundum se*, and the *ens per aliud*, but at this point we need a more detailed understanding of these notions than has been required previously. In metaphysics the ens per se is that which has separate being or being by itself. The corresponding distinction in a transcendental philosophy is between that which can be known by itself and separately, and that which can only be known in accordance with its relations to other things. The exact scope of these two distinctions will depend upon the framework of metaphysical or transcendental assumptions which we are prepared to accept. One obvious and familiar example of the effect that metaphysical assumptions can have on the scope of the metaphysical distinction is furnished by the famous dispute between Platonists and Aristotelians. Plato appears to have conceded a separate being to entities that Aristotle categorized as properties and treated as having being only in some substance. Hence we find that when Saint Thomas uses that expression *ens per se* in one place, he can write:

Et sicut ponebat Ideam hominis et equi separatam quam vocabat Per Se Hominem et Per Se Equum, ita ponebat Ideam entis et Ideam unius separatam quam dicebat Per Se Ens et Per Se Unum.

And just as he believed in separate ideas of man and of horse, calling them Man Himself and Horse Itself, so also Plato believed in separate ideas of being and unity, called Being Itself and Unity Itself.[26]

In another place, where the context of the relevant metaphysical assumptions has plainly shifted, Aquinas can—without any terminological contradiction —consider an objection that is based upon the popular, loose, and inadequate definition of substance as "simply that which has separate being": "Sub-

---

[24] *Ord*. Id. 2n. 394 (Vives, II, p. 352); cited in Zielinska, p. 661.
[25] Thomas F. Torrance, "Intuitive and Abstractive Cognition from Duns Scotus to John Calvin," in *De Doctrina Ionnis Duns Scoti*, IV, p. 292.
[26] *Summa Theologica* (Blackfriars, 1964) PPQ 6 Art. 4.

stantia enim est ens per se subsistens."[27] The clear and obvious point about these passages is that the scope of our concept of what has being *per se* will vary as our metaphysical assumptions vary.

The concept of what has separate being either is or is very close to the concept of what has absolute being—as contrasted with what has being only in relation to other things. Thus, for example, the text of A.C. Pegis's selections from an English translation of the preceding passage from Saint Thomas renders the "man *per se*", "being *per se*", and so on as "absolute man", "absolute being" and the like.[28] Consequently if we require a second illustration of how metaphysical assumptions can alter our opinions about the scope of the notion of the *ens per se*, we need only consider the controversy that raged in Kant's day between those who held that there are absolute points in space (or points *per se*) or absolute moments of time, and those who denied that points and moments have any being *per se*. It should be sufficiently obvious that this dispute turned on a large number of complex metaphysical and logical issues; the idea that the dispute could have been resolved by consulting the proper definition of the phrase *ens per se* is preposterous. The same illustration also serves to remind us for a second time that *ens per se* or separate being does not necessarily mean substantial being, and that *ens per aliud* does not necessarily mean *ens secundum accidens*, even though these explanations retained their popularity from the time of Thomas to the time of Kant. An example of the long tradition is provided in the edition of 1775 of Walch's *Philosophisches Lexicon* where an accident is explained as that which does not subsist *per se*. Yet the great majority of those who argued that space is absolute probably would not have agreed that space is a substance or that the points in space are substances. The example of Newton serves as a sufficiently plain reminder of that historical fact about the defenders of an absolute space.

We have yet to see whether the underlying transcendental assumptions made by Scotus could have been responsible for his belief—so unlike Kant's— that an intuitive cognition or a cognition of something present as present can also be a cognition of a *thing-in-itself*. One general assumption which Scotus appears to have adopted is that an intellectual cognition—whether intuitive or discursive—can occur only if the intellect grasps a nature or a real essence in its object. If this general proposition is combined with the further assumption that the nature of an object is what determines the object as something which falls under a general concept or a category, the consequences are certainly not favorable to the Scotistic position. Yet this second assumption

---

[27] *Ibid.*, PPQ 3 Art. 5.
[28] *Basic Writings of Saint Thomas Aquinas*, ed. A.C. Pegis (New York, 1945), I, p. 55.

is one which Thomas found it natural to make in his refutation of the objection that we must have a metaphysical knowledge of God since God is pre-eminently *ens per se* and an *ens per se* is a substance. Replying to such an objection, Thomas writes:

The word 'substance' does not mean baldly that which exists of itself, for existence, as we have seen, cannot determine a genus. Rather 'substance' means that which is possessed of a nature such that it will exist of itself. But this nature is not itself the thing's existence.[29]

When Scotus reached the opposing conclusion that we can have a metaphysical knowledge of God or, indeed, of any being as being, he apparently retained the general assumption that an intellectual cognition of something is possible only on the condition that the intellect can conform its representation to the nature of the thing that is cognized. The assumption he apparently discarded is that every nature determines a generic conception as its valid and proper representation. Instead he introduced his well-known distinction between the common and the distinctive nature of a thing. His novel doctrine of the distinctive nature allows him to maintain that an intuitive cognition is not only cognition of the thing in its present and evident existence but also is cognition of the thing in its own nature (*sicut et in se*). Since the distinctive nature of the thing gives the thing its separate existence, he is able to maintain that an intuitive cognition grasps the *thing-in-itself* (*ens per se, Ding an sich*). If this analysis of the situation is correct, then we are dealing with a conclusion that goes well beyond any definition of intuition itself and that involves the assumption of new metaphysical elements to account for the possibility of the disputed knowledge.

We know that Kant did not accept either the general or the special assumption that was made by Scotus. Kant denies that we can account for the cognizability of the object by referring to what the object is, and by postulating a conformability of our representations to the common *or* the distinctive natures of things. We have already seen that for Kant the fundamental philosophical problems surrounding the cognizability of objects are problems concerning the jurisdiction, the competence, and, in general, the rights of the intellect in making judgments about the object. When the pretensions of the intellect have been made the subject of a challenge, the challenge cannot be dismissed by any metaphysical account of the nature or the natures of the object—because a question about our cognitive rights cannot be settled in that manner. This is the transcendental assumption introduced by Kant. It effectively cuts him off from the Scotistic conclusions about the objects of

[29] *Summa Theologica* PPQ 6 Art. 4.

intuitive cognition and, in particular, from the conclusion that these objects can, by virtue of their distinctive natures, be known *per se* or in their separate existences. Parenthetically, it should be remarked that it also cuts Kant off from any speculation about whether our intellect is naturally fitted for an intuition of God and whether beings such as ourselves, but with a different status from ourselves, have a vision of God and of one another in commerce with God. But the essential point to carry away from this comparison of Scotus and Kant is that their differences do not extend to the definition of intuition itself. Considering the interval that separated the one from the other and considering the prevailing opinions about the origins of Kant's terminology, some will find it incredible that Kant used the term in a way that preserves the sense of its origin as a term of art. But there are absolutely no grounds for asserting that Kant uses the term in any other sense. Intuitive cognitions are intellectual representations or representations by the understanding (of which sensibility and understanding are parts), and these representations are representations of an object that are based upon the presence of this object, here and now.

This account of the history of Kant's notion may become more plausible if it is recalled that we are not discussing some abstruse and remote corner of philosophical terminology but a set of distinctions which can be given continuous documentation from Scotus to Kant. Kant did not need to forage for himself in the manuscripts of the Latin schools. For example, the philosophical lexicon prepared by Rudolph Goclenius in the seventeenth century uses language that unmistakably derives from Scotistic sources. In distinguishing intuitive concepts from abstractive concepts, Goclenius explains the former as being "of the present thing, as something which is present."[30] He employs similar language in distinguishing intuitive from abstractive cognitions. Walch's German philosophical lexicon was even closer to hand for Kant; Henning's revised edition appeared in 1775. Walch gives a threefold division of concepts, dividing ideas into singular concepts or ideas of individual things, particular concepts or ideas of the particular accidents of things, and universal concepts of things. His examples to illustrate the division are the idea of Peter "an sich selbst", the idea of the learnedness of Peter, and the idea of Peter's human nature, which Peter shares with all other men.[31] These very examples can be traced back through earlier sources.[32] Walch's editor notes the fact that the Cartesians and the Leibnizians do not accept these

[30] Rudolph Goclenius, *Lexicon Philosophicum* (Frankfurt, 1613), entry under *notitia*.
[31] J.G. Walch, *Philosophisches Lexicon*, ed. and enlarged by J.C. Hennings (Leipzig, 1775).
[32] Thus, Peter appears in the same roles in the seventeenth century in Stephanus Chauvin, *Lexicon Philosophicum* (Dusseldorf, 1967; reprint of the second edition of 1713).

distinctions of concepts, preferring instead their own divisions of ideas into the clear, the distinct, the adequate and the complete. Kant repeats that very point in the transcendental aesthetic and elsewhere. Baumgarten's *Logic*—a work which we can assume that Kant had a working knowledge of—retains the term *Anschauung* for the singular concept or idea of the individual thing; but the term does not appear in Meier's *Logic*—a work that Kant used many times in his college courses. Instead, Meier follows a Cartesian tradition which adopts the terminology to a slightly different sense:

Die erweislichen Urtheile sind entweder bloß durch die Erfahrung gewiß oder nicht. Jene sind *anschauende Urtheile* (judicium intuitivum), . . . *Das anschauende Urtheil besteht aus lauter Erfahrungsbegriffen*, und ist eine unmittelbare Erfahrung und ein einzelnes Urtheil.[33]

Meier's use of the term *Erfahrung* for an empirical judgment illustrates a point that was made earlier about the existence of many precedents for Kant's use of the term. But the point which must particularly interest us is Meier's explanation of intuitive judgments. The grandfather of his explanation is almost certainly Descartes, who admitted that when he introduced the term *intuition* to stand for the natural light of reason he was departing from the scholastic precedents. The term appears most frequently in Descartes's early writings; at that time he held the rather striking belief that all cognitions can be resolved into cognitions of simple natures; and hence he certainly had no need for a distinction between representations of the individual and representations of the nature of the individual. Instead, he needed a term to describe our capacity to have a well-grounded and fully justified judgment which is not drawn by reasoning from other judgments. If Descartes was the grandfather of Meier's explanation, Wolff was undoubtedly the father. According to the testimony of his devout follower and compiler of a Wolff-lexicon, Wolff was the one who had freed the idea of an intuitive judgment from its connection with Descartes's theory of a natural light of reason. Meisner tells us that Wolff introduced the definition of the intuitive judgment as an immediate judgment which can serve as the reason or the ground for other judgments, themselves to be called discursive judgments.[34] Meier, in the passage just quoted from his *Logic*, makes the relatively minor adaptation of this definition to an empiricist framework. Now the basic sense of an intuitive representation for Kant is, as we will see when we take up his actual definition

---

[33] *Gesammelte Schriften*, XVI, p. 674.
[34] Heinrich Meissner, *Philosophisches Lexicon* (Düsseldorf, 1970; reprint of the edition of 1737).

in the *Critique*, the earlier sense of a representation that refers to an existing individual, but in his discussion of intuitions he frequently manages to combine the two traditions. For example, he explains in one place that "The intuition is the immediate representation of an individual object. The concept is the mediate representation of an individual object." [35]

I have already called attention to the fact that Kant uses the term *understanding* in a wider and a narrower sense. There is a parallel observation to be made about his use of the term *concept* (*conceptus, Begriff*). In his Latin writings Kant regularly used the term *conceptus singularis* as an alternative designation for intuitions. Thus, he contrasts intuitions with the *conceptus generalis*, just as Baumgarten, Walch, and countless others had done before him. Two passages from the *Dissertation* of 1770 illustrate this point:

Aliud enim est: datis partibus *compositionem* totus sibi concipere, per notionem abstractum intellectus, aliud, hanc *notionem* generalem, tanquam rationis quoddam problema, *exsequi* per facultatem cognoscendi sensitivam, h.e. in concreto eandem sibi repraesentare intuitu distincto.[36]

Intuitus autem purus (humanus) non est conceptus universalis s. logicus *sub quo* sed singularis *in quo* sensibilia quaelibet cogitantur ideoque continet conceptus spatii et temporis.[37]

The special concept which Kant discusses in this work is the concept of this world—a concept to be contrasted with a general concept of merely logically possible worlds—and this concept of the world is obviously not a likely candidate for the status of an abstract or general concept, yet Kant consistently describes this representation as a concept. Kant's usage in the *Critique* almost always reflects the narrower sense of the term *concept* (*Begriff*) by which every concept is abstract or general. However, there are some obvious exceptions to this rule, in the form of passages where Kant retains the earlier and very long-standing practice of using *concept* to cover both general concepts and concepts of individual things. For example, after he has demonstrated that our representations of space and time are pure intuitions, not concepts, and after he has isolated the pure concepts of the understanding, he remarks: "Wir haben jetzt schon zweierlei Begriffe von ganz verschiedene Art, die doch darin miteinander übereinkommen, daß sie beiderseits völlig *a priori* sich auf Gegenstände beziehen, nämlich, die Begriffe des Raumes und der Zeit, als Formen der Sinnlichkeit, und die Kategorien, als Begriffe des Verstandes." (B118) *Concept* is a genus term in this passage. The first species

---

[35] *Vorlesungen über die Metaphysik*, p. 26.
[36] *Gesammelte Schriften*, II, p. 387.
[37] *Ibid.*, II, p. 397.

of concept is the intuition, described in the traditional language as a *conceptus singularis*, while the second species of concept is the general concept or what is simply called a *concept* through most of the *Critique*. The passage that has just been quoted has a more fundamental importance than its use to illustrate the way in which an ancient tradition survives in the language of the *Critique*. The phrase Kant uses to mark out the relationship of representations to their objects is a matter of great importance: representations "refer to" the objects.

Kant's first attempt to define *Anschauung* in the *Critique* occurs in the opening lines of the aesthetic:

Auf welche Art und durch welche Mitteln sich auch immer eine Erkenntnis auf Gegenstände beziehen mag, es ist doch diejenige, wodurch sie sich auf dieselbe unmittelbar bezieht, und worauf alles Denken als Mittel abzweckt, die Anschauung.

The critical verb phrase in this explanation is *sich auf etwas beziehen*. Kemp Smith and Meiklejohn both translate by the colorless phrase *to relate to*; Muller gives *to reach*. Nevertheless, the original has a slightly different and somewhat more specific sense. The better translation is *to refer to*—a translation that Muller adopts when the same phrase appears later in Kant's explanation of the different species of representation at A320. Smith adopts a less defensible strategy in this later passage; he translates by *to relate to* for as long as the genus being divided contains intuitions, but when it passes over to concepts he switches to *to refer to*. Since Kant had launched that division with some remarks about the importance of accurate terminology, the reader is justified in niggling a bit about the details of a proposed translation. The evidence about Kant's terminology in these passages supports the following interpretation of the basic sense of his terms: Intuitions are representations through which our judgments are referred directly to objects, while concepts are representations that are referred to objects only indirectly and by means of other representations.

Kluge's etymological dictionary gives a brief indication of the history of the verb phrase used by Kant to define intuitions:

Sich beziehen an wird in der Rechtssprache 1450 . . . 'den Rechtszug nehmen, appellieren.' An die Stelle des *an* ruckt *auf*, der Sinn lockert sich, der papierne Klang bleibt: 'ich beziehe mich auf mein gestriges Schreiben.'[38]

---

[38] Friedrich Kluge, *Etymologisches Wörterbuch der Deutschen Sprache* (Berlin, 1957), entry under *beziehen*.

We get additional and supporting evidence about the sense of the phrase in Kant's day from the entry in Adelung's *Grammatisch-kritische Wörterbuch* of 1793:

Sich auf etwas beziehen, sich darauf berufen. Er bezog sich dabey auf Zeugen. Ich beziehe mich auf dich. Ich beziehe mich auf mein voriges Schreiben. Imgleichen auf etwas verweisen.

Both sources confirm that the basic idea is that of referring to someone or something. In the light of my earlier arguments concerning the normative character of Kant's transcendental premises, we might conjecture that he selected the phrase to define intuitions because of the legal connotations of the term. At any rate the relationship of referring to something is not merely a factual affair. Instead, the special legal sense was that of appealing to someone or to something as that which will confirm or justify one in what one represents before the court. As the use of the phrase became more generalized, so that, for example, it covered an appeal to earlier writings, the same flavor still attached to it. The main condition for success in an appeal is that a ground or a source for the appeal be present. If the appeal is successful, then the validity of one's representation or one's right to represent things in the given way must be granted.

The room for debate over the correct translation of Kant's phrase is considerably narrowed by a very fortunate circumstance. This case is one of the many ones in which he provides us with his own translation. Thus, for example, in a note which the editors of the Academy edition of his writings place in the 1750's Kant wrote:

Repraesentatio est determinatio mentis interna, quatenus ad res quasdam ab ipsa nempe repraesentationes diversas refertur. Ist diejenige Bestimmung der Seele, die sich auf andere Dinge beziehet.[39]

The same phrase is repeated thirty years later to define intuitions as representations by means of which we refer or appeal directly to objects.

III. INTUITIONS AS FORMS AND AS CONDITIONS

Several of the phrases which Kant uses to characterize the transcendental status of certain intuitions are also puzzling, until his usage is put into its proper historical perspective. It will be recalled how the sarcasm of De Quincey was provoked by the phrase, "forms, *a priori*". It is also true, and

[39] *Gesammelte Schriften*, XVI, p. 76.

can be verified from several recent discussions, that when Kant speaks of universal or necessary conditions of knowledge, his words are no longer familiar items for his reader. Yet neither set of words deserves De Quincey's epithet, "cabbalistical". Both phrases have a meaning that can be made sufficiently plain if we will consult the appropriate sources upon which Kant depended for his terminology.

The phrase which apparently puzzled De Quincey has the clearest roots in the language of the schools. If we remember that the essential features of the objects of an intuition are existence (or presence, as opposed to absence) and uniqueness, then we can easily appreciate what Kant has in mind when he discusses the form of an intuition. It is that which confers being and distinctiveness upon a thing. The scholastic maxim which Kant was fond of quoting is that "forma dat esse rei"—the form gives the being of the thing.[40] The sense of this ancient principle had been explained for Kant in Walch's treatise: "Thus several canons or rules pertaining to the form are still given: for example, *forma dat esse rei*, *distingui et operari*, the form brings it about that a thing has its essence, is distinguished from other things, and that it acts." What Kant retains from this teaching is clear enough. The form is not that which constitutes the nature of a thing, but rather the form of intuition is what makes one thing be distinguished from another thing.

When Kant teaches that space and time are the forms of intuition, he may well have had in mind a second sense of *form* which has been present from the Pythagorean beginnings of philosophy. In this second sense form is that which contributes order or structure to things. When space and time are conceived in this way in connection with a theory of intuitions as those representations which refer to things, the resulting thought is modern, or, at least, is post-Cartesian. Whether or not Kant had the thought when he used the term *form* is one question. Whether or not he had the thought is a second question. We know more definitely how to answer the second question because of another, and very technical expression, that Kant had employed. The term *co-ordinatio* which had appeared in Kant's dissertation was a neologism in Latin that had been coined to describe space and time as organizing forms that provide the basis for a system of references. The system is what has come to be called a Cartesian or co-ordinate system of reference. We know from the *Dissertation* that when Kant speaks of space and time as forms of intuition, he did have in mind the role of space and time in co-ordinate systems, but we cannot say for certain that he used the word *form*, itself, in anything more than its primary sense. A form is that which makes a thing exist or be present

---

[40] An extended discussion of the principle in Kant is to be found in Hans Graubner, *Form und Wesen* (Bonn, 1972).

and that which makes a thing be different from other things. These are precisely the features of the objects of reference, as objects of reference, which Kant's doctrine of reference requires him to account for.

The basic sense of *esse* for the schools is *being present*—a point which will be defended and amplified in connection with my discussion of the conditions of knowledge. The majority of scholastics, accepting that basic understanding as a deliverance from logic, also held that what the presence of a thing with other things or the sharing of a world with other things confers upon a thing is the possibility of acting upon other things or of affecting them in some way or other. Kant evidently retained this earlier understanding, because no sooner has he defined intuition in the *Critique* than he gives a definition of *Empfindung* as the effect of an object on our capacity for representation so far as we are affected by the object. (B34) His next step in this chain of definitions is to use *Empfindung* to explain *empirical intuitions* and, finally, he introduces *appearances* as the undetermined objects of empirical intuitions. This language deserves the utmost caution and respect. It has given rise to a very widespread impression that there is a causal theory at the base of Kant's account of sensibility. There are more modest and more daring versions of the causal theory. The modest version simply holds that Kant accepted a causal theory of sense perception and that the language of the passage records that commitment. Unfortunately, the key terms in the passage which give rise to the causal hypothesis are used by Kant to define the faculty of sensibility in general. Accordingly, there is a certain logic compelling the passage to a stronger theory. That is, since the sensibility is defined as a faculty of representations that have their source in the way we are affected by objects, since the faculty of sensibility is one of the indispensable roots in all human understanding, and since intuitions which have their source in the understanding are an element in all synthetic knowledge, *a priori* as well as *a posteriori*, Kant seems to be committed to giving a causal account of our pure *a priori* knowledge in metaphysics and in mathematics. The stronger versions of the theory are necessarily accounts of a double causation: either there are two ways in which the object of sense perception acts upon us or there is causation by something other than the cause of our sense perceptions. But before we are justified in accepting any of these theories, we must consider carefully the key terms in Kant's definitions.

First we must consider the term *to affect* (*afficieren*). We have seen that this term is undoubtedly used by Kant to convey what is conferred by the form of a thing. The form confers being, distinctiveness, and the capacity to affect other things—as we have already seen in the account of the form provided by Walch. According to Kant's theory of the forms of intuition as the transcendental conditions of the object of knowledge, the presence of the object in space or time gives the object its existence, uniqueness, and capacity to affect our knowledge. The question we must ask, however, is whether the conformity to this transcendental condition implies or presupposes the existence or the possibility of a causal connection between the object and our representation. When the object affects our knowledge in accordance with this transcendental condition does that mean that there is a causal, a metaphysical, or a factual relationship between the object and its representation? It would appear that, at least in the case of our empirical representations, the answer must be affirmative, but to interpret Kant in this way is to misconstrue the critical nature of his definition of what is empirical in our representations. The empirical representation is "borrowed from" what we see, hear, and so on, in a sense of "borrowed from" that is intended to call attention to the source of a right rather than a sense that is intended to provide an explanation of a psychological fact. What Kant means by the "borrowing"—as his contrast between empirical concepts and concepts which require a deduction of our right would suggest—is that our right to empirical representations is not anything like a "right of original possession" which can be established only by reference to what we have done or to our own, individual acts of purely spontaneous conceptions. Instead, our right to empirical representations depends upon our being able to refer or to appeal to the presence of the object that is represented. When the appeal or the reference is to that which is an empirical object, the witnesses to the validity of the representation are present and can be called; they do not need to have been brought before the bar and actually examined. Thus, there is nothing in Kant's discussion of empirical representations that suggests that the validity of an empirical representation is contingent upon how we happen in fact to have been related to objects. There is no reason in the nature of the case why he should want to say that.

The preceding remarks reflect a general understanding that transcendental philosophy is concerned with the normative aspects of representations, and a specific understanding of the term *empirical* as qualifying a representation the validity of which can be established by appeal to the objects of the senses. To say that a representation is empirical is to declare a certain kind of right in the representation and not to describe the factual causes of the representation. Assuming the general understanding, we should look for confirmation of the specific claim in other passages in which Kant discusses rights. One particularly interesting passage occurs in Kant's account of the conditions under which something different from myself (literally, something external to myself) can be mine by right. He argues that in order for something to be my private property I must be capable of being affected if the object is used contrary to my will. But since he wishes to extend my jurisdiction over property beyond the things that are physically within my possession, he makes it very clear that when he uses the word *affects* he does not mean to imply any causal or factual connection between me and the change in the object. I am affected in my possession, even though nothing happens to me in any causal sense. I am affected in my status as an owner and that is a legal or a normative qualification of me; I am not causally acted upon in my nature as a physical or psychological being. In connection with the same point, Kant argues that I cannot actually possess something by right in a state of nature. The possession of something by right presupposes the existence of a set of positive laws or of established norms which will be violated if someone uses my property without my consent.[41] Each of these points can be extended in an obvious way to the case in which *empirical* is used to qualify a representation within a transcendental context—under the same assumption as before that a transcendental context is a context in which the grounds of my rights to have and employ representations are under discussion. If anyone denied this assumption and prefers to believe that Kant's characterization of a representation as *empirical* is a merely factual characterization with no implication about the rights we have with the representation, then of course the information about how Kant uses *affects* in the discussion of rights will be of no interest.

There is a second term in Kant's chain of definitions that has often been given too narrow an interpretation. The term is *Empfindung* (*sensatio*), which is usually translated by *sensation*. An alternative needs to be found for that translation but the obvious candidates are impractical or verbose. The expression that I will defend as a better and more accurate expression of Kant's thought is a verbal monstrosity: An *Empfindung* is a representation with content that is justified by our capacity to take note of the object of the representation. When we say in ordinary English that so-and-so caused a sensation—meaning that so-and-so caused others to take some special notice, we use *sensation* in a way that is closer to Kant's sense, but philosophers do not usually have that sense in mind. The difficulty with the ordinary translation and the reason why even a linguistic barbarism might be preferable is that Kant uses the term to cover empirical concepts as well as empirical intuitions. Thus, the person who causes a sensation may come to my attention through the descriptions that are offered to me by a third person observer but the agitation that results in me is still part of the general sensation that was

---

[41] The important stipulation about a sense of *affects* that implies no actual causal interaction will be found in Kant's discussion of *Das Privatrecht* in *Metaphysik der Sitten*.

caused. Kant's employment of the term *Empfindung* to include empirical concepts reflected the common practice of philosophers in his day, and the existence of this common practice is the first of my reasons for supposing that it was Kant's practice. Three examples will illustrate this first point. First, there is the fact that Gottsched's work on logic is divided in the traditional way into three parts. The division reflects the three basic faculties of the understanding: conception, judgment, and reasoning. What Gottsched's logic has to say about our faculty of conception is contained in the first section, entitled "Von den Empfindungskraft und den Begriffen". The first sentence of the section reads, "Empfinden heißt, sich in Gedanken eine Sache vorstellen oder abbilden."[42] That is, *Empfinden* means to represent or to copy a thing *in thought*. If *Empfinden* is translated here by *to sense*, the meaning of that should be understood to be a taking note of or being sensible of. Certainly everyone must agree that it would be very misleading if the title of the section were translated without any further explanation, as though it were concerned with our faculty of sensation.

In Meier's work the actual definition of *Empfindung* is somewhat more equivocal. It reads "Eine *Empfindung* (*sensatio*) ist eine Vorstellung einer gegenwartigen Sachen, . . ."[43] That is, an *Empfindung* is the representation of a thing that is present. That could conceivably be a sensation in the ordinary modern sense. However, in accordance with his belief that all our representations are concepts, Meier goes on in a later passage to remark that all our *Empfindungen* are concepts.[44] Lambert also uses the term as an alternative for concepts, and in contexts where it is clear that he has in mind abstract concepts rather than sense impressions.

If one were seeking to draw a sweeping conclusion from a small and niggling terminological point, one might well call into question the common assumption that Kant presupposes a sensationalism or phenomenalism of the Humean variety in the first *Critique*. I do not propose or intend any general conclusion, but I do call attention to the fact that Graham Bird has offered a very persuasive reconstruction of the arguments of the transcendental analytic. Bird's discussion attacks the common view according to which Kant's theory of knowledge rests upon a Humean analysis of sensory perception— that is, of seeing, hearing, and the like. My own conclusion about the aesthetic is a narrower point. If sensations are defined or are understood in accordance with some physical, physiological, or psychological account, by which they are effects in the mind of a physical or a psychological cause that explains

---

[42] Johann Gottsched, *Erste Gründe der Vernunftlehre* (Leipzig, 1766).
[43] *Gesammelte Schriften*, XVI, p. 493.
[44] *Ibid.*, XVI, p. 542.

what we see, hear, and so on—if that is the hypothesis about sensations, then Kant's term *Empfindung* (*sensatio*) in the aesthetic does not pick out sensations. *Empfindungen* are not defined by him in connection with any factual account of anything. Instead, Kantian "sensations" or, better, the sensory content of our representations, is that part of any representation which can be referred to, or validated by appeal to, the objects of the senses. Kant explains, "Das in der Vorstellung was auf der Gegenstand der Sinne an sich bezogen wird, ist Empfindung."[45] That is, *Empfindung* is that in the representation which is referred to the object of the senses *per se*.

When Kant introduces the term his objective is to draw a contrast between one part of our intuitions and concepts, the empirical part, and another part of our representations, the *a priori* part. This contrast is not a contrast between a part that is caused by the object and another part that is justified *a priori*. The contrast is between a part that is justified in one way and a part that is justified in another way. In the one case the validity of our representation or our rightful possession and use of the representation depends upon the presence of the object to the senses. The representation rests on the testimony of the sense that can be summoned in its behalf. In the other case, the validity of our representation can only be established indirectly, because the validity of the representation in these cases depends ultimately upon a proof of our rightful or lawful employment of our own capacities. In these latter cases, the critical account is indispensable and must be supplied upon demand. Criticism, as Rutherforth and other predecessors of Kant explain it, is that branch of the law which concerns the validation of laws, wills, and other legal documents from the point of view of establishing their genuineness.[46] The central question for criticism is always whether or not an act in the legal sense can be said to have been properly executed. Kant's term in the transcendental analytic for the fundamental act of the understanding, *Aktus*, is not the ordinary term for a mental act; he has borrowed the term for an official or legislative act.

In those cases where criticism is necessary, the absence of causes—rather than the existence of causes—is sometimes an important factor in establishing the validity of something. For example, in the probate or the official proof of a will, which can fairly be compared to what Kant calls the *deduction* of the

---

[45] *Ibid.*, XVIII, p. 616.
[46] Thomas Rutherforth, *Institutes of Natural Law* (Cambridge, 1756), II. Rutherforth actually limits criticism to "the art of determining which parts of the law are genuine" (p. 309); but later when contrasting criticism with the art of interpretation he uses the example of testaments as well: "It is one thing to determine whether a writing, that is before us, is the genuine will of the person, whose will it is pretended to be; and another to determine what was the intention of the testator in that will. The former of these points must be settled before the latter can properly come into question." (p. 310)

validity of *a priori* concepts, the absence of coercion has generally been held to be a necessary presumption. By comparison Kant lays great stress upon his so-called "metaphysical deduction" of the pure concepts of the understanding. This part of the *Critique* has two functions. First, it follows what Lambert had described as the process of the "discovery of the clue" as to the content of conclusions which are to be established by a synthetic method. This discovery of the clue was called a middle way between the synthetic method that Kant follows generally in the *Critique* and the analytic method of exposition that he adopts in the *Prolegomena*. The metaphysical deduction viewed in this way has the function of making known to us the categories whose validity as *a priori* concepts is to be made subject to probate. The second function of the metaphysical deduction is to lay the basis for the claim that these concepts arise out of the spontaneity of the understanding, and to lay this basis by tracing them to their origin in the forms of judgment.

The situation in the aesthetic is altogether more simple. Here, too, there are representations that lay claim to validity and among these there are those that are *a priori*. The validity of the *a priori* representations are subject to transcendental criticism, but, if the proof of the validity of the pure concepts of the understanding can be compared to the validation of a will or a statute, the *a priori* validity of the forms of intuition might be compared to the validity of a confession in those jurisdictions that will accept a confession as valid even though it may have been extracted by the fear of a long prison sentence, by the fear of eternal damnation, or by whatever coercion. My point is that where the issue concerns the validity of our *a priori* representations, Kant holds that the element of pure spontaneity—the absence of a causal story—is important in the case of our pure concepts of the understanding. But it does not follow that he believes that the presence or absence of a causal account is indispensable in evaluating every claim to validity in our representations. The *a priori* form of intuition rests its claim to validity on what can be shown to be a proper and lawful exercise of our receptive capacities. It is important not to allow Kant's undertaking to be twisted out of shape. The lack of any necessity to show the absence of causal influence in these cases should not be interpreted to mean the necessity of showing the existence of causal influences or of providing a causal account of the representations. A court which will accept a confession even though the prosecutors used force (on the ground that the causes of the confession do not necessarily destroy its validity) is a different court (in principle, if not in fact) from one that will only accept a confession if the prisoner has been "shown the instruments".

The idea that we must construct a mode of causation of the phenomenal object in a theory of "double causation" or that we must impute causal efficacy to things in themselves, or that we must in some other way account for the causal origins of pure intuitions is an idea that has its roots in a misunderstanding of our faculty of receptivity. The source of the error is the false contrast between the empirical in our representation and the *a priori*. The empirical representations or empirical parts of our representations are those whose validity depends upon our being able to refer them to the objects of the senses. We must only be able to "name" or to "cite" the objects as the witnesses for what we have represented. The possible presence of the object affects us in our rightful employment of these representations in the same sense that my neighbor's unlawful use of my property affects me. That is, it affects me whether or not there is any supposition about a causal interaction between the object and myself. Now Kant will argue in the aesthetic that the forms of intuition, which confer upon the objects their capacity to affect us in our empirical representations cannot themselves be the objects of merely empirical representations. His precise reasons for holding that these forms are *a priori* will be considered in the next chapter. The point at the moment is that these forms are not introduced as a part of any causal account of the way in which the objects actually do interact with us. They are introduced as part of a critical account of the validity of our empirical representations.

The second phrase in the aesthetic which has given readers difficulty occurs when Kant describes these forms of intuition as *conditions* (*Bedingung*, *conditio*) of the possibility of our empirical cognitions. For example, Kant says that outer experience is itself possible at all only through the representation of space. (A31) He says that the principles concerning the relations of time are valid as rules under which alone experience is possible. (A37) And he speaks of space and time, as "the necessary conditions of all outer and inner experience." (B66) De Quincey astutely observed that our first reaction to these remarks is not to ask "What are your reasons?" but to ask "What is your meaning?" This need for a clarification of the phrase "necessary condition" can be illustrated by reference to R.P. Wolff's treatment in *Kant's Theory of Mental Activity*.

Wolff explains what the phrase means in modern logic or, more accurately, what it means in the introductory chapters of a modern logic text that deal with the elementary truth-functional logic of unanalyzed propositions. "Q is a necessary condition of P" means that if P, then Q. It also means that P is a sufficient condition for Q. Having clarified the notion to his own satisfaction in this way, Wolff goes on to argue that Kant gave a confused and misleading account of the structure of his argument in the *Critique*. Kant simply confused necessary conditions with sufficient conditions. On Wolff's view what Kant set out to provide in the first *Critique* were universally accepted premises from which the propositions of Euclidean geometry and of Newtonian mechanics can be deduced. Wolff prefers to suppose that Kant, who knew that Lambert and others had discovered notorious difficulties in the search for a proof of the parallels-postulate, nevertheless imagined that he had discovered the proof for that postulate and for the other postulates and axioms in Euclid. Wolff also appears to believe that for Kant the best evidence for Newtonian mechanics consisted in a set of transcendental principles.

Everyone is free to judge for himself the plausibility of Wolff's reconstruction of the argument of Kant's analytic, but what should specifically be noted is that it relies on our present understanding of the phrase "necessary condition", and, thereby, it obscures several features in the way Kant and his contemporaries employed the expression. First, the general concept of a condition cannot be analyzed as a relationship of implication or even of entailment between propositions. The evidence is manifold. One obvious point is that Kant, Baumgarten, Lambert and others speak of the conditions of things which are not propositional and which do not stand in deductive relationships. Kant's highest principle of all synthetic judgments gives an example of this: The conditions of the possibility of our knowledge of objects are said to be conditions of the possibility of objects themselves. Lambert's discussion of conditions includes examples of conditions for the possibility of questions and of commands, among other things. For example, the question whether the conclusions of the fifth-figure syllogism are affirmative or negative is said to be impossible, on the ground that the question does not satisfy the condition that there be a fifth-figure syllogism. Lambert's discussion also confirms that when the conditions are conditions for propositions, it is not the truth of the proposition, but the possibility of the proposition, that is in question. That is to say, condition (*Bedingung, conditio*) was commonly understood to be defined in such a way that "condition of the possibility of A" is a reduplicative expression of what is already implied by "condition of A". Perhaps there is an exception to this rule among the common texts of the period, but none comes immediately to mind. A second thing which Lambert's discussion makes clear is that the phrase "necessary condition" does not contrast with "sufficient condition" in the manner that Wolff's discussion might suggest. Instead the contrast is with conditions that are illusory (*scheinbar*) and superfluous (*überflüssig*).[47]

Another indication that we are not dealing with a simple deductive relationship between premises and conclusion is that all judgments whatsoever are said by Kant to have the principles of logic as conditions of their possibility.

---

[47] Johann Lambert, *Neues Organon* (Leipzig, 1764), I, p. 84.

When he says this, he does not mean that any given judgment (or a modal judgment to the effect that the given judgment is possible) can be deduced from the laws of logic as premises. He means that conformity to the laws of logic is indispensable to the possibility of the judgment. We must bear in mind that for Kant the laws of logic do not teach us how we do think but how we ought to think, and that the most that can be derived from an *ought* is a *can*. If a condition which is a *sine qua non* of a judgment is omitted, the result is not the *de facto* non-occurrence of the judgment but rather the *de jure* non-occurrence of the judgment. We no longer possess the judgment by right, though as a matter of psychological fact (if, for example, a contradiction is not too obvious) the mental process might very well have occurred. Again, when we say—following another of Lambert's examples of what has a necessary condition—that the *sine qua non* or necessary condition of a question is not satisfied by the question "Are the eclipses of the moon in the first quarter total eclipses?", we do not contradict ourselves, as a clever reader might suppose we do. We are in fact in physical possession of a question—as something that can be subjected to linguistic and other study. The necessary condition of the question is that which we are not permitted to omit in the asking of the question. The penalty that is assessed against us in logic when we dispense with a formality or omit that which we are not permitted to omit is not the factual non-occurrence of the question—as though the laws of logic were sanctioned by a strange inability to speak or to think. The penalty that is assessed is that we are no longer in rightful possession of a question that can be supplied with a rational or logical reply. Thus, we do not have a question that we can convey to the astronomer for an answer, but we certainly do have a question that we can give to a practical linguist for translation back into German. The importance of these remarks will become clearer in the next chapter when we consider an argument that Kant adopts for regarding the representation of space as an indispensable formality. I once had a professor who taught Kant and who read the argument in a psychological sense. Since he was a very competitive and combative type, he naturally took Kant to be offering him a challenge to perform an intellectual feat that Kant had never seen performed and did not believe that anyone could perform. What I am doing is in preparation for a less heroic assault on the passage.

Kant thinks of the conditions for the possibility of synthetic *a priori* judgments as determined by a transcendental logic which is analogous to formal logic with its conditions for the possibility of thought in general. Only one difference need concern us here. A transcendental logic unlike ordinary formal logic can supply us with conditions for the possibility—the real possibility—of the objects of knowledge. The question of concern is not why Kant believed this but what he meant by it. What he meant is that the only valid conception of the objects of knowledge is a conception of them as conforming to certain transcendental conditions. The original understanding that Kant had had of this relationship of conformation of thought and object was given by his "picture-theory" of the representation—a matter which has been discussed earlier. This original account of the relation of conformation was an account of a factual relationship according to which, as Kant went on to say, a possible representation is one that derives its nature from the nature of that which is represented. The critical account of the relationship of conformation views the self as lawgiver to nature. That is, Kant takes the way in which things become subject to the authority of a court or a legislature as his model for an understanding of the way in which things become subject to our cognitive powers. This model quite evidently influenced his conception of the types of necessary condition which are conditions of the validity of representations.

Kant's working notes call attention to the important distinction between necessary conditions which are restrictions and necessary conditions which are limitations. Kant's published works contain numerous references to a closely related distinction which is also drawn in the language of jurisprudence. A clear and typical example is his statement of our general objectives as philosophers: "The philosopher must be able to determine (1) the sources (*Quellen*) of human knowledge, (2) the scope (*Umfang*) of the possible and useful employment of all knowledge and, finally, (3) the limits (*Grenzen*) of reason."[48] More likely than not Kant uses *source* in the technical sense which Wolff had first given it in the discussion of knowledge and by which it means that which validates or supplies the ground.[49] In any event the distinction which matters for us at the moment is between the scope and the limits of knowledge. The distinction could be put more fully and more perspicuously as the difference between the limits of our jurisdiction and the scope of our competence in knowledge.

The idea that courts or legislation have validity only within certain boundaries or jurisdictions is a familiar idea to all of us today. Thus, one obvious type of condition on the person or the events that are subject to the legislation or to the acts of the court is that the person or event fall within the limits of the court. The court is restricted to verdicts about what is within its jurisdiction. The only point which is at all subtle about the idea as Kant deploys it is

[48] *Gesammelte Schriften*, IX, p. 25.
[49] In accepting this claim for his priority I rely on the accuracy of his disciple, Meissner, in his *Philosophisches Lexicon*.

that the philosophy of the law in Kant's day tended to treat jurisdiction or domain as a type of property and to discuss it along with that which belongs by right to the legal agent.[50] The point which corresponds to this in the *Critique* is of course that being in space and time "as necessary conditions of all (inner and outer) experience are mere subjective conditions of all our intuition." (B66) That is to say, the question of who or what falls within the jurisdiction of a court or of a legislature has nothing at all to do with the way in which that person or event is to be conceived. The jurisdiction "belongs" to the being that has authority in the jurisdiction and is not constituted out of the properties or relationships of those over whom jurisdiction is exercised.

This reflects a contrast between jurisdiction and scope which may be harder for us to appreciate today, but with administrative courts, student courts, military courts, and the like the contrast is still retained to some degree in our own legal system. Johann Klüber writing a little later than Kant on the public law of the cities and the states of the German Bund remarks that the limits (*Grenzen*) of a court may be accompanied by limitations (*Einschränkungen*). These limitations are what serve to define the special courts: ecclesiastical, military, university, and the like. As he says, the competence or power (*Competenz*) of these courts is not of the same scope (*Umfang*).[51] The reason this contrast is hard for us to appreciate is because we are not accustomed to the idea that the way in which an individual is categorized determines whether the individual is subject to a court within whose jurisdiction he finds himself. But here we see the Kantian language applied to set forth a second, necessary condition for the validity of the judgment of the court. And here, of course, the necessary condition is one which must be presumed to have objective validity. That is to say, contrary to what will seem to many of us to be the obvious or the only sound legal doctrine, the question of who you are is relevant to a determination of whether the judgments of some court about you are valid judgments.

Two points need to be emphasized in reflecting on how this model from the law will translate into a discussion of our cognitive powers. First, the relevant kind of limitation on the powers of the court is not determined by how the facts about the person are to be conceived but rather by how the rights of the person must be conceived. When lords were tried before their peers, the lords were not noticeably larger than life. Or perhaps it would help to consider the recent trend in student courts in which members of minorities have gained the right to be tried before a jury of like individuals. If the member of a minority

---

[50] *Institutes*, II, p. 471.
[51] Johann Ludwig Klüber, *Öffentliches Recht des Teutschen Bundes und der Bundesstaaten*, third edition (Frankfurt a. M., 1840), p. 548 and p. 569.

within such a jurisdiction waives that right, then the mere fact that he belongs to that minority does not prevent him from falling within the scope of a valid verdict rendered by a jury constituted at random. This type of consideration leads directly to a second point. The question of the classes or categories of person, things, or events that fall within the competence of a court is primarily and in the first instance a question about how the courts are constituted and not a question primarily of the nature of the individuals that will be subject to the jurisdiction of the courts. This point has an obvious relationship to Kant's thoughts about the type of necessary condition that is a category of thought and that reflects the special powers of the subject in judging. These brief remarks will suffice to indicate my central thesis: There are a number of important and interesting differences between necessary conditions that are restrictions affecting the limits of the law and necessary conditions that are limitations affecting the scope of the law.

Restrictions determine limits of jurisdiction; limitations determine the scope of competence or power. Since this terminology had an established role in the juridical discussion of the validity of judgments in Kant's day and since his subject is criticism, or the science concerned with the validity of legal instruments, we are not strictly obliged to speculate about Kant's knowledge of the esoteric sources of his terminology. If that is understood, it is also true that the ultimate origin of his language is to be found in the logic of the schools and our understanding of his doctrine of space and time as restrictions on knowledge can be improved by the comparison with the earlier sources. From the days of Peter of Spain and before logicians were accustomed to say that a restriction on a sentence or a judgment is something that contracts it to a lesser domain.[52] A comparison of Kant's idea of restrictions with the doctrine that was already in place reveals a general likeness and some specific differences. The basis of the general likeness has already been exhibited in the discussion of space and time as forms of intuition. Kant calls the representations of space and of time the formal (*das Formale*) in intuition or formal intuitions. If we merely suppose that Kant applies these terms in the ordinary and commonplace sense that was listed by Walch, then the formal in representation means the more specific as opposed to the more general.[53] Thus, in an example given by Peter of Spain, where "white" contracts "A white man is running" to its lesser supposition, the more generic representation of a man is said to be material and that which makes it more specific is said to be the formal element.

[52] Peter of Spain, *Tractatus* (*Summulae Logicales*), ed. L.M. de Rijk (Assen, 1972), p. 194.
[53] Cf. the entry under *Form* in Walch's Philosophisches Lexicon.

The same example reveals the most interesting and important difference. The tradition—or at least the part of it that we assume Kant to be familiar with—tacitly assumes that the restrictive condition or the formal element is itself a general concept, just as "white" is a general concept. The clearest specimens of restrictive conditions which are offered by Walch are his illustrations of the so-called "reduplicative sentences". For example, the king of Sweden, conceived as the king of Sweden, has to rule in Uppsala. Walch contrasts such sentences to "specificative sentences" in which the truth or falsity of what is predicated of the subject is independent of the description by which the subject is specified or picked out. For example, the student is a painter. In this example it is presumed to be an accident that the subject is a student. Now Walch merely assumes that both the reduplicative condition and the specification can be given using terms of general description. This assumption gives Walch a position that is closer to the rationalists than to his earlier predecessors or to Kant.

The concept of a restriction in modern quantificational logic is a closer neighbor to Kant's idea of a necessary condition than is the modern concept of a necessary condition. But the modern logician frequently makes the same assumption as Walch. Thus, what is called a "many-sorted" system of quantification is one in which the domain or domains of the things to which predicates are applied are restricted in one or more ways. The assumption is that the restriction can always be expressed in general terms within the system and can in this way be removed. The effect of this assumption can be illustrated for an abbreviated system: Suppose that the scope of the quantifiers is limited to red things. In this case, if "R" is a predicate in the system which describes red things and if "(x)" is the quantifier by which the predicates are referred to everything in the domain of the system, then "$(x)Rx$" will be a necessary truth in the system, even though it is not analytic in the system— that is, the denial of the expression does not yield a contradiction within the system, even when conjoined to whatever definitions we may suppose in the system. For the logician the existence of these types of necessities is trivial and proves nothing about the possibility of non-analytic necessities. The logician finds the example uninteresting because he supposes that he can provide us with a general rule for converting the many-sorted systems into an unrestricted system. The rule is to make a predicate, or a term of general description, out of each restriction. The appropriate predicate is then affixed to each existentially quantified predicate on an additional conjunct and to each universally quantified predicate as the antecedent of a (formal) implication having that predicate as the consequent. Thus, in our tiny example "$(x)Rx$" with "(x)" restricted to red things becomes "$(x)(\text{if } Rx, \text{ then } Rx)$" without restriction. The latter is pretty obviously something that can be shown to be a necessary truth by drawing a contradiction from its denial. The importance of this illustration comes from the fact that Kant denies the assumption that every restriction can be expressed in predicates. Hence, he denies that the relation of every necessary condition to what it is a condition of can be expressed meaningfully as a relation of truth-functional or formal implication. In particular, he denies that a relation of implication can be defined between a singular concept or intuition that restricts us to things that are present in this world and the general predicates which the formal intuition restricts. By the same token he denies that the restriction to what has present existence or to what has a position in this world can be expressed by a predicate. The upshot is that any necessary truth whose possibility depends upon those restrictions would not be analytic—in the modern sense of the term. It will be a synthetic necessity.

Kant gives us several examples of the way in which the condition that objects be present in the world—present, that is, in space and time—can affect the discussion of the validity of concepts. Lambert had anticipated Kant's general concern for the question of how we can show the real possibility or the objective validity of a concept. One of the ways he discusses depends for its plausibility upon the theory that concepts do sometimes as a matter of fact have their origin in a process of abstraction from what is experienced. Lambert assumes that wherever the origin of a concept can be shown to be of this sort the possibility of the concept is certain, since the concept can at least be applied to the things from which it was abstracted. Kant's objection is that the concept may have been abstracted beyond the limits of the conditions for its possibility—which are the limits of any possible valid employment of our understanding. Kant gives as an example the concept of the everlastingness or eternity of God. Since God is not a being in space or time, our concept of his magnitude of existence cannot be subject to the restriction that it be the longevity of a being in time. Hence, the fact, if fact it be, that we have formed the concept by abstraction from those long-lived beings we have encountered in our experience is not a fact that establishes the objective validity of the concept. A second example shows the way in which the existence of restrictions on concepts will give rise to trichotomies in transcendental logic to replace the dichotomies that occur in the division of concepts in formal logic—a discipline that can ignore the effects of these restrictions because it is not concerned with the real possibility of concepts or with their objective validity. Kant tells us that neither the judgment that God moves nor the judgment that God does not move (it is not the case that God moves) is true. The reason, as he explains it, is that a necessary restriction of the objective validity of the concept is its restriction to beings in space and time. Where the predicate is applied to something that is not in space and time the resulting judgment is neither true nor false.[54]

There is an interesting similarity between Kant's views on the restriction to what has present existence and the views of earlier logicians. First, there is an agreement on the way in which the tense of the verb of predication can reflect a restriction on the subject matter that confines it to the things that exist. Thus Peter of Spain: "Terminus communis supponens vel apponens verbo presentis temporis simpliciter sumpto, non habenti vim ampliandi nec ex se nec ex alio restringitur ad supponendum pro huis qui sunt sub forma termini supponentis."[55] The significance of their agreement on the way present existence can be expressed will become clearer in the next chapter as we contemplate an argumentative use that Kant makes of the point. But, secondly, Peter is just as clear as Kant about the fact that the restriction to what has present existence does not depend upon the nature of the thing or upon what the thing is. It depends entirely upon the temporal position or location of the thing. "Et sic, 'esse' non restringit ad existentia sed ad praesentia, cum iden tempus sit utrobique, quod est causa restrictionis."[56] The distinction between this type of necessary condition and the condition which limits the competence of our judgments to certain categories of object has the most profound importance in the structure of the *Critique*. Modern logic has, by and large, not found any use for the idea of representations that cannot be converted into predicates, so the agreement between Kant and the earlier logical tradition is a matter of some interest. There are two ways to interpret this lack of modern interest; at the end of the next chapter I return to the problem with a Kantian proposal about something that is lacking in modern logic.

[54] *Gesammelte Schriften*, XVIII, p. 715–716; XVI, p. 637–638.
[55] *Tractatus*, p. 216.
[56] Peter of Spain, *Summulae Logicales*, ed. J.P. Mullally (Notre Dame, Ind., 1945), p. 58.

CHAPTER FIVE

ARGUMENTS IN THE AESTHETIC

I. KANT'S STRATEGY

The central arguments in Kant's aesthetic are two arguments for each of two main conclusions about our representations of space and time. Since the two pairs of arguments dealing with the representation of time reduplicate the arguments about time, my analysis will mainly be confined to the arguments about space. In each case the first pair of arguments attack a dogma of the empiricists by seeking to establish that the representation in question is *a priori*. The second pair attacks a dogma of the rationalists by seeking to establish that the representation is an intuition rather than a general concept.

Kant must have thought through the organization of these arguments with much care. The ordering of the arguments indicates a fine sense for tactics and for strategy. On the tactical side it should be noted that the successful refutation of the empiricists supplies Kant with a lemma that is necessary for at least one of his two arguments against the rationalists. We can appreciate the necessity for the premise if we recall that the major rationalists had never claimed any more than that everything that can be known can *in principle* be known *a priori*. The other side of that opinion is the view that *in practice* many of our objectively valid representations will always be merely empirical. Hence, the rationalist doctrine that everything which can be known can be known through clear, distinct and adequate ideas, or through a conceptual definition of the subject matter, is a doctrine that applies only to what in practice can be known *a priori*. Now one of Kant's arguments against the proposition that our representation of space is a general concept depends upon the fact that there are an infinite number of representations involved in that given representation. Hence, there is more represented in it than we could achieve in practice by the method of clear and distinct ideas. Kant's tactical exercise reflects a general point about arguments concerning the impossibility of infinite regresses or concerning the impossibility of given, infinite sets: The successful arguments tend to depend upon a preliminary maneuvering to get it established that the existence of the infinite regress or of the infinite collection would presuppose a performance that clearly outstrips our abilities or that the infinite set would depend in its membership upon our having accomplished something which in practice we cannot accomplish. These tactics are very obviously adopted in the spirit of Kant's overriding transcendental strategy—a strategy that retreats from the direct consideration of what is possible in *theory* or in *fact* in order to consider what is possible in our epistemic *practice*.

The particular strategy of the aesthetic may also reflect Kant's sense that in these matters and contrary to the case in the analytic his quarrel with rationalism involves the deeper and the more profound levels of reflection. The strategic situation today, when every denial of empiricist dogma is apt to be greeted as scandal or as provocation, would seem to be different from what it was in Kant's day. Thus, even the first set of arguments to show that the cognition of space is *a priori* has only been understood in the most superficial way if it is regarded merely as the denial of what the empiricists had affirmed, namely, the denial that every valid representation is empirical. Kant has a positive doctrine, and with the consideration of that doctrine we move from the level of tactics to the deeper level of strategy. The doctrine concerns not some representation or other, but the specific representations of space and of time. In arguing that *these particular* representations are *a priori*, Kant affirms something that Leibniz had denied. Space and time for Kant's magnificent predecessor had the status of what the *Critique* defines as mere appearance—not appearance, it should be noted, but mere appearance. Appearances, as we have seen, are the subject matter of our empirical cognitions. (More precisely, appearances are the undetermined objects to which empirical representations are referred in intuition.) Leibniz took the view that to the extent that our cognitions of what is spatial and temporal these are always only empirical representations. The attitude concealed in that position is comparable to the attitude that was characterized in the first chapter as a sickly version of Platonism that wishes to withdraw from the world of change and becoming in order to contemplate a different set of realities. Should we succeed in replacing those empirical representations with *a priori* cognitions, the latter will be representations of things that are not by nature spatial or temporal. The Kantian view by contrast is that the objects of scientific knowledge are the realities in appearance. As a result and paradoxically, rationalism is a major target of Kant's attack even where he is arguing the case for the *a priori* character of our knowledge of space and time.

In discussing Kant's strategy up to this point, I have tried to stress the historical context for the arguments. If his problems are to be considered in the context of our modern contentions and disputes, the contemporary reader deserves a different type of briefing on what Kant is about: In the first place, the two sets of arguments concerning space occur in the course of what Kant describes as a metaphysical exposition of the representation of space. Kant has in mind a contrast between two types of discussion or exposition of concepts. The first type merely attempts to describe or to expound what in fact has been thought or represented in a given concept. If the representation is that of space, the question for this first type of discussion would concern what it is that men have represented space to themselves as being. Lambert pointed out long before Hilbert that the axioms of Euclidean geometry can be taken as a definition of the ordinary conception of space. Whether or not space is Euclidean has nothing to do with this first investigation, which concerns what it is that men have thought in thinking about space. Kant calls this first type of exposition a verbal definition (*Namenerklärung*). Some of his contemporaries, using terminology in a way that varied from earlier custom, called these explanations nominal definitions.[1] The terminology is perhaps unfortunate because where the representation is a general concept the nominal definition states—or is intended to state—the essence of the thing represented. Thus our nominal definition of space would tell us what space is and does tell us, at least, what space as a logical object or object of a logically possible representation is. In the same terminological tradition the real definition of a concept is an exposition that makes clear the source or the origin of the real possibility of the object. Kant's metaphysical exposition has approximately the same import as an inquiry into the real possibility of the object, but, as we have seen in the definition of the transcendental turn in philosophy, Kant prefers to seize the opposite end of the stick. His metaphysical exposition is concerned to establish two things: that a representation of space has objective validity as an *a priori* representation and, secondly, that the

---

[1] J.G. Walch, *Philosophisches Lexicon*, ed. and enlarged by J.C. Hennings (Leipzig, 1775). Hennings's commentary on *Definition* reads in part: "Das Wort *definitio nominalis* (Worterklärung) und *definitio realis* (Sacherklärung) wird anders bei dem Alten, und wieder anders bei dem Neuen genommen. Die Alten verstunden unter der Nominalerklärung, eine Entwickelung des Worts, nach der Herleitung, nach den gleichvielbedeutenden Worten, und nach den verschiedenen Bedeutungen. Die Realerklärung aber bestunde in einem vollständig deutlichen Begriff der Sache, wodurch man selbige jederzeit von allen andern unterscheiden konnte. Und diese Ideen der Alten schickten sich auch recht wohl zu den Benennungen: Nominal- und Realerklärung. Es ist aber bei allen Neuren nunmehr gebräuchlich, mit diesen Worten ganz andere Begriffe zu verbinden. Denn Nominaldefinition heißt bei ihnen eben das, was die Alten Realdefinition nenneten. Hingegen Realdefinition, welche auch eine genetische heißt, soll diejenige Erklärung seyn, da man den Ursprung einer Sache zeiget und erkläret."

way in which it has objective validity is as an intuition, rather than as a concept.

Throughout the previous discussion I have put great stress on the second of these objectives. It gives the entire doctrine of the transcendental elements a different look. But Kant's modern reader remembering Hume's enquiries and perhaps not being fully in sympathy with Kant's transcendental turn will have large difficulties in developing some enthusiasm for Kant's first objective. The currents of empiricism are too swift and too strong to be dammed by a few words. But can anything at all be said in defence of the plausibility of Kant's strategy? The following thought-experiment will help to convey the seriousness of Kant's proposals both in the aesthetic and the analytic. Let us select a philosopher well-endoctrinated in the spirit of Hume's empiricism. Let us set him the task of drawing up two lists of terms. For simplicity at the outset we ask him to ignore the problems connected with singular terms, and we ask him to proceed as follows: The first list is to be restricted to possible descriptive predicates (or to representations that the Kantian will characterize as ones that have objective validity in conformity with the conditions for validity that are set out in formal and transcendental logic). His task therefore is to place on this first list all and only those terms which can be employed to describe something which we can experience—to describe, that is, in descriptions that may be either true or false. Every other term is to go to the second list. Now we have endowed our mental creature with the conscience of a Humean, so we can imagine that he recalls the famous "appeal to experience" and he goes to work. His appeal to experience will not, of course, allow him actually to complete the task but we imagine him a man with the patience of centuries as he works away at the task. Is there any other problem he will encounter? The Kantian opinion is that he has a serious problem and that his methods are defective in conception and not merely in execution. Why?

Confronted by a given term and asked to dispose of its fate, the man who appeals to experience has a way of answering the question, "Do I, or can I, experience what this predicate describes?"—Or possibly he even confines himself to a narrower, more retrospective, and less experimental attitude by asking himself, "Can this idea in fact be traced back to what I have experienced?" But the appeal to experience, past, present, or future, gives no *direct* and *immediate* answer to the question that was asked, viz., "Can this predicate be employed to describe something that I can or do experience?" Our imaginary Humean was set the task of answering one question and he has actually answered a quite different question. For instance, if the specific issue is whether "cause" can be employed to describe the sun in a description such as "The sun is a cause of a warming of the rock," our Humean will dutifully review what he experiences when he experiences the sun. If on that basis he rejects the predicate from the first list, he only shows that he mistook the issues. What he requires to justify his rejection is not a closèr look at what he has experienced, but an argument or a transcendental deduction that will carry him from what he experiences to a conclusion about the lack of objective validity in the term.

This very elementary point—so very elementary that it may even escape our attention—cannot be asserted too vigorously. In recent years the Anglo-American philosophical world has been divided into the great mass of virtuous empiricists and the tiny band of intrepid Kantians. The divisive issue is usually construed as the peculiar belief of Kantians in the possibility of trans-cendental deductions. But transcendental deductions are proceedings designed to settle our rights in the employment of certain representations, where our rights have been disputed. Anyone at all who reaches a decision about where to list "causes" must do so on the basis of a transcendental argument. If Hume reaches a different conclusion from Kant, that is because his *assumptions* are different. If we look to the historical sources of Hume's argument, we will have a better conception of the relative strengths of the two arguments than if we foolishly believe that the Humean answer exhibits a virtuous and hard-headed empiricism. Hume's transcendental deduction is an offshoot from the method that Descartes and the logicians of Port-Royal had codified as a method for becoming clear about the content of our ideas. Thus, it is a method for supplying what we have called verbal or nominal definitions. If the general method of clarifying an idea is to attend carefully to the content of the idea, or to attend to what is implied by the idea, no great novelty was required for the British empiricists to say that the clarification of the empirical content of an idea can be achieved by the appeal to experience. Hume's novelty is to argue that the method for determining the empirical content of an idea is also a method for determining the objective validity of an idea. That is, the fact—established by empirical observation—that "causes" has no empirical content is taken as a premise in an argument designed to reach a conclusion about my rights and obligations in employing the term. In particular, I am to reach the conclusion that the predicate cannot be employed by me to describe the things that I do experience.

The conclusions from the transcendental aesthetic have a direct bearing on our confidence in this Humean deduction, because our assessment of the empiricist argument will reflect our views on the conditions under which predicates can be referred to what is experienced. Hume does not appear to have perceived any important difference between the limits of the employment of a term—the class determined by what the term can be referred to—and the scope of the term—the class determined by what the term specifies through its content. And underlying every empiricist deduction concerning the objective validity of terms, the presupposition which justifies the appeal to experience is that terms are restricted to what can be experienced by means of the representations that determine the scope of the empirical predicates. In the deduction offered by the empiricist there cannot be room for a distinction between the conditions for reference to what is experienced and the conditions for description of what is experienced. Thus, if one had become conscious of the empirical content of the various elementary ideas and if one had accounted for the possibility of association of simple ideas in complex ideas, then one would have no additional question to ask concerning the objective validity of our representations. The counterpart of the Humean assumptions about the representations of objects shows up in Hume's belief about the objects of scientific knowledge. For Hume as for the rationalists the objects that are known are always things *per se* and cannot be appearances. The reader may be inclined to protest this description of Hume's situation, unless he recalls what Kant means by an appearance. An appearance is the undetermined object of an empirical intuition. Hence, a philosopher cannot make the Kantian distinction between appearances and things *per se* unless he is willing to make the distinction between intuitions and concepts which Hume's analysis fails to admit. The air of paradox in the description of Hume's position as one that seeks to analyze scientific knowledge as knowledge of "things-in-themselves" comes from that other and more familiar sense of appearance which is associated with Hume's analysis of the object as a bundle of sense impressions. But precisely this analysis should serve as evidence that Hume cannot make Kant's distinction between the appearances that result when the water is spinning in the pail and the appearances that result from the pail spinning about the water. Or, confining ourself to the difference between mere change in appearance and change both in appearance and reality, if we were confronted by a house on large, invisible roller skates, there would be no difference between what we would experience when the house spins in front of us and what we would experience by walking around the house.

Hume is as unable to make out a distinction between appearances and things *per se* as the rationalists had been, *precisely because Hume has never gone beyond their formulation* of the task of an analysis of knowledge. Each supposes that the central task is to account for the *scope* and the *content* of our knowledge. But we cannot account for the possibility of knowledge merely by accounting for how and why we *do* know that which we *do* know about the objects. This analysis fails to provide any coherent account of the limits of our knowledge. Kant's discussion of intuitions provides this account of the *limits* of knowledge, and thereby Kant is able to explain how there can be things about the object of scientific knowledge—things such as the mere change in appearances of the object—which are not reflected in what I can know about the object. The real and substantial object of scientific inquiry is not merely what can be known. The real and substantial object of scientific knowledge is also in part a "that which I do not know" or—to use Locke's phrase in what may or may not be his sense—the object is in part "un je ne sais quoi". As a result, any discussion of knowledge which merely accounts for the scope and content of knowledge without also accounting for the limits of human knowledge is defective. If Locke's analysis of the material substratum was intended to explain why the object of knowledge is not merely a thing *per se* or thing as we are able to conceive it, then Locke was probably the last major philosopher before Kant to deal with the limits of knowledge in a serious way.

II. SPACE AS AN A PRIORI REPRESENTATION

Kant gives two arguments to show that our representation of space is *a priori*. In the first edition of the *Critique* Kant drew out the transcendental implications of this conclusion in a paragraph which he very wisely withdrew to a separate section in later editions of the *Critique*. The paragraph had made it appear that the considerations in favor of the view that space is represented *a priori* embodied a form of argument that Kant did not use and which he knew he could not use. Since the form of argument is one that modern readers have been given to suppose they will discover in Kant, it is important to understand what the argument is supposed to be and why Kant is barred from using it. As to the first point, we might expect that Kant will argue in this way: Adopting the idea of Lambert, we can take the first principles of Euclidean geometry as a determination of the nature of Euclidean space and thereby as a nominal definition of our representation of space. Consequently, if we suppose that our concept of space is empirical, we must regard geometry as an empirical discipline. But geometry is an *a priori* science. It follows that "space" must be an *a priori* representation.

Kant never employs this argument in the aesthetic—contrary to a popular impression about his thoughts on the subject. Kant does regard geometry as an *a priori* discipline, and, after he has settled the point that "space" is an *a priori* representation, he does bring forward that conclusion to explain the possibility of geometry as *a priori* knowledge—that is the thrust of the re-positioned paragraph. But his metaphysical exposition does not simply assume the existence of geometry as a body of *a priori* knowledge. Why? The answer reveals much about the direction of his thinking throughout the metaphysical exposition. The short answer is of course that he anticipated objections from the side of empiricism concerning the nature of geometrical knowledge: If it is possible at all, it is empirical. But the way some recent empiricists have flaunted this objection shows that they have not grasped the direction of his reflections. The more up-to-date version of an empiricist refutation is often put this way: First, geometrical propositions, *qua* geometrical, do not give a description of real space. Hence they are neither true or false. Secondly, any description of space which *is* true or false is subject to confirmation or disconfirmation by observations. In support of this analysis it will be pointed out that recent advances in our physical understanding have underscored the empirical character of our assertions about space by making it possible to theorize that physical space is not Euclidean. The thrust of this last remark is to suggest that experience is teaching us, or even perhaps has taught us, a better understanding of the nature of space than Kant had—a suggestion that is the cap on the head of an empiricist rebuttal of Kant.

What is the most striking feature of this argument? Not the fact that it fails to join issue with Kant, but that it rests on a premise accepted by Kant. Kant did not anticipate the development of alternative geometries—though we will see in connection with the third argument how little their development affects his position. But Kant had been forced to the key assumption which these developments were later to force upon Carnap and the other distinguished modern empiricists. Kant *knew* that he could not assume that geometrical statements give a description of the nature of space.

The reason why he was forced to dispense with the naive confidence in geometry as an *a priori* discipline is that an impressive series of Platonic idealists had defended a radical scepticism about the objects of geometrical description. We need only recall the last figures in that ancient tradition which extends almost from Plato himself. Geometrical statements cannot merely be assumed to give a description of the nature of space because space itself is nothing real—or so Berkeley teaches us. Geometrical statements cannot merely be assumed to give a description of the nature of real things in space, because the geometrical relationships between things are nothing real—or so Leibniz teaches us. *A priori* knowledge which characterizes space or describes things in space cannot be assumed to be possible, because it does not exist—and Kant never in fact supposed he could show the contrary.

Kant diagnosed the failure of the earlier attempts to provide for the possibility of an *a priori* science of geometry as efforts to soar too high and to prove the possibility in a way that would transcend the limits of possible experience by rising to an understanding of the natures of things through pure concepts alone. Any judgment that is not restricted to the things that can be referred to within the limits of possible experience is what Kant calls a transcendent judgment—meaning thereby that it exhibits a tendency to soar in a flight of Platonic enthusiasm. More prosaically, Kant says, "If therefore a subject is a thing in general and the predicate is space and time or a concept built thereon, the judgment is transcendent. (Every thing is somewhere or at some time.) I do not say that the judgment is false; it just does not follow, *non liquet*."[2] Instead of commencing his discussion of geometry with an analysis of the possibility of a pure geometry, Kant's discussion of the objective validity of the representation of space begins with an analysis of the possibility of an applied geometry, and only later takes up the question of a pure geometry. The result is that the objects which are described in pure geometry are always objects which can be taken in fact, or at least in our imagination, as objects to which empirical predicates can also be applied. To illustrate this point we can use Kant's example from the section on the schematism: This round thing which can be given intuition can also be subsumed under the empirical concept of a plate; that is, having seen a circular thing or even having only drawn a circle in my imagination, I can frame the judgment that this circular thing is a plate. Kant's point in this later section of the *Critique* is worth making explicit in order to avoid any confusion about the example. The thing which is round is subject to certain conditions under which it is given in intuition as a possible object of applied or of pure geometrical description. These restrictive conditions are what concern him in the aesthetic. In the later section Kant's point is that our freedom to imagine the round thing to be a plate is also subject to a qualifying limitation or condition. The thing which we spontaneously—as a pure conjecture or even only as a playful whim of our imagination—conceive to be a plate cannot be a mere circle that has been imagined by us in the course, let us say, of an abstract investigation of conic sections. Suppose we have drawn a circle in the course of such a study. Are we perfectly free to interrupt our mathematical researches with a flight of the imagination in which we say to ourselves that it is a plate, or that it is a flying saucer? Kant's point is that our freedom is *subject to* a second type of condition—namely, that the description can be objectified through our categorization of the thing. In the case in hand, we must classify the thing as a substance in order to think it to be a plate. Hence, from the fact that for Kant pure geometry is restricted to a study of the things that are within the limits of possible experience, no one should draw the unwarranted and fallacious conclusion that it is limited to the things that are within the scope of competence of our empirical judgment. Kant holds

[2] *Gesammelte Schriften*, XVI, p. 637–638.

precisely the reverse to be the case. The doctrine of the transcendental ideality of space and time is the doctrine that space and time are not within the competence of empirical judgments. In geometry we do not permit conclusions about the subject matter to be based upon experience. The significance of this fact for Kant's metaphysical exposition will become apparent as we discuss Kant's third argument—the first of his two arguments to show that space is represented in intuition. But subject to this understanding about the complexity of the conditions that are involved in accounting for the possibility of an applied geometry, the point to be emphasized here is that Kant's discussion of the *a priori* character of our representation of space attacks the problem from the point of view of an applied geometry first, and only subsequently passes to a discussion of the possibility of a pure geometry. Our analysis of Kant's first argument for the *a priori* status of space should help to clarify what is meant by saying that the discussion begins with the possibility of an applied geometry.

We have an example of a judgment which can be possible as an empirical judgment in "This round thing is a plate". Kant wishes to argue that such a judgment *is* possible as an empirical judgment only if the representation of space is added to the judgment as an *a priori* representation, or as an element in the judgment which cannot be based upon the evidence of our senses in observing the thing. More generally, our representation of space is *a priori*, Kant argues, because our empirical representations of external objects are representations of objects that are differentiated by their size, shape and position, and because they can be differentiated in this way only if we have an *a priori* representation of space. In the judgment that this round thing is a plate, our empirical concept of a plate is not applied to ourselves or to the content of our minds; it is applied to something other than ourselves. Also the empirical concept of a plate can, like any general concept, be applied to things that differ from one another; it can be applied, let us suppose, to this round thing here and to that unusual square plate over there. The key phrase in Kant's first argument is usually translated "external to ourselves and external to one another". But if Kant gave us no guidance about how to understand the phrase, *außer uns und außer einander*—if we were translating entirely on the basis of the terminological conventions of Kant's day, we could say "extrinsic to us and extrinsic to one another". Thus Hennings explains the phrase so that it means being different from us and different from each other, and we have had several close looks at the reigning views on what it means to say that things are different. Before Kant and in his tradition, to say that two things are different is to say that the one is not what the other is, or that the nature of one is not involved in the nature of the other. But Kant takes note of this earlier sense in which one thing had been said to be extrinsic to another and says that it is not all that he means. Experiences of extrinsic or adventitious objects are ones in which judgments apply empirical predicates to objects that are not merely different. The objects must be represented as having different positions in space in order for the objects to be differentiated in the ways that they *are* differentiated—namely, on the basis of shape, size and position. And in order for the objects to be represented as having different positions in space a representation of space that is *a priori* must be added to the empirical description in the judgment.

Why must objects be represented as having different positions in space in order to be differentiated as they are in our empirical judgments about extrinsic objects—i.e., about objects that differ in shape, size and position? We know already why Kant *desires* this conclusion: if the manifoldness or diversity of the objects of empirical judgments always depended upon the way the objects are thought in the judgments, then inductive reasoning and synthetic *a priori* judgments about the objects would be impossible. But philosophical desires milk no cows. What we are concerned with now is his reason for insisting on this distinction between mere difference in what things are and a difference that depends upon our representation of the space in which the things are located. It might be supposed that, contrary to Kant's desires and Kant's contention, if we do not think of ourselves as plates, or of our thoughts as plates, the reason *is* only that plates are different from you and from me. What I am is certainly not what a plate is. Furthermore, why not suppose that experience has taught us this difference? The empirical concept of a plate involves the concept of a thing that either is or can be circular. The occasional square plate that we encounter is something that can have its corners trimmed. It seems to follow that if we imagined ourselves to be circular or to have circular thoughts, we might suppose ourselves to be plates. Why not? Children are exposed to books in which people are represented as circles, and, so long as we are only considering what is possible, we must agree that nothing is easier than to think of any circular thing as a plate. What this feat of the imagination shows is that if experience had taught the child to think of himself as one sort of thing—as an angular thing—experience could *not* have taught him that when he has a set of representations of a circular thing these representations are to be referred to something different from himself. It is not because the child knows himself on the basis of experience to be something which is not circular that he is able to refer the representation of a circular thing to something other than himself. To be sure, if he knew on the basis of experience that, while square plates can be trimmed a bit, angular people cannot be made circular and made to sit over there on the table, then of course he would be able to differentiate between himself and the plate on the basis of perceived shape. But experience only teaches him that the circular thing is a plate, not that it must be so, and that the angular thing is an arm, not that it must be so.

We have been exploring the suggestion that things which are differentiated by size, shape and position are merely differentiated by what they are—as experience has disclosed what they are. The reader might suspect that the last clause is the one that should go and that if it went then the solution to the little puzzle would be obvious. How is it possible to differentiate the objects of extrinsic experiences, or the objects which differ in shape, size and position? Answer: because there are categories that are involved in what we think of ourselves and other things. That is, we bring to our empirical judgments a conceptual ingredient which tells us not merely what the various objects are, but also what they can and can not be. Some of my representations can be referred to the plate as something different from me or from my thoughts and impressions because person and thoughts are not the sorts of thing that can be circular. That is, we know *a priori* from our concept of persons and our concept of thoughts that a thing to which the concept of a circular thing is referred must be different from us or from our thoughts.

Despite the attractions of this solution Kant is justified in rejecting it for three very good reasons. First, we are only justified in asserting of the objects of empirical judgments that they are actually to be differentiated on the basis of shape, size and position; we are not justified in asserting this of things as they must be—not even of things as they must be by virtue of the way they must be conceived. After all, Leibniz had taught us that if we could form a more adequate conception of that round plate over there on the table, we would not conceive it as a flat, roundish, white thing at all. No! We would conceive it as a hive of spiritual beings droning with the activity of representation. If Leibniz's view seems capricious or fanciful, he can at least make one telling observation in his own defence. If the question under discussion is what the properties are which distinguish different kinds of objects in reality and independent of the vagaries and fluctuations of our experience, the shape, size and position of objects make poor candidates. After all the observed properties of souls—or at least of things that think—are not so obviously subject to a kind of change that is independent of any variance in what the object is. The primary qualities of the objects of empirical judgments, on the other hand, are notoriously subject to merely apparent change as well as to real change or change that must be reflected in our conception of what the objects are.

Still and all, the possibility of the Leibnizian conception of that plate may seem inconclusive as an objection to the proposed solution in terms of categories involved in the judgments about different things.

There is a second difficulty in the suggestion that we bring to experience conceptions of what objects can and cannot be and that the content of these conceptions is what explains how we are able to differentiate between ourselves and plates. We have seen in an earlier chapter that Spinoza had a valid *deduction* to show that things cannot be differentiated, because there is a valid proof or *demonstration* that if things are to be differentiated only on the basis of what they are of how they are to be conceived, they cannot be differentiated at all. One thing, God or the world, will serve as the ultimate subject matter of all our predications. It appears from this line of argument that something is possible in the contingent world of experience, namely a differentiation of objects, which is not only not to be explained by the concepts we bring to experience, but which is not even possible in the domain of those pure concepts. The second objection therefore is Spinozistic.

There is a third and decisive objection to the suggestion that the differentiation of objects on the basis of size, shape, and position is possible because of the content of our conception of different objects. This third (Cartesian) objection which is at the heart of Kant's problem in the aesthetic is concerned with the actual details of the way in which the representations of size, shape and position are achieved in our empirical knowledge of objects. In order to deal with this we must return to the topic of an applied geometry. Pure geometry as a discipline that supplies us with conceptions of things like circles contributes nothing to an understanding of how the plate can be differentiated from me on the basis of size, shape, or location. But the Cartesian analytic geometry which teaches how a conception of a plate can be referred to a circular thing does supply us with insight. This reference to a type of geometry that is applied to the objects of cognition is not to be taken as part of some extended analogy or metaphor for the problem which Kant is required to solve. The entire thrust of Kant's argument in the aesthetic, including this first argument, is in the direction of his ultimate conclusion and his basic conviction: There is only as much knowledge in any area as there is of mathematics in it. The paradigm of an empirical judgment in our discussion (that is, this round thing is a plate) has been inadequate because it does not adequately expose the mathematical aspects of any paradigm of empirical knowledge.

The question, to repeat, is how, when we think of an empirical object as a plate, can the object be represented as different from some other object on the basis of shape, size, or position? The first point which emerges from the recollection of Descartes's analytic geometry is a confirmation of the point we have just been pursuing: *The way in which the object is conceived, described or otherwise judged to be does not establish that object to be circular, to be big, or to be in some definite location.* It will be recalled from our earlier discussions of Kant's terminology that the objects to which empirical predicates are referred are called appearances and that the latter are defined as "the indeterminate objects of empirical intuitions." In Descartes's analytic geometry, the empirical representations of circles are given by representations that are called "empirical equations in two unknowns". Now *prior to Descartes these equations in two unknowns were not taken to be descriptions of circles at all.* On the contrary, because they contain two variables—or, in Euler's later analogy two generic concepts—the objects of such equations were said to be indeterminate objects. The plain truth is that even though you may fully understand the conceptual or mathematical content of such a judgment you cannot take it as having any empirical employment at all until something is added to it that solves the problem of what it is about. No one can solve such equations in two unknowns and thus, no one can say on the basis of what they contain whether they are equations of circular things or angular things or even of dimensionless spiritual things. Two things have to be added to the judgment before it becomes the possible empirical equation of the shape of a plate. First, we must supplement the representation with a representation of space— something which is certainly not contained in the equation and something which hardly anyone before Descartes had even connected with algebraic expressions. What Descartes added was of course a representation of a space in which the positions in the space are distinguished from one another in some way—usually, but not always, by their relation to a set of imaginary lines that are taken as normal to one another at some point of origin. The second thing that must be added—and care must be taken to separate the two steps—is the idea that the two variable quantities or the two generic concepts in the equations in two unknowns can be taken as representations of sets of points in the space. Until we have added the representation of the space and until we have made a decision about the domain of the variables, we do not have an equation that has any geometrical significance of any kind. Nothing could be clearer than that the ways in which the objects of these equations are represented *in the equations themselves* does not determine the "size, shape, or position" of those objects.

The proposal for an interpretation of Kant's first argument is that we take the equations of applied geometry as our paradigm in interpreting Kant's remarks about the empirical knowledge we can have of objects that vary in size, shape, and position. One advantage of this paradigm is that it enables us to make a more careful separation of the two steps in Descartes's contribution than we might be inclined to do with ordinary empirical judgments. The mathematicians who have discussed Descartes's work have indeed been very clear about the importance of a sharp distinction between the two elements.[3] Before we turn to the reasons for their concern and the transcendental implications of their point, we should be clearer about why the separation of the two steps is easier to achieve in the case of empirical equations than in the case of empirical judgments in general. The reason is that prior to Descartes the variables of mathematical equations were understood to be concepts of numbers and the association of these numbers with positions in space to give them geometrical significance required an act of thought on Descartes's part. The mathematicians are well aware of the importance of this act of synthesis or of association as an indispensable ingredient in the process of formulating and of verifying sets of empirical equations. The case is different in our ordinary empirical judgments, where our concept of the subject matter may already contain—or appear to contain—a concept with a purely geometrical significance. Leibniz may infect us with doubts about the soul of the plate, but, as I have already remarked, most people find these objections inconclusive and they continue to suspect that if the object in question is a plate then it is the sort of thing that can be circular. It should be noted even here however, that if the ordinary conviction about ordinary empirical judgments is sound then that only means that such judgments contain concepts with a pure geometrical meaning. The concept of circularity, for example, can be given a meaning as a concept in pure geometry. The usefulness of separating Descartes's two contributions comes when we see that even if the equivalent of his second step had been taken, we would not know how to formulate or to verify our judgments as empirical judgments until we had supplied some equivalent of his first contribution—namely, some representation of the space in which the circular thing is to be located. Until both steps have been taken, the concept of the plate—even though it may contain the idea of something that can be circular—lacks all analytical significance. I use the phrase *analytical significance* in this discussion to characterize our representations of the so-called primary qualities of objects—size, shape, and position, and I say that such representations have analytic significance just in case the shape, size, or the position which an object is represented as having is a size, shape, or position that will differentiate one

<hr />

[3] The distinction between Descartes's two steps is marked very clearly by B.N. Delone in the Russian work, *Mathematics: Its Concepts, Methods, and Meaning*, ed. A.D. Aleksandrov, A.N. Kolmogorov, and M.A. Lavrent'ev (Cambridge, 1963), I, p. 184.

object of knowledge from another object of knowledge. The two steps whereby our representations of size, shape and position gain their analytic significance are, first, the addition of a representation of the space in which the objects are to be located as objects of knowledge, and secondly, an act which associates some feature or features of the given representation of the object with positions in the space.

Descartes seems to have been aware of certain implications that follow from the separation of his two contributions and that show very clearly the necessity of separating them. He realized that even if a theory embodies concepts which have a *geometrical* significance and content, the *analytic* significance of that content varies with the representation of the space that is supplied for the theory. He realized in this connection that objects which would from the point of view of a pure geometry be differently conceived objects can be regarded as mere variants of one and the same object of knowledge varying under different projections of the object into space. As we will see, he used this circumstance to give an ingenious defence of an otherwise heretical conception of the world. But it is also true, and here we are aware of more possibilities than Descartes could have been, that even if the mathematical representations of two objects may be the same, the objects may nevertheless have to be differentiated as objects of knowledge because differing representations of space have been added to the equations of the same form. If we supply one co-ordinate system for an equation of a given form, what is described by the equation may have a circular shape. If we vary the co-ordinate system by varying the way in which the variables are associated with positions in the space—for example by skewing the co-ordinates from the normal or by/letting the co-ordinate system rotate around the object, then the appearance of the object in that given space will change accordingly. But by the same token, if we vary the representation of the space in which the objects are to be located, then the effects can be compared to the effects of a variance in the co-ordinate system for given space. In both cases equations of a given form will represent objects with different shapes. The idea that a mathematician can determine the shape of an object merely by studying the form of some equation that represents the shape is too simple. He cannot simply look at an equation and tell us, "That is the equation of a circular thing."

In discussing Kant's argument we are concerned with the possibility of empirical knowledge and here, of course, the equations do not merely drift before us from out of nowhere and ask to be inspected. But the preceding remarks have an obvious bearing on the interpretation of the significance of empirical judgments. For suppose that we have picked out an object in space as a thing with a circular shape and suppose that we have formulated the empirical equations that describe its shape. From what has just been said about the purely mathematical aspects of the equations, we know that we can alter the apparent shape of the plate without altering the real shape and that we can make this change in two ways. First, we can act on the plate and cause it to rotate in the given space. To be strictly and entirely accurate, we must concede the physical possibility that every such real change of position causes some slight deformation of the object so that the real shape as well as the apparent shape must be changing. But we can abstract from this physical possibility here since we are only concerned at the moment with the geometrical appearance or image of the shape. One and the same shape which is projected in a given space with changes of orientation in the space will assume a succession of different appearances. This truth is a truth about the applied geometry of the object and should be kept distinct from any thoughts we may have about the physics of the situation or about the psychology of perception. The elliptical appearance of the shape, or the projection of the shape into the space as an ellipse, *just is* the circular shape of the object in that particular way of appearing of the circular shape. We can produce exactly the same result by a different method. Instead of rotating the object in the space so that its position changes in the space, we can rotate the co-ordinate system around the object. One and the same shape will again assume a succession of different appearances, as we vary the way in which the shape is given representation in the space. Now, for an understanding of Kant's first argument, it is essential to realize that these second changes, even though they resemble the first from the point of view of the pure geometry of the situation, are nonetheless changes in the mere appearances of the objects and they have absolutely no analytic significance. The geometry of the object has not changed at all. If we know what the original appearance of the object was and if we know how we have chosen to vary the representation of the object by varying the way in which it is combined with our idea of the space, then we can deduce from our understanding of the geometrical effects of such a transformation what its subsequent appearance will be. We do not need to abstract from the physical or psychological aspects of the problem because there are no such aspects to the problem.

If I know that an equation describing an object of which I have some knowledge is the equation of a circular object, or if I have empirical knowledge of something like a plate to which the pure geometrical concept of a circle applies, and if you tell me that the pure concept of what is elliptical applies to the object with which you are acquainted, you and I are *not* in a position to conclude that we are acquainted with different objects. We may well be considering different appearances of the same shape and hence we may be describing one and the same object. Before we can compare the objects on the basis of their shapes with a view to differentiating them or identifying them, you and I have to agree on a representation of the space and we have to agree on a normal or standard way of orienting the objects within the space. The fundamental points to be stressed about this agreement concern the applied geometry of the situation, but these points are easily confused with other points which are not relevant to Kant's argument and which are not in themselves very major points. The first of these misleading issues is that our choice of a word in the language to describe the given shape of an object is constrained by certain conventions. If the objects are oriented in a normal and conventional way in a co-ordinate system and if the shape of the object in that appearance of the shape is circular, then you would be using English in a very misleading way if you described the object to me by saying, "The object is elliptical." Nevertheless, that very shape can be represented in the equation for an ellipse and the pure geometrical concept of an ellipse can be applied to that object. Kant's point is that objects *cannot* be differentiated from one another on the basis of our *concepts* of size, shape, and position, *unless* a representation of space is added and unless the concepts are given analytic significance in the space. His point is a point about the representations in any applied geometry of our concepts of primary qualities, and it is not a point about English usage. (In truth, the point about English usage is only a point about a certain popular use of the term "elliptical" in any event, since geometricians use English when they describe circles as degenerate or non-paradigmatic ellipses.)

The second potentially misleading point is that we sometimes use the word "appearance" in philosophical discourse in English to describe the object in its orientation to some percipient or, more generally, in its relation to some percipient. Thus, if I say that the appearance of the object *to me* or *from where I am located* is elliptical, the shape of the object which I intend to describe may very well be circular. In such judgments the word "appearance" (or, in strict analysis, the phrase "appearance of . . . to . . .") is not being used precisely as Kant defines or employs it in the aesthetic, and it is not being used precisely as the applied geometricians had earlier used the term. Kant and the cartographers before him employ the term in such a way that the representation of the appearance of an object presupposes the representation of some space and the representation of the object within the space. Appearances in the geometrical sense are always oriented in a space, and it is from a knowledge of that orientation of the object that we are able to determine what the analytic significance of an appearance is or to determine whether the appearance lacks analytic significance. For example, we might ask whether the size of the objects can be determined from their appearances or whether the size has no analytic significance in the given representation of the object, and the answer we receive will be determined by the underlying presuppositions. Lambert and others had made very sophisticated mathematical studies of the type of case in which a change in our presupposition about the space underlying the representation can affect the appearance of the object represented. This case occurs when we map the earth, which experience has taught us to be an object in a space of three dimensions—an object shaped like a pear, in a space of two dimensions. In this transformation some appearances of the object, for example, appearances of the size of the object, have to be sacrificed to preserve other appearances of the objects, for example, appearances of the shape or the relative position. (Kant's friend was the first to describe a general rule for changing the space in this projection of the earth in such a way as to maximize the information that is retained in the map that represents the earth.) If, on the other hand, you merely say how the object is in relation to you, your remark only presupposes that you or your listener can add a representation of space and can locate you in space. Your remark does *not* presuppose that you or that anyone else can locate that object in space in relation to you and can determine the analytic significance of your remarks about the object.

The aesthetic deals only with empirical judgments, and for our present purposes we may think of these as judgments in which the descriptions are restricted to objects in space by an underlying representation of the space and where the descriptions are subject to the conditions that reflect our way of associating the descriptions with the positions in the space. What has just been said reflects the limitation of our present interests to judgments about objects that can be extrinsic to one another; the remark is not offered as a definition of empirical judgments, or even as a general characterization of them. (We can get a general characterization that will be true for all empirical judgments whatsoever, if we substitute "time" for "space" in the preceding.) In a later work in which Kant gave a popular exposition of some of the results in the *Critique* he marks a distinction between the empirical judgment and the judgment of perception, where the latter is one which describes the object as it is in relation to some particular subject who is viewing the object. While nothing is gained by importing the distinction into the aesthetic, where it is not needed, the distinction is useful in the analytic. Thus, instead of imagining the rotation of a co-ordinate system around an object, we might imagine our own position as that which fixes the origin of the co-ordinate system. Then as we move around the plate, the sense of the space will change and the result will be changes in the appearances of the object that correspond to changes in what we will actually see. The change of these appearances cannot be distinguished from changes in the appearance of the object that result from giving the plate a real spin, so far as the argument of the aesthetic goes. That is, nothing in the pure or the applied geometry of the situation allows us to distinguish these changes in appearances from one another. Instead, we can only distinguish the two types of change on the basis of a physical investigation which seeks to detect the existence of real causes and effects of the change of appearances in the plate, or by a psychological investigation which seeks to detect the existence of real causes and effects of the changes in our sensations. Thus, for example, only a force acting on the plate will cause it to begin spinning. If the plate is in real motion, then we will experience certain effects when the motion is impeded. It follows, or would seem to follow, that if the physical investigation is to be able to differentiate between what is real in appearance and what is merely appearance, something more is required than an *a priori* representation of a space in which the objects are located. What must be added is a set of categories, which includes in this case the category of causation.

How such a categorization of objects is possible, or indeed whether it is even possible, is a matter for separate argument. The important point to notice is that there are two entirely different conditions on the possibility of knowledge and that there are corresponding distinctions to keep straight in the objects of knowledge. On the one hand, there is a distinction relevant to the aesthetic between objects of pure geometrical conception and images or appearances. If the former were to be considered as possible objects of cognition through concepts alone they would be a species of thing *per se*. The latter are the objects of a geometrical representation that has acquired an analytic significance through being associated with a representation of space. On the other hand, there is an entirely separate distinction between something which is a mere appearance and something which is real in appearance. The value of distinguishing these different notions of the object can be argued from the case of Descartes. It is well known that he defended the Copernican hypothesis against objections based upon the fact that it denies a fixed position to the earth. When the opponents learned that he espoused the heretical view that the earth moves, they raised the standard objections. Descartes's defense is instructive because it shows that he understood very clearly one of the points which Kant argues in the aesthetic, namely, that the analytic significance of an ascription of primary qualities like shape, size, and position depends upon the choice of a frame of reference. Thus Descartes was able to reply that his earth is no different from the earth of the theologians, and if anyone should desire to represent the Cartesian earth as an object with a fixed location, he can do so by suitable alteration in his frame of reference. But this reply does more than illustrate the fact that Descartes was aware of the difference between things *per se* and things as appearances in the mathematical sense. The reply also illustrates the fact that Descartes, unlike his opponents and unlike Kant, felt he could ignore the difference between what is real motion in the appearances and what is only apparent motion in the appearances. Descartes was only justified in this second move because he had nothing to say about any dynamic effects of motion or dynamic forces causing motions.

The aesthetic deals with the conditions for the possibility of empirical judgments and with the distinction between things *per se* and the appearances of things. Here we have no need for the concept of a judgment of perception, in which concepts are applied to some subject matter only as that subject matter is conceived to be in relation to a possible percipient. Having conceded that the latter may have some use when we turn to the categories of understanding, I should stress this point that neither the distinction of the aesthetic between things *per se* and appearances nor the distinction of the analytic between what is real and what is merely apparent in appearances requires us to draw the distinction between empirical judgments and judgments of perception. The essential point about Kant's definition of empirical representations has already been made, and it is that when Kant says that they are representations which belong to us in our status as recipients, or that their validity is that of representations borrowed from the object, or that we are affected by the object in these empirical representations, Kant most emphatically does not mean that the objects which are conceived as the gift of our senses have all been delivered in through the door of the senses. We can be affected in our representations in the sense that we gain a lawful dominion over a sphere of objects without being brought into any actual relationship to the objects in sensory experience. Therefore, I think it is useful to have in mind a range of models of Kant's two distinctions which do not invite us to concentrate on the changes in the condition of some human percipient but which nevertheless allow us to illustrate how the two sets of distinctions in the objects are related to differences in the nature of the representations of the objects. When the mathematicians or the physicists wished to illustrate the terminology of the various distinctions that Kant borrowed, they asked the reader to consider the appearances of a candle in a flexible mirror. A number of points are obvious in this model. First, it will be clear that as we change the geometry of the mirror by flexing it, we produce a succession of altered appearances of one and the same shape. The standard or the normal appearance of the object in the mirror might be conceived by the layman to be the appearance that is most nearly congruent with the thing *per se*—in this case with the candle that is *not* itself appearance. When the mathematician or physicist uses the model to make Kant's distinctions, however, he may tell us, as Kant tells us, that we are not to suppose that we can get at the candle *per se*. The scientist may make this stipulation about the model for the same reason that the Kantian will—namely, to make the point that there is no way to get at the object free from its involvement with the geometry of the space in which *it* is represented.

Kant's first argument stands or falls on the truth of this observation as a point about the condition under which our empirical representations of objects can have an analytic significance. If we are confined to a knowledge of the appearances of sizes, shapes, and positions, and if these can vary in ways that reflect distortions in their representations, then it is natural to think that the standard or the normal shape, size and position are to be identified on the basis of the appearances of the thing in itself in a perfect mirror, or a mirror without curvature. The question of what geometrical conception of flatness is appropriate for the characterization of our perfect, or non-distorting, mirror is unexpectedly difficult to answer. In the next section, I will discuss the implications which these recent discoveries have on other aspects of Kant's discussion in the aesthetic, but it is clear that they can only reinforce the point of his first argument: questions about whether two objects are congruent in their primary qualities presuppose some agreement about the space or spaces in which the objects are being represented to have those qualities.

It is also clear from the example of the mirror that the basis for Kant's distinction between what is real in appearance and what is only appearance does not depend upon any relation of the objects that appear to beings that have eyes and ears. Physicists call attention to the same distinction using mirrors where Kant places the person who knows on the basis of experience. If a mirror is flexed to a parabolic form and positioned at an appropriate distance from the candle, the physicist will tell you to expect a real appearance of the candle; but if the appearance is an appearance in a flat mirror, the physicist will tell you to expect nothing but an appearance of the candle—a mere virtual image. He means by this that if you put your finger where the real appearance is predicted, you can expect to experience the physical effects of the appearance of the candle in that position; but if you put your finger where you see the mere appearance of the candle, nothing else will happen. His distinction is nothing but a specialized illustration of the same distinction that Kant makes in the *Critique* by a more generalized reference to causation and to other categories as well. Our categories, as concepts of the object in general, are concepts that objectify appearances and that thereby introduce a distinction into the appearances which the aesthetic alone does not teach us.

What the aesthetic does teach us is that the objects of empirical judgments are appearances or objects whose unity and diversity have a different basis from the unity and diversity of things *per se*. The representation of appearances presupposes a representation of the space of the appearances and without this representation of the space no empirical representation of what the appearance is (as an object with primary qualities such as size, shape and position) would have any analytic significance. Kant's conclusions in this matter are no great novelty, but merely extend to empirical knowledge in general things which mathematicians and phycisists had known from the days of Descartes about the conditions for the possibility of empirical equations that describe primary qualities.

Kant's first argument deals with a restriction on the condition under which things can be *one or many* as objects of empirical cognition; his second argument will deal with a restriction of the condition under which things can *exist* as objects of empirical knowledge. In each case, the indispensable restriction is itself determined to be *a priori* rather than empirical. In turning to the second set of arguments, I will consider the argument as it applies to representation of time rather than the representation of space. The reason for this substitution is that we can be clearer about the historical roots of Kant's arguments in the work of earlier logicians on the representation of time. The justification for the substitution is that the only important logical difference between the two arguments is in the strength of the conclusion reached. The argument about time appeals to something true for every empirical representation whatsoever, in order to conclude that the representation of time is *a priori* as a condition for the possibility of every empirical cognition. The argument about space only seeks a conclusion about the conditions of the possibility of the empirical knowledge of extrinsic objects—that is, of objects that can co-exist with one another. Whatever can co-exist with something can exist, but the reverse is not necessarily true.

Kant's argument to show that the representation of time is *a priori* can be stated as follows: If the representation of time is empirical, then the judgment that time exists must be possible as an empirical judgment. If it is possible as an empirical judgment, it is contingent and therefore will have a contingent denial. But it is not possible to think the non-existence of time. Therefore the representation of time is not empirical. On the other hand, the representation of time must be possible, because the representation of the existence of appearances or of the objects of empirical intuition is possible only as the representation of things that are present in time. Since the representation of time is possible and cannot be empirical, it must be possible or have validity as a representation *a priori*. If this is Kant's second argument, its soundness turns on Kant's assumptions about empirical representations, about the existence of appearances as presence in time, and about the judgment that time does not exist.

We have seen that an empirical representation, by definition, is one which has a certain type of objective validity. To say of any representation that it has objective validity means that the existence of something to which the representation can be referred must at least be a possibility. This first observation merely turns on the meaning we have come to attach to the idea of a representation having objective validity. Now when we form a judgment about the existence of any object of an empirical representation, the judgment will be an empirical judgment about its existence. And any empirical judgment is contingent; that is, without regarding the existence of the object of any empirical judgment as more than a possibility, we can say that if the object does not exist it might not have existed, and if the object does not exist it might have. Nothing that has been said about empirical representations so far is anything but a commonplace in a dozen schools and traditions. The controversial doctrine concerns the answers to questions about whether and how the existence of the objects of empirical judgments is possible.

Earlier metaphysicians had thought the existence of things in general through the idea of act and were accustomed to say that only God has an underived or uncaused act of existence. All other things have a dependent mode of existence, so that their existence is to be understood under our general conception of all existing things other than God as *creatures* of God. Later metaphysicians had continued to think the existence of things through the category of causation, or, more commonly, through the category of causal interaction. We have seen that some believe that Kant continued this metaphysical tradition by conceiving the existence of appearances through the idea of causal effects that are actually produced in us through the senses. But we have also seen that Kant breaks with the metaphysical formulations of his problems when he takes his transcendental turn. How is the existence of appearances or the objects of empirical knowledge possible? Kant's answer depends upon an investigation of what is involved in the possible *knowledge of* appearances. But it must not be supposed that because Kant breaks with the views of certain earlier metaphysicians that he invented a new doctrine in connection with his second argument; this aspect of his argument is firmly rooted in an age-old doctrine affirmed by logicians. The teaching of logicians had been that when "being" or "non-being" are added to any representation, these representations do not contract or restrict the given representation to what has being or to what has non-being. Instead, they restrict the representation to what is temporally present or absent. The logicians realized that an existence that can meaningfully be denied of an object cannot be involved in the representation of that object *per se*. The existence or non-existence must add something to what is involved in the representation of the thing *per se*, because otherwise no restriction of the scope of our concept of the thing would occur in the judgment of existence or of nonexistence. The logicians's solution to this set of requirements on the interpretation of what is involved in adding a representation of existence or of nonexistence to a given representation was the one adopted by Kant: The possible existence is a possible being in time, and the existence is present being in time. "And thus," says Peter of Spain, "*esse* does not restrict to existing things but to present things, since the time-element, which is the cause of the restriction, is the same for both."[4] The judgments which express these possible judgments of existence and non-existence are judgments in which "exists" is a tensed verb rather than a tenseless verb. That is, in the verbal formulation of such judgments the contrast between what is now and what was or what will be is a marked and significant contrast. Conversely, Peter argues that wherever the verb is taken in the present tense, the judgment is possible only if it is restricted to what exists.[5] Kant affirms this ancient doctrine as true for every empirical judgment whatsoever. Whenever anyone purports to convey to you his empirical knowledge about some subject matter, it always makes sense for you to make inquiry concerning the time-parameters affecting his knowledge.

We have seen in earlier discussion that Kant employs the concept of an intuition in the same general manner that Duns Scotus had when he introduced the concept into philosophy. A representation which is an intuition is a representation the very possibility of which depends upon the existence of the object to which the representation makes reference. The logicians' point about the manner in which representations are restricted to what exists or to what does not exist had been preserved down to the time of Kant in the textbook formulations of the Scotistic distinction between intuitive and abstractive cognitions. Thus, Goclenius defines the one cognition as "rei actu existentis praesentis" and the other as "rei actu existentis vel non existentis, sed absentis". From the foregoing observations on the roots of Kant's analysis, we can say with confidence that there was absolutely no novelty in Kant's explanation of how the existence of the objects of empirical knowl-

---

[4] Peter of Spain, *Summulae Logicales*, ed. J.P. Mullally (Notre Dame, Indiana, 1945), p. 59.
[5] Peter of Spain, *Tractatus (Summule Logicales)*, ed. L.M. de Rijk (Assen, 1972), p. 216.

edge is possible. The existence of these objects can only be represented through the restriction of the subject matter of these judgments to what has present being. But, says Kant with a show of novelty, the restriction of the subject matter to what has being in time involves the representation of time. The novelty of Kant's argument and the feature he stresses in the aesthetic is what the preceding analysis forces one to say about the representation of time itself.

The representation of time itself is not an empirical concept and it does not make sense for us to think the representation of time contracted or restricted to what has present being in time. Kant's way of bringing home this point, and with it the *a priori* nature of our representation of time, is by asking us to consider the denial of the judgment that time exists. His technique of reasoning is a familiar one, but it is employed here to establish a transcendental impossibility rather than a formal, logical impossibility. We know that if a representation which is possible is empirical, the judgment asserting the existence of something to which the representation applies must at least be possible. We also know that such a judgment will be contingent, and hence, we know that if the representation of time is empirical then the judgment that time does not exist must be possible. Now there is a timeless sense of "exists" or "has being" in which every logically possible representation contains or involves the idea of existence. But judgments in which this idea contained in the representations is itself predicated of them obviously cannot be judgments in which a given representation is contracted or restricted to things that exist. What we want to consider, by contrast, are those judgments of existence in which a representation is restricted to something that exists, because only these judgments have a consistent denial and do not merely exhibit an idea of being that is involved in every representation whatsoever as a mark or indication of its being a consistent representation. "Not only a consistent judgment, but one with a consistent denial" says more about the type of existence of the object of the judgment than does "A consistent judgment". In contingent, empirical judgments something is posited or affirmed that has being or status in the world, or that is absent from the world. The representation of something as having being in the world involves the representation of it as having being in space and in time. Hence, if the representation of time itself is empirical, then the judgment that time does not at this moment in time exist must be possible—the contraction or restriction of a representation to what is absent is a restriction of it to what does not exist at this moment in time, according to the ancient doctrine of logicians. But the judgment that at the present time time is not is not possible; it is absurd. Hence, the representation of time, since it is possible but not empirical, must *be a priori*.

The absurdity or the impossibility of the judgment that time does not now exist requires a further word of clarification. It seems sufficiently obvious that Kant does not intend to call our attention to a mere psychological impossibility or to a psychological incapacity on our part to perform the feat of thinking the non-existence of time. That is, everyone can see that there is a logical oddity or impropriety of some type or other in attempts to attribute non-existence to time—or, at least, everyone will see that who is prepared to agree that Kant interpreted predications of contingent existence in the way that the earlier logicians had explained these predications. What is not so clear, however, is that the logical impossibility in question belongs to transcendental logic rather than to ordinary formal logic. Transcendental logic concerns itself with the relations of representations to objects, while formal logic deals with the relations between representations themselves insofar as these relations are said to be possible or impossible, valid or not valid. The reason why the issue is clouded is that a representation of existence *can* be involved in other representations and *can* be made into a predicate. That is, the idea of existence that is contained in other ideas can appear in judgments which the formal logician permits as logically possible acts of predication. Now the representation of time which Kant has identified in the argument under discussion has a role in the job of specifying appearances or the objects of empirical description as objects which are either present or absent. If we could imagine that it performed this task through the addition of one more general idea to the given description of the object, then the logical impropriety of thinking that time itself does not exist could be analyzed as the impropriety of a logical contradiction.

The definitive response to this way of interpreting the significance of Kant's remark about the impossibility of representing to ourselves the non-existence of space and time comes when Kant proves that the representations of space and time are intuitions rather than concepts. If they are possible only as intuitions, then they do not contract our empirical ideas to appearances in space and time by adding some further general description which restricts the given empirical idea by narrowing its scope. However, this line of argument by Kant is already anticipated in his second argument, and most explicitly in the argument about space. The representation of space is identified as the ground of all intuitions of things which are extrinsic to one another and to myself, and thus which not only can exist but can co-exist. The ground of an intuition, it will be recalled, is that which justifies or makes possible the intuition. Since an intuition involves the reference to some one object, the possibility of an intuition is not the merely formal, logical possibility of non-contradiction. That which grounds the intuition must supply it with credentials in its relationship to its object. Thus, from the fact that we are taking up the question of the possibility of the representations of space and time in connection with intuitions and with appearances or the objects of empirical intuitions we can anticipate that the possibility or the impossibility in question belongs to transcendental philosophy rather than to formal logic.

The representation of time is presupposed as a restriction on the possibility of all empirical knowledge whatsoever. The representation of space is only presupposed by the possibility of a certain class of empirical representations. This asymmetry is reflected in English (though not in every language apparently) by the fact that, while we have words to express the form of reference to the position of things in space as well as to the position of things in time, we do not have any grammatical form for the sentence that will express the modes of co-existence of things in the way that tenses can be used to express modes of existence. Throughout the *Critique* Kant is concerned with the conditions of the *possibility* of knowledge, and the possibility of knowledge only restricts the judgment to things that are or are not present when considered in relation to their representation. The idea of space when understood in the Leibnizian way as the idea of the order of the co-existing is an idea which shows up in *any actual* knowledge which is empirical, whether the actual knowledge is of me, of my representations, or of things extrinsic to me. Thus, even if the thing which I represent as present happens to be myself conceived as empirical substance, and even if the representation in which I represent myself as present is conceived as a predicate of myself as thinking substance, an idea of the co-presence or the co-existence of two things must be involved in this actual knowledge of myself. If we do turn from the logical and transcendental inquiry into the possibility of knowledge—the conditions of its validity—and turn to an inquiry into the actuality of some experience of myself as substance, then the earlier and more metaphysical discussion of what is involved in the existence of the empirical representation again becomes a matter of relevance in the discussion. When the question concerns the empirical representation as an actuality, we must be prepared to tell a causal story about the empirical representation. Since the causal relation (like the relation of reasons that was discussed in Chapter One) is a relation contained in diversity, and since the diversity of the relata (unlike the relata of the reasons-relation) is a diversity of things that we must be capable of thinking of as existing, the representation of our own thoughts as actualities presupposes the possibility of things that are extrinsic to these thoughts. In a later section of the *Critique* Kant takes advantage of these metaphysical principles he has by that time won back, and he argues that, although the representation of time is the only restrictive condition on the possibility of all empirical knowledge, nevertheless, an idea of space and, with it, an idea of material substance is required if we are to be able to account for any actual exercise of our competence in making empirical judgments. The line of argument can be summarized by saying that, if the question about empirical knowledge is critical and concerns only its possibility, then being in time is the only general restriction on the objects of empirical knowledge, but if the question about empirical knowledge is factual and concerns its actual causes, then we must be prepared to posit the existence of causes that are extrinsic to the representations themselves. But, as our consideration of Kant's first argument has shown, the idea of space is presupposed by all empirical representations that represent objects that are extrinsically different from one another.

III. SPACE AS AN INTUITIVE REPRESENTATION

Kant gives two arguments to prove that the representation of space is an intuition or singular representation, rather than a general concept. The first argument is a lineal descendant of Spinoza's proof that no substance other than God can be or can be conceived. If the line of descent is not always obvious to Kant's modern readers, there are undoubtedly two major reasons. First, the transcendental aspects of Spinoza's own argument have not always been sufficiently apparent. Of course everyone can see—as an abstract possibility—that the question of the validity of some author's argument may be related to the logical or the transcendental doctrines which one holds concerning the possibilities of representation. But not everyone will immediately see the corresponding point about Spinoza's valid metaphysical conclusion that there is only one object that will satisfy a certain possibility of representation. The corresponding transcendental conclusion is reached by inverting the direction of the argument, and is the conclusion that any possible representation of such an object must be an intuition rather than a general concept. I trust that enough has been said in earlier discussion to make that aspect of the historical background more familiar to readers of the aesthetic.

The second major reason why the Kantian argument is difficult to follow is that it reflects the results of certain technical developments in philosophy between Spinoza and Kant. These developments show up in the specialized terminology which Kant uses in order to summarize the Spinozistic analysis of ideas like the idea of God. Kant's argument is that the representation of space must be an intuition because one can represent to oneself only a unitary space (*einen einigen Raum*). In this argument the term *unitary* (*einig*) is sometimes translated by the too colorless English "one", but it is a technical expression which was employed by Baumgarten and others to mean much more than that. Adelung's dictionary at least can be trusted to mark the difference between ordinary and technical senses of a term in Kant's day, even if it cannot be trusted to give the best analysis of the technical terms as they were then employed. Adelung's entry informs us that for recent philosophers —that is, for those in the 1770's and 1780's—a unitary essence is one in which all the characteristics which one thinks in the essence are united to a common set of consequences which are grounded in that essence. This should not necessarily be regarded as a proper working definition of the motion—I will re-state that in a moment—but it should instead be regarded as a summary of some developments in post-Spinozistic philosophy.

Spinoza had defined God as something which is pre-eminently substance. Few of his successors defined God in precisely the same way, but the leading exponents of a rational theology did wish to preserve the central features of his definition. In particular, they were anxious to conceive God as a being which (a) has no accidental or contingent features and (b) is such that from a knowledge of its defining attribute a knowledge of all its other properties can be deduced. As Kant remarks, anything which can be thought of in either of these ways is a unitary being. Thus, he writes in one note: "God has attributes from which all the others can be deduced. Such a thing can not belong to a species but rather is possible only as an individual thing: concept of a singular thing (*conceptus singularis*)." [6] The characteristic in question was a source of concern for the rational theologian for an easily understandable reason. If he had proved that there is a being which satisfies his conception of it as, for example, a most real being, he wished to be able to show that that same thing is what has been known to others under some other, possibly more familiar, conception such as that of a most powerful being. Or, if the proof were based upon the omnipotence of God, how did the theologian show that the being in question is not a trifle malevolent? Baumgarten had taken these questions seriously and had offered an extended discussion of the unitary aspect of God's essence or definition.

We have already seen how Spinoza built this unitary aspect of God's essence into his definition of God. He could not, of course, actually think in his definition all the unlimited aspects of God, but he could and did summarize them all as the properties which a thing must have if it is substance. Generalizing this solution to include other conceptions of God, or, indeed, other conceptions of anything that has a unitary nature, we get the following: The representation of S is the representation of a unitary thing just in case anything which is S is such that any property which it has is a property which

---

[6] *Gesammelte Schriften*, XVIII, p. 331.

a thing must have if it is *S*. On the basis of this explanation we can say that the crucial step in Kant's argument is borrowed from Spinoza in precisely this sense, namely, that Spinoza exhibited a valid argument to show that if something, *x*, is *S* and something, *y*, is *S*, where *S* is unitary, then *x* and *y* must be identical. This is the Spinozistic side of the argument, and as we saw in Chapter Two, it is perfectly sound. But since a general or discursive concept, by its definition, is a concept which it must be possible to predicate of many things, a representation which is possible and is unitary must be an intuition rather than a general concept. Since the argument which Kant gives in the text of the aesthetic is certainly valid, our only question can be a question about whether he was justified in taking the representation of space to be unitary.

The idea that our representations of space and of time must have a transcendental logic that resembles our representations of God is one that appears very early in Kant's work. Indeed when he seems to suggest in one note that from reflection on our concepts of space and time we can appreciate the nature of our concept of God, we cannot be certain whether he has worked his way to a more advanced conception than Spinoza had or whether he has not merely returned to a deeper understanding of his own sources and roots in Spinoza's thought. It has sometimes been the fashion to play down the significance of the way in which Spinoza displayed his thoughts, but who can be certain that Spinoza had no conscious knowledge of this connection between his own decision to employ the method of geometry and the actual content of his main and radical conclusion about God?

But whatever may be the truth about Spinoza's own understanding of that connection, we do know that the path back to geometry and to an appreciation of the significance of its way of representing space had been smoothed for Kant by two considerations. First, Kant conceived of representations, or concepts and judgments, in such a way that there is not much difference between concepts and judgments. Thus he says that it is all one whether you call the understanding the faculty of judgments or the faculty of concepts. Secondly, we know that Kant had the specific authority of his friend, the mathematician Lambert, for regarding the axioms of geometry as providing a definition of the concept of space.[7] Thus for both the particular and the general reason, Kant would have found it natural to say what the ordinary modern reader will admit very readily. The first principles of Euclid's geometry present Euclid's concept of space.

---

[7] Johann Lambert, *Anlage zur Architectonik* (Riga, 1771), p. 8ff.

Is a geometrical conception of space a representation of something which is unitary? Of course it is. And given our *methodological* understandings about the way in which geometrical knowledge is to be possible, the object must be unitary. There can be only one Euclidean space because Euclidean space does not have any accidental properties. *All its properties must be derived from its geometrical definition.* Hence if that space whose representation has been shown to be possible as a presupposition of empirical knowledge is Euclidean space, then the real space or space of real possibilities must be unitary—and precisely the same conclusion will follow if the given representation of space is defined in any of the non-Euclidean systems of geometry. The underlying point here is not a metaphysical point but a transcendental or critical point concerning *what we will admit* as possible knowledge of space and its properties. Until geometricians had arrived at the proper cognitive standards, much of what they learned about the nature of space they probably learned empirically in the course of land surveys and the like. Also, even after they had become aware of the requirement that something can be known to be true in geometry only if it can be deduced from the proper definitions and axioms, geometricians sometimes continued to appeal to experience in order to make discoveries about geometrical objects. Thus, for example, there are illustrations from the post-Euclidean history of geometry of geometricians who were unable to solve certain problems about the areas of figures. Thwarted in their efforts by the regular means at their disposal, they resorted to such devices as cutting the figures from materials of equal density and thickness, and weighing the two pieces to determine which had the greater area. The existence of these examples and of others like them shows that when one says that geometrical objects cannot be conceived to have contingent properties and that one cannot learn about space by appeal to experience, the "cannot" does not have the force of a metaphysical or a psychological impossibility. It has a transcendental and normative force: the transcendental principles in conformity with which the objects of a geometrical science are thought being what they are, a space which is conceived in some geometry will never have accidental properties or properties to be learned through experience. The particular principle of the possibility of geometrical knowledge that gives space its unitary character is, of course, the principle that in those geometrical researchers in which the knowledge will be up to the very best standards a space is to be regarded as having all and only those features which follow from a set of axioms for that space. Assuming that it has been established from prior argument that a representation of a space is presupposed as a possibility in empirical knowledge and assuming that that space of real possibilities can be given definition in a geometry, what we have to ask is whether there is evidence for such a transcendental principle as the requirement for any such geometry.

The best evidence comes from developments in geometry and physics since Kant wrote the aesthetic. These developments are often cited in attempted refutation of Kant's position and it may seem willful to argue the same evidence in support of his position. But Hermann Cohen and Paul Natorp were already aware by the turn of the century that the development of non-Euclidean geometries is a powerful vindication of Kant's views. Love of the truth will lead one to that assessment whether one begins from the side of Kant's anticipation of the results or whether one begins from the side of what is novel in those developments and could not have been anticipated by anyone in Kant's day and age.

It pleased Wallace Stevens to draw a distinction between philosophers and poets according to which the former give the official view of being and the latter an unofficial view of being. It pleased Stevens to draw the contrast in these terms because he was a poet in an age that smiled upon Bohemian gestures. But there can be a touch of the poet in any writer, and the historian of philosophy should be scrupulous in distinguishing between the philosophy and the poetry in Kant's writings. Too frequently, the badness of Kant's ear for poetry has been judged against the quality of his philosophy. He undoubtedly did believe that the theorems of Euclidean geometry give a true description of that representation of space that he had isolated in his first two arguments. We can chide Kant, if it pleases us, for being too unimaginative to conceive the possibility of what are today called non-Euclidean geometries. What we cannot do, or have no business in doing, is to criticize his official view in the aesthetic for such a failure of his imagination. What he had attempted to do in the aesthetic is to establish the possibility of Euclidean geometry as a discipline *a priori*. There is not a line which establishes or purports to establish the truth of Euclid's postulates. What he says is that only his finding "makes the *possibility* of geometry as synthetic *a priori* cognition comprehensible"; and in saying this, Kant himself emphasizes the word "possibility". Now since evidence that the theorems of Euclidean geometry give a description of physical space that is false will be evidence that Euclidean geometry is possible, anyone who is justified in chiding Kant for his bad poetry will be someone with reasons to support Kant's official verdict.

Some will remain sceptical and will suspect that Kant's opinion about Euclidean geometry must have had a greater bearing on his philosophical doctrines. There are several reasons why that is improbable. In the first place, Kant knew of the unsuccessful attempts to establish the parallels-postulate or some equivalent to it. If he had supposed that the philosophical conclusions he set out in the aesthetic committed him to the truth of Euclidean geometry, he would necessarily have had to suppose that he had solved an important problem that had vexed so many, and, among others, his correspondent Lambert. Yet he reached the main conclusions in the aesthetic before the death of his friend and without attempting to communicate such a fact to him. Also, long after the *Critique* had been published, Kant noted that the problem of the parallels-postulate had never been solved. In the second place, it must be stressed that Kant did know of the possibility of geometries that are not Euclidean geometries and he did know that the space presupposed in empirical science might be defined in one of these alternative geometries. This historical point is one that must be acknowledged in very careful language in order to avoid any possible misunderstanding about what is being claimed on behalf of Kant. The geometries in question are other than the Euclidean geometry which Descartes and other modern physicists had begun to employ in the applied mathematics of a modern mathematical physics, but these alternative geometries with which Kant was familiar are not the non-Euclidean systems that were developed in the century after his death. Also, if we were to conceive of a geometry as a science that sets out the properties of physical space or of the space of the things that belong to the world of appearances— that is, if we think of the geometry as engendered in the course of physical research, then perhaps the concepts that caught Kant's attention cannot be called geometrical. But the point is that Kant had been aware from a very early point in his career of the fact that we can frame logically consistent conceptions of something that a modern geometrician would call a space and that are different from the Euclidean conception. In Euclid's concept of space the geometrical properties of a thing have been full determined when, but only when, we have oriented the thing in three dimensions in the space. Yet Kant was aware of the legitimate and interesting puzzle as to why space does not have only two dimensions or why it does not have more than three. Kant knew that there is no logical contradiction in the thought of such spaces. Indeed, he could hardly have thought that the former is inconsistent, since the essentials of the conception are contained in the Cartesian conception of space. In his pre-Critical writings Kant's solution to the question of why space must have three dimensions is to deduce this necessity from assumptions that formed a part of his physical theory. In the aesthetic he does not withdraw this earlier belief that the adoption of a physical theory will always entail geometrical consequences. He continues to maintain that this is so, but he notes that the geometrical propositions—such as the proposition that space has only three dimensions—will only be empirical cognitions if they are merely deduced from what is known through experience as a part of our physical theory. His own critical solution, as we have already seen in discussing his first two arguments, is that the geometry is entailed by the physics for the reason that the representation of space as a co-ordinate system of reference is already presupposed by the objective validity of the physical judgments. Now it may be true that contemporary physical theory does entail a non-Euclidean conception of space, but that fact can be argued against Kant's position in the aesthetic only if the position which he adopts in the aesthetic can be collapsed into a position that he considers and explicitly rejects.

Kant evidently bases his judgment about the unitary character of space on the fact that a geometrical conception of space is brought fully formed to our empirical judgments. It is a pure geometrical conception that has objective validity within the domain of experience because it articulates in its axioms and theorems the representation of space that underlies the possibility of reference in empirical judgment. The events that have occurred in geometry and physics since Kant's day confirm that space does have this unitary character. The axiomatic development shows that the methodological program of any geometry demands that the geometry of a space be subject to characterization in a set of axioms and postulates. What that space is conceived to be is not subject to progressive change and refinement as a part of the program of physical research. The central point about things with a unitary character is that everything that is said about such things is necessary; there are no contingent discoveries to be made about such an object. That is Kant's point about Euclidean space and *the fact that we can meaningfully say that we are no longer certain that space is Euclidean proves him correct.* If Kant were mistaken, what we would have to say is that subsequent physical research has corrected our conception of Euclidean space. But it would be absurd to say this because it badly misrepresents the course of our historical development beyond the physics of Kant's day. What has happened is not that observation has led geometricians to make corrections in the Euclidean account of space; what has happened is that one unitary conception of physical space has been replaced by another. The alternative conceptions have been set out axiomatically and in complete independence from experience. Indeed only the very wisest souls among the geometricians who developed these alternative geometries had any suspicion that they might come to be useful in physical research.

Kant gives an explanation of how a conception that has been developed in this manner can be a conception of the space of empirical objects. His explanation is that it is given objective validity when we take it as the conception that we supply *a priori* in providing a system of reference for empirical descriptions.

There may be a better explanation of the real possibility of a geometry, but the idea that the geometrical conception is possible because it is itself a part of the empirical description of the objects is an idea that would make our idea of space be contingent and be subject to change in the light of experience. There is a serious flaw in this latter proposal which becomes apparent when we consider that according to the argument of Kant's *Dissertation* and according to the best contemporary physical opinion the fundamental frame of reference in giving physical descriptions is supplied by a world-concept. The concept of a world gives our references a temporal dimension as well as the three spatial dimensions. Now suppose we are told, in accordance with the view that our conception of the properties of the space is empirical, that the Cartesian and Newtonian description of real space must be altered in the light of contemporary observations. How do we know what interpretation to place on that suggestion? There are two possibilities. Either the Newtonian description of space was incorrect and must be altered for that reason—the assumption underlying this first interpretation being that the physical descriptions offered by Newton and by some contemporary physicist are descriptions of one and the same world. Or we could react to the necessity of altering the Newtonian conception of space in the light of experience by saying that the space and perhaps even the world described by Newton is different from the world described by Einstein—the assumption underlying this interpretation being that the physical descriptions offered by Newton and some contemporary physicist include nothing but the descriptions of contingent, empirical objects. Now the point of calling attention to these two possibilities is to observe that *only the first* interpretation of the reason why Newton's description of space must be revised is consistent with *the use of an historical record* in physics to refute Kant and yet the first interpretation presupposes what Kant presupposes about the frame of reference for empirical descriptions. On the second hypothesis there will be no common record.

Kant gives us a second argument to prove that the representation of space is not a discursive concept and that there are not many worlds in the same way that there can be many species of animal. Kant argues that this conclusion about space follows from three assumptions. First, it is possible to represent space as an infinite given quantum. Secondly, we can represent space as an infinite given quantum only if the representation contains within itself representations which form an infinite set. But, thirdly, no general or discursive concept can contain within itself representations which form an infinite set. This argument seems valid, but, as in all the other cases, we have to ask ourselves whether it is sound. The soundness of Kant's reasoning is displayed most convincingly when it is considered in the context of our own contemporary discussions of space and time, but fidelity to the historical record compels one to ask first about the reasons that Kant's contemporaries had for accepting his argument. There are two ways to analyze what lies behind Kant's argument as its unspoken and tacit assumptions. I begin with the historical construction that seems to be more probable on the basis of what we know about Kant's beliefs and the beliefs of his contemporaries, and I then will turn to a construction that presupposes more historical understanding of discussions of the infinite than Kant may have possessed—but which compensates somewhat by offering a more elegant synthesis of the given argument and the preceding argument.

One way of interpreting Kant's reasoning will turn on the things that it would have to be possible for us to do in order for us to be able to represent space and time as infinite given quanta. We know from the first two arguments that the space which it is possible for us to represent is a space that can be represented by us *a priori*. That is to say, we do not have a situation in which some object which is given as the object of a possible representation also merely happens to be an object which is infinite. On the contrary, the object in being given through its representation is given through that representation as an object that is infinite. The difference between what an object which is represented can be and what an object which is represented can be *as the object of a possible representation* is the difference elucidated for us in Kant's second premise. Any representation can be said to be possible—that is, to be really possible or to be possible in the sense of having objective validity as an *a priori* or an empirical representation—only if something exists which the representation can be taken as representing. The representations which are contained in a given representation are the ones whose possibility must be conceded if the possibility of the given representation has been conceded. The representations which are contained under a given representation are ones which can be added to it, provided they are possible; but, since they are not actually thought in thinking the given concept, their possibility is not assured by a proof of the possibility of the concept which they are contained under. If it is possible to represent space as one whole that is infinite, then, since each of the representations of a part of space must be possible if the representation of the whole space is possible, an infinite set of representations is contained within the representations of space.

If Kant's argument is understood to be directed against his rationalist predecessors, as I think it most plausibly is, then the impossibility in question is an impossibility in our being able to complete all the acts that are required to think such a general concept as an *a priori* concept. Here the key facts are the fact that the representation in question has already been shown to be *a priori* and the fact that his predecessors would concede that whatever is contained within an *a priori* concept must be something we are actually capable of having thought in the course of having justified that concept on the basis of an appeal to explicit definitions. The assumption here is that whatever one knows *a priori* has been established by the method of clear and distinct ideas and this assumption is thus being pitted against the rationalist's concession that no human can actually complete the definition of a representation which requires an infinite analysis for all its parts to be clearly conceived.

The foundation for such an argument is supplied within Kant's own system in the *Critique* by his views about the origins of our general concepts in the understanding. Every concept that is general has its source in the spontaneity of our understanding and is subject to any limitations on our competence to frame judgments about things. A representation which has been declared to be possible *a priori* is a representation that is possible on the basis of what can be given to us and can be represented by us independently of any empirical judgments. (The discussion is of course limited here to what is a pure *a priori* judgment.) If such a representation is a general concept, then we must be able to complete the act of thinking each of its parts because the possibility of the given representation cannot have been established in any other way. It cannot have been established without establishing the validity of the representations contained within it and the validity of any *a priori* concept has as a condition that the understanding is competent to form that conception. Since, as Kant says elsewhere, the understanding must be supposed to have a complete insight into whatever derives its possibility solely from the legitimate exercise of the understanding itself, we are justified in requiring a definition of any pure concept of the understanding. Here the Kantian view joins hands with the rationalist view and the argument continues as before. The understanding cannot complete the act of setting out everything contained in the representation of space and so we are not justified in saying that this ought to be the case. The impossibility on which the argument turns is the impossibility of exhausting the members of an infinite set of representations through acts of the understanding in which each of the representations is separately and clearly conceived. If the assumption is that the validity of a representation has its source entirely in acts of the understanding and if that assumption gives rise to such an infinite regress, then I believe it will be agreed that in this case the regress is vicious and the assumption must be false.

In the case of each of the four arguments we have considered, the validity of the argument is easier to establish than the soundness of the argument, because Kant does not give us the reasons behind his reasons. He does not tell us, in the case at hand, why a general concept that is to be possible *a priori* cannot contain an infinite set of representations within itself. We have to supply his probable reason on the basis of what we know about his views on the nature of concepts and on the basis of what we know about his views on the nature of the infinite. Now in our earlier discussions we have seen that Kant actually supplies us with two ways of distinguishing between concepts and intuitions. First, he says that concepts belong to us in our spontaneity as thinkers, while intuitions belong to us in our status as possible recipients of evidence. This first way of characterizing concepts is at the base of the preceding reconstruction of the background to the fourth argument. But, secondly, Kant says that there is a logical distinction between representations: Intuitions represent just one thing, while general concepts are possible predicates of many things. There is a way of reconstructing the reasons behind Kant's reasons which will turn on this second way of characterizing a general concept. However, this second reconstruction also involves a different way of thinking about the infinite, and although the historical tradition would have provided Kant with this way of thinking about the infinite, I am not able to supply definite evidence that he took notice of this tradition. The second reconstruction has the merit of bringing the second argument to show that the representation of space is not general into a closer coordination with his first argument, and it deserves a brief glance for that reason if for no other.

When philosophers of the tradition prior to Kant conceived the infinite as something which cannot be constructed or completed in a sequence of successive acts, they were of course giving expression to a popular and well-known conception of the infinite as something potential and not entirely determinate. But when they defined the infinite as something *given* or as something actual, they defined it as a plenum. Their idea of a plenum was the idea of something that is already so complete or so full that it cannot be added to by any further determinations of it. Walch's entry—which Kant might well have taken notice of—reflects this tradition when it explains that something is infinite in respect to its essence or infinite in the philosophical sense, if the thing has every perfection and the accompanying powers in a way that is not subject to any limitation. Walch explains that in the corresponding philosophical sense a thing is finite if its perfections are limited and restricted. By the perfections of a thing he means of course the possible determinations of a thing, and he conceives these determinations in a traditional way as limitations of the things which they determine. We know that for Kant every concept of the understanding has limitations that determine the scope of the concept. We also know that for Kant every general concept applies to many things and hence, that every general concept can be subject to further limitations which will narrow the class of things to which the concept applies. That is, every general concept must be capable of containing other concepts under itself. Hence, if we could say for certain that Kant thought of the representation of an infinite *given* quantum as the representation of something that is complete in its existence and is not subject to any further addition, then we could reconstruct his reasoning in a way that makes it complementary to the first argument: Consider the representation of space that we have shown to be possible *a priori*. That representation can be defined through the axioms and the postulates of a geometry. Every property which can be applied to space or to the parts of space themselves (in contrast to the physical objects which may occupy those spaces) can be shown to be possible within the geometry itself, because in order to be possible its concept must be constructible in the space with the aid of the axioms. Just as the axioms frame a representation of a unitary essence, so the postulates frame a representation of an infinite given quantum, something that is not capable of being provided any additional present existents beyond the ones to which reference can be justified in accordance with the postulates. But every general concept must contain an unlimited number of representations under itself and therefore must represent something which is not infinite in essence or infinite in present existence. Thus space—like every attribute of Spinoza's God—is unique because it is represented as being perfect in its own way. As such, the representation of space is an intuition not a general concept.

So far we have merely been contemplating the historical background to Kant's fourth argument. The most convincing case for accepting his argument can be furnished by starting from the assumptions of Kant's most dedicated modern critics. One of the clearest and hence one of the most disingenuous attacks on Kant's aesthetic comes in an elementary text on the philosophy of science written by John Kemeny. He describes Kant's well-known view that the propositions of geometry and of arithmetic are synthetic *a priori* propositions and then very forthrightly declares: "This is one of the most ingenious theories ever invented; it is a pity that Kant was quite wrong."[8] "The reasons," we are told by this distinguished logician and educator, "will be given later in this chapter," but there it develops that, ". . . if we recognize these two [the axiom of infinity and the axiom of choice] as legitimate logical principles—as most logicians do—then all of Mathematics follows and becomes just advanced Logic." Kemeny's observation can fairly be called disingenuous because they conceal from the reader the divided state of opinion among contemporary logicians, most of whom probably do not think that the axioms are analytic. It is also less than candid about revealing what Kemeny

[8] John Kemeny, *A Philosopher Looks at Science* (New York, 1959), p. 17.

knows to be the case from his reading of the *Critique*, namely, that Kant's opinion that mathematics is possible as synthetic *a priori* knowledge is supported in part by Kant's views on possible representations of the infinite. Finally, it is unfortunate but true that Kemeny only tells us that the two axioms are analytic; he gives no argument to show that this is so. Still, for all these reservations about what he says, we can mark out a considerable area of agreement between Kemeny and Kant from which to begin the discussion.

First we can agree that only a limited fragment of classical mathematics can be developed without assumptions that are equivalent to the axioms of infinity and of choice. Secondly, if we choose to do so, we can express Kant's assumption about the representation of space as a whole in the form of an axiom that holds for its parts—parts that are represented when we represent space as a whole. For example, we might assert that no part of space is a proper part of itself (that is, a part not identical to the thing of which it is a part), but that every part of space does have a proper part. If we add that the relation between proper parts is transitive, then Kemeny will agree with us that the conjunction of the three assertions is a version of what he means by an axiom of infinity. Under the given set of assumptions it is not possible for the space to exist and to have parts unless the set of parts is infinite. Since the form, rather than the particular content of these assertions is what really matters, the example can easily be modified to give an illustration of a similar axiom in the domain of numbers.

If the two assumptions which are agreed to be indispensable for the full possibility of mathematics can be stated in the manner in which Kemeny refers to them—namely, as axioms, I believe he would agree that they *can* also be stated as rules of inference. If the rules are constructed so that whenever a universal proposition is given, the universal can be instantiated with any one of an infinite set of terms that refer each to a different individual, then it seems clear that we are dealing with rules of inference that have a force comparable to Kemeny's first axiom. A version of the axiom of choice has likewise been formulated in the rules for instantiating particular propositions, or propositions in which the reference is to some individual or individuals in the domain to which reference is made. The latter possibility supplies the basis for an instructive comparison between the views that Kemeny attributes to logicians and the views that are revealed by their practice. The late John Lemmon once published a set of rules for logical inference, including a rule for instantiating particular propositions. When he subsequently discovered that by inadvertence his rules amounted to a version of the choice-axiom, he felt obliged to publish an additional note calling attention to that fact as evidence of a legitimate defect in a system purporting to give rules of pure, formal logic.

What do we gain by centering the discussion on a rule rather than an axiom? First, it becomes plain that if the rules of formal logic are intended to permit us to reason about objects in every logically possible domain, then no one can seriously maintain that these equivalents of Kemeny's axiom are valid rules of formal logic. Secondly, the formulation of an axiom of infinity as a rule for instantiating universals makes it clear that the soundness of the assumption can be related to the restrictions we are willing to admit on the scope of the universal quantifier—the latter being understood to be an operation by which a predicate can be converted into a proposition by being referred to everything that is within its scope (referred, it is necessary to add, in one or more applications of the operation). The point to consider is this: Whenever the rule *is* valid as a rule of inference it is valid because the possibility of the references to the infinite set of individuals is already presupposed as a restriction on the operation of generalization and the rule does nothing more than to tell us how that which is already contained in the universal statement is to be specified. If the reader is prepared to concede the connection between these issues, then he will be receptive to these final reflections on the dispute between Kant and Kemeny over the problem of the infinite.

There is a widespread, if not unanimous, agreement that where a universal statement is understood as having this restriction, the force of the restriction cannot be achieved by a conjunction of statements in which the predicate is expressly applied to each of the individuals separately. This, under the given presupposition about its domain, the force of "Everything is red" cannot be expressed by saying of the individuals, A, B, and so on, "A is red, B is red, and so on". Two arguments are usually advanced against this translation. First, if the domain is infinite, the required translation cannot be completed. Now we have already seen that, from the point of view of formal logic, individual constants are superfluous—in the given case, we can imagine the terms, "A", "B" and so on, replaced by a set of predicates that apply uniquely and respectively to A, to B, and so on. What we are dealing with, therefore, is nothing more than a linguistic restatement of Kant's argument, on our first reconstruction of that argument.

Since the days when Ramsey first advanced these objections against Wittgenstein's view on the foundations of mathematics, there has been a second line of argument against the proposed translation into the express content of a theory of something that can be presupposed about the range of its general references. The objection is that even if the translation could be completed, it would be inexact. First, it would say too little unless we add that the individuals to which reference has been made are all the individuals there are in the domain. But if we do add that provision, then we have re-expressed the notion which we are trying to translate out. Secondly, the translation would say too much. It would tell us how many individuals there are—in the original that information was contained in the presupposition of the statement rather than the statement itself. It would identify each individual for us. And, if we have adopted a radical translation in which everything is conveyed by the predicates, it would give us a uniquely characterizing description of each individual. This objection does not correspond to anything in the Kantian argument that is under active consideration. I have mentioned it, in the first place, to give a fuller picture of the serious reservations which modern logicians have expressed about the proposed translation. I have mentioned it, in the second place, in anticipation of an argument that I will propose in the final section on behalf of Kant's views. The idea that there may be more that is contained in the presuppositions of a statement than is conveyed in .the statement itself is an idea that has applications which go beyond any that Ramsey contemplated.

Ramsey's line of argument will apply to every universal judgment or set of judgments that can be interpreted as involving a reference to an infinite set. *A fortiori*, the remarks apply to Kemeny's axiom of infinity or to any such axiom. If the universal quantifiers can not be assumed to range over an infinite domain, then the axiom itself is not possible. But if the quantifiers can be assumed to have such a range, then the axiom only makes explicit part of what is presupposed in every generalization and this will be something that can be clearly seen to be contained if we add the appropriate rules of inference for construction of individual instances of the generalization. Kant believes that there are rules of this type and that they are presupposed by every empirical science. However, they are not understood by him to be rules of inference in formal logic. Instead, as we have seen, Kant has in mind the type of rule which was articulated by Descartes as a rule for the geometrical construction of the empirical judgments—in the case of our physical judgments, or as a rule for the location of objects in time—in the case of all empirical judgments. In view of what has been said, Kant's fourth argument may be said to be insufficient but it cannot be said to be simply wrong-headed or to be unintelligent. There is more to be said in defence of Kant against the objections of modern mathematical logicians such as Kemeny, but what more there is to be said requires us to be somewhat bold and speculative in exploiting the difference between Kant's rules for the construction of concepts and the ordinary logical rules for instantiation. For that reason, I prefer to complete the defence in a separate section where there will be no danger of confusing the mistakes of others with the mistakes of Kant.

There is a final point to be made here about Kant's fourth argument. Sometimes it has been thought that there are objections that can be brought against the axiom of infinity on grounds of modern physical theory. If the number of elementary particles is finite, we are sometimes told, then the axiom and its equivalents must be false. As an objection to Kant's views about the objective validity of statements in mathematics and in the empirical sciences that presuppose an infinite domain, the objection misfires for two reasons. First, the objection would have us assume that Kant gains an infinite domain for these statements by a presupposition that multiplies the number of different things in the domain, but of course his presupposition by itself only tells us about the appearances of the things, not about the things *per se*. Secondly, his critical inquiry into the ground of the objective validity of judgments does not require him to defend a presupposition about the actual presence of any thing, even as an appearance. In the case of empirical judgments, as we have seen, he argues that their objective validity only presupposes a presence in space and time, not an actual presence to us. If we are able to know where to look for the appearances that will support or falsify the empirical judgments that is sufficient. In the case of mathematical judgments, the presupposition of their objective validity is merely the constructibility of their concepts and judgments in space or time. The empirical discoveries about the dimensions or the total mass in the universe do not count against either presupposition.

IV. FORMS OF INTUITION IN FORMAL AND TRANSCENDENTAL
LOGIC

My objective in this brief concluding section is to throw up a bridge between Kant's aesthetic and on-going work in formal logic and in transcendental logic or logic of cognition. Some of the research to which I shall allude was initiated by Kant, some by others, and some undoubtedly remains to be pursued. The reader will correctly assume from this that I am not concerned in these final remarks with the interpretation and defense of Kant's own words I am concerned with the still living truth in his analysis of the forms of intuition. The first, and perhaps the most controversial, application of his results is in the area of recent work in formal logic. Most of what I have to say concerns this area of prospective research and it is highly tentative in nature. My other observations return to the topic of the logic of science. Kant's aesthetic presents an interesting challenge to certain views in the history and logic of science which have recently become very influential.

The Kantian doctrine of the forms of intuition has roots in the Cartesian discoveries. Descartes realized that certain mathematical forms of expression which have one type of significance in themselves can be given an added and, even, a different significance. In order to do this, we must add a representation of space and must construe the expressions through references to locations in that space. Now we have just seen that Kant's ideas about the construction *in concreto* of the objects of mathematical and empirical description can be compared to the rules of the formal logician for instantiating universal propositions. This comparison between the Kantian construction of objects and the formal rules of inference has been developed by Hintikka in a series of compelling and brilliant publications. There is no doubt at all that the analogy is a comfortable and tempting analogy for partisans of Kant to adopt. It allows some of the huge prestige of modern formal logic to be radiated back upon Kant's doctrine of reference. But apart from certain historical defects which are incidental to my present purposes, the great defect of the comparison is that it does nothing to destroy the complacency of logicians about the adequacies of modern logic and, in particular, about the adequacy of some version or other of what is called "first-order predicate logic". In the opinion of some, this just *is* formal logic. The truth of the matter is that it is only a part of logic—the part which has developed under the influence of one of several possible forms which the mathematicization of logic could have taken. If we wish to disturb this complacency in formal logic, we might begin by assuming that Kant's doctrine of construction has its own independent virtues, that it derives its peculiar strength from a different part of the mathematical tradition from the part that was mainly exploited in the nineteenth century development of the predicate-calculus, and that Kant's doctrine can be applied to the subject matter of logic itself.

The theories of the formal logician have variously been taken to be about judgments, propositions, statements and sentences. Whatever the choice from among these, the objects can be construed as objects that appear and re-appear in time or in space and that can thereby be made the subject of mathematical treatment. It will be recalled that on Kant's view all knowledge of objects in space and time can be given a mathematical treatment, and that he even anticipated an algebraicized branch of the metaphysics of the categories that he developed in the *Critique*. If every science can and should be made mathematical, Kant did not suppose that the same parts of mathematics will furnish the useful and natural framework for each discipline. If we treat the objects of formal logic as objects that can be constructed in time in accordance with the *a priori* conditions for reference to objects in time, then this alternative will lead to a mathematicization of logic that exploits the potentialities of applied algebra and analysis. As I noted in the first chapter, Kant was aware of this possible development in logic and he was aware also that it inevitably makes the mathematical concept of a function or operation the central idea in the presentation of the science of logic. The reason for this is that the idea is central in the mathematics that is being applied to logic. Kant urged this mathematicization of logic as a way of making logic a "technical" discipline, and a flowering of logic unquestionably did occur under the impetus of these developments in mathematical logic.

Instead of referring to the first appearance, the second appearance, and so on, of the objects under investigation, we can develop the set of logical rules as rules for the construction of the premises and the conclusions of the arguments as objects in space, which present the same or different appearance depending upon what they are and how they are constructed in the space. Kant had a very rudimentary awareness of the possibilities in this direction also, since Euler, Lambert, and others had already taken the first step in the development of what are now known to every school child as Venn diagrams. There are some interesting exercises in Kant's working notes in which he tried to use the spatial models of judgments to represent the differences between analytic and synthetic judgments, which may be compared with the more common exercises in which he used the symbolism of algebra to represent those forms of knowledge.

The logical symbols which belong to the elementary theory of deduction have a natural model in spatial relationships, because the relation of antecedent and consequent holding between propositions or between predicates can be constructed in space as the relationship between the parts of a surface, one of which is spatially included in the other. Progress in this line of development of modern logic appeared to be a dead end and came virtually to a halt until the role of the quantifier in the theory of reference had become better understood. The quantifier and its associated symbolism (the quantified variable) makes possible the expression of a type of connection between predicates which is not only independent of the content of those predicates (as reflected in the geometrical or other likeness of the predicates), but is independent also of the logical relationships between the predicates themselves. Quine gives the obvious spatial model for what is basically a Kantian understanding of the role of the quantifier: He asks us to imagine the universal quantifiers and the positions in the predicates on which they operate to be replaced by a system of lines connecting the given places in the predicates.

The American logician Charles S. Peirce was apparently the first to combine the method of the Venn diagram with such a spatial construction of the universally quantified variable. Now Peirce was aware that the familiar algebraic approach to the mathematicization of logic throws the emphasis on the general properties of functions or operations. For example, modern logicians refer to certain laws in logic as De Morgan's laws. These laws are used in abstract algebra to illustrate the specialized application to logical operations of a general algebraic principle which holds for a wide class of operations—including the familiar arithmetical operations of addition and subtraction. No one is surprised by this family-relatedness of these two sets of operations, of course, because we remember that the modern calculus of logic was inspired by the example of arithmetical computations. But when Peirce had developed his spatial representation of the central ideas of modern logic, he realized that the result is to embed the mathematical logic in a different branch of mathematics. The central ideas of his spatial model are the ideas that are studied in combinatorial topology or the theory of graphs. The foundation of this mathematical science go back to Euler and beyond. (If the main thrust of my present argument is sound, there is an odd coincidence in the fact that the first great mathematical problem which led to main results in combinatorial topology is the so-called "Konigsberg-bridge problem".)

When Pierce presented an equivalent of modern first-order predicate logic as a part of the applied theory of graphs, he represents the quantificational identity of objects by a line of connection or a bridge connecting different parts of the space—the logical relationship between predicates themselves being represented by inclusion between the parts of the space, where the discovery of those relationships may involve a geometrical transformation of the appearances of the parts. Thus, the graphing of the line of identity or of the possible ways of being connected of different parts of space is what turns the dead-end of Venn diagrams into a vital area of research. An associated idea in combinatorial topology is the idea of a disconnectedness in the space or a "cut". This idea has become quite familiar to modern logicians working in the theory of proofs.

There are two ways in which the mathematicization of a theory can help to vitalize the theory, and this is true whether the theory is mathematical logic, mathematical economics or any other field that makes use of mathematical models. First, as already noted, the mathematicization can help to dispose of technical problems. In the case of the application of combinatorial topology to logic one anticipates the same type of results that have made this branch of mathematics interesting to those designing electronic circuits, laying out airline routes and the like. The question about the shortest route connecting various cities is not so different from the shortest proof connecting various propositions, from the point of view of the mathematics that can be applied. In the last several years there have been very interesting results along these lines.[9] The second gain to be anticipated from the mathematicization of a discipline is a gain in the fruitful and effective generalizations of the theory. It is necessary to add the terms "fruitful and effective", because there can be

---

[9] Richard Statman, *Structural Complexity of Proofs*, Ph. D. Dissertation (Stanford, 1974).

great controversy over the novel applications and extensions of the theory just as there can be controversy over any challenge to the existing order of ideas. An example of the depth and persistence of these controversies is provided in the history of the algebraic development of logic by Peirce's generalizations of the logic of ordinary "two-valued" truth-functions (which he and Frege developed independently) to the three-valued case, and to the many-valued case. The mathematical possibility of a many-valued logic has been haunting modern logic for more than half a century, without full agreement having been reached about whether it is fruitful for logic.

When Peirce developed his theory of logical graphs as an alternative to the predicate-calculus, he was able to exploit almost immediately a very interesting potential for generalizations. The full predicate-calculus for individuals can be represented in graphs in a plane, even though the purely geometrical possibility goes beyond that. If predicates are represented as parts of a space and if the device which indicates the common identity of individuals possessing the predicates is a line of identity in the space connecting the different predicates in the space, what happens if we allow the line to leave the space of the predicates and to return to the space of the predicates? The geometrical model that is being applied allows for the possibility of leaving the world of actual objects (whatever its dimensionality), entering some other world, and returning again to the world of the actual objects of the theory—whatever those objects may be and whatever the dimensions of the world of those objects. And yet, the mathematical aspects of the theory in question will change if we exploit this abstract possibility. Recalling the original application of the theory of graphs, we see immediately that the Sunday walker who wishes to know how to visit all the parts of Konigsberg clearly has a different problem if he has routes in four dimensions rather than the customary three dimensions. The relevant question, therefore, is whether there is any way in which the mathematical logician can exploit the possibilities that are made available to him. In order for this to be so, he must perceive an inadequacy or an insufficiency in any logic equivalent to ordinary predicate-logic. Until that has been perceived, he will be justified in thinking that the possibilities of fiddling with the lines of identity in the mathematical model are only an interesting curiosity.

Since the chief task of the deductive logician is to analyze correctly the difference between good and bad deductions, we need an example or examples of deductions that ordinary predicate logic classifies incorrectly and we need an analysis that connects the defect in predicate logic with its representation of the identity of the objects of quantified variables. When Peirce discovered both of these things, he became excited about the possibilities of his theory of logical graphs. One of his illustrations of deductive connections that are not correctly represented in predicate logic concerns these two sentences: "There is an x and there is a y such that if x fails in business then y commits suicide" and "There is an x such that if x fails in business then x commits suicide." If these two are symbolized in the obvious way *in predicate logic, they are deductively equivalent.* That is, one can construct what is supposed to be valid deductions from each of these to the other. Yet the two statements are quite obviously not equivalent: The x in the first sentence might be Johnny and the y might be Johnny's sorrowing father.

The diagnosis of what is wrong is obviously a matter of controversy, since first-order predicate logic provides us with a very touchstone of logicality. Also, diagnoses of where and how to amend predicate logic that seem to be dissimilar may turn out on closer examination to be dealing with different symptoms of a common disease. Nevertheless, a very clever student who had listened attentively to the usual patter that accompanies the introduction and explanation of the logical quantifiers might form a shrewd guess about one source of the difficulty. He will be told that when he has to interpret universal quantifiers that are given in succession, or when he makes successive instantiations of a given universal quantifier, he can pick the same individual twice, but it is not necessary for him to do so. Yet when he makes the moves in question, he necessarily picks some determinate individual which either is or is not the same as some other individual. That is, the idea of a possible identity and possible non-identity of objects under discussion is an idea that is present in almost all systems of modern logic in the informal and heuristic discussion that surrounds the logic, but is an idea that cannot be expressed in the standard logics. Yet, in order to deduce the second of the statements from the first in Pierce's example, we can form the denial of the second—a denial of a particular that is equivalent to a universal—and we can instantiate it in two terms that are simply different. By this means, we can easily derive the denial of the first, and, thereby, we establish the counter-intuitive implication of the second by the first.

The Kantian model of our formal logic is supplied by adding a representation of space to the judgments or propositions that are studied in logic and by adding a way of constructing those judgments or propositions as objects in the space. As in the Venn diagrams, the actual individuals which are determined by the predicates in the judgments will be represented by the parts of some space. But, following the Kantian insight into the nature of all such constructions, we will realize that the sameness or the difference of objects in the construction is determined in part by the spatial conditions that are added to the representations that are under study. We will realize, in other words, that the domain of the quantified variables does not need to be the same, or even to have the same dimensions as, the space that represents the scope of the predicates. One way to approach this possibility is through the observation that ordinary predicate logic interprets the objects within the domain of quantification as though they always form proper Cantorian sets or classes of objects. What I have in mind is Cantor's basic intuition concerning the objects upon which mathematical operations can be performed. Cantor imagined every such class as something composed of determinate individuals which can be "spread out, as it were, before one's view." The members of a Cantorian class have definite identities. Since they do have definite identities, and as a sign or a mark that one is dealing with a proper Cantorian class, it always makes sense to ask about such a class "How many members does it have?" Even though there are Cantorian classes that can be described for which we cannot give the answer to this question, the question itself always makes sense for the types of classes one wants and one needs to do arithmetic, algebra and analysis. But there are classes of objects for which the question does not make sense and which are not proper Cantorian classes—by the proposed criterion. As Quine has pointed out, it does not make sense, for example, to ask how many possible fat men there are in the doorway. When we are talking about individuals that are the same *as possibilities* or that are different *as mere possibilities*, the question does not make sense because the sameness or difference of the individuals is not entirely a function of what the individuals are, but is a function also of how the individuals are picked out or constituted by us the same or as different. Now the moral which Quine draws from his example of the fat man in the doorway is a moral designed to save the purity of first-order predicate logic from contamination by what he regards as deviant logics. But that is absurd. Peirce's example would hardly be convincing if we were not capable of distinguishing informally between valid and invalid forms of reasoning in cases in which two individuals are only either possibly the same or possibly different—reasonings where we instinctively see that we will go wrong if we are forced to narrow the references to definite and actual individuals. If ordinary systems of logic misrepresent those forms of reasoning, then it is simply a sign of the beliefs of the youth of modern logic hardening into the dogmas of its middle age when logicians cling to their inadequate theories.

A mathematically rigorous treatment can be given of reasonings that are about possible objects, where the references to one and the same or to different possible objects are not necessarily references to objects that are identical or not identical as the determinate objects of Cantor's vision. Cantor may not, in other words, be able to tell by looking at these objects whether they are the same or different; and the reason that he may not be able to tell is not the relatively trivial reason that he may not know all there is to know about the objects. The reason is that the sameness or difference of the objects is not determined by that which makes the object a determinate object for Cantor to view. The possible objects of reference in our valid reasonings include objects that do not necessarily belong or not belong to partciular Cantorian classes or even to the most general categories. *A fortiori*, questions about how many such objects there are will not make sense, because the objects in question have not necessarily been brought under any scheme of classification. Now an object that has been given a location in space or in time in accordance with the restrictions on such references that are acknowledged by Kant is still only a possible object in this sense. It is not a determinate object. That is, we can mark a clear distinction between its location as an object of reference and its membership or non-membership in any Cantorian class. Also, we are able to retain the Kantian idea when we construe the predicates or the Cantorian classes which are extensions of our (categoreally possible) predicates as parts of the space. Kant's distinction between the conditions on judgments which are restrictions and those which are limitations is a distinction between forms of intuition which are indispensable for reference to objects and categories which are indispensable for connected description. In the algebraic logic the force of this distinction is not preserved, or not preserved in the obvious way in which the logical graph of judgments can preserve and display it. If the dimensionality (the "worlds") of the objects of reference is determined by the space of the predicates, then we have, as already noted, an equivalent form of the predicate-calculus. But if the dimensionality of the objects of reference is different from the space of the predicates, then we have a modal extension of predicate logic. These modal logics differ from the ordinary modal systems. The latter have been sponsored by basically Aristotelean intuitions about the reality of natural kinds of things and about the existence of necessary, but non-analytic connections between predicates. The standard semantics of ordinary modal logic is Cantorian.

Even as recently as ten years ago, the exploitation of Kantian insights and motivations in the mathematicization of logic was hindered by the blinding dogmas of the foundationalists in mathematics and in logic. In the first chapter we reviewed the dogma of the latter and discovered that there is no truth or substance to the claim that all of mathematics can be unified and put on a secure foundation by reduction to logic. The corresponding claim of the old foundationalists within mathematics was the claim that one branch of mathematics contained the foundation and the source of all the other branches of mathematics. The usual candidate for that role was, of course, Cantorian set theory. Any modal logician who retains that conviction will, of course, not feel comfortable in his mathematical reasonings concerning modal systems until he has provided such an interpretation for his system. But he should realize that there is nothing that is uniquely mathematical about the branch of mathematics that deals with sets, and there is growing evidence that the unity of mathematics is not provided by deduction from a single set of assumptions, whether they be about sets, or about anything else. Instead, the unity of mathematics is more like that envisioned by Kant. That is, there are several different branches of mathematics, each with its own structure of reasons and its own appeals to evidence in its objects; the unity of mathematics consists in the existence of correspondences between these parallel structures. This idea is one that has passed from modern mathematics into the history of philosophy and has been applied to Leibniz in a very provocative study by Serres. As the idea gains greater currency among those concerned with mathematical logic, the practical influence of Kantian ideas is bound to increase—if not in the way I have outlined then in some comparable way.

The construction *in concreto* of the ideas of the logician as that construction has just been discussed depends upon the distinction between two types of possibility. There is the mere logical possibility of an object as something that is the object of a consistent description and there is the possibility of an object as something that falls within a domain of reference. This distinction reflects the difference between what is possible if the object that is represented is given an identity in time or in space, and what is possible if abstraction is made from the conditions under which the object can be given in intuition. The difference and its implications for a transcendental logic of the categories can be illustrated by an elaboration of one of Kant's favorite illustrations: Suppose someone asks the nurse on duty at the clinic whether it is all right to visit the man with measles in the room at the end of the hall. Suppose also that the nurse says in reply, "The man with measles in that room is well and is at his home." How can we expect the nurse's remark to be interpreted? The visitor might retort that it is logically impossible for a person with measles to be well. However, we will expect this reply only if we have the additional information that the clinic is located in the vicinity of one of the great universities. Everywhere else, we can expect a choice between two other interpretations. The point of the example comes from the fact that there *is* a choice and that the existence of the choice shows that we are dealing with neighborly alternatives. Each of the two alternatives preserves the consistency of what would otherwise be a logical incompatability in two descriptions. The first plan for preserving the nurse's reputation for good sense alters the force of her references by introducing a modal notion that changes the way in which the description is referred to the objects. There are a large number of such notions that might be supplied. For example, the nurse might be interpreted to mean that the man whom the questioner *believed to* have measles and *inquired after* as a man with measles did not in fact have measles. There are other, similar interpretations that will serve to straighten out the nurse's remark. But in ordinary situations the second line of interpretation is more natural. This line consists in applying a category to the object which permits the descriptions to be employed without contradiction. If we think of the man as a substantial thing who can persist through change of properties, then the nurse can be interpreted to mean that the man who did have measles has now recovered and has gone home. Now, Kant observes that there is an affinity between these two constructions of the predicate, the one by way of a kind of "subjectification" of the predicate by means of notions such as "It is believed that," "It is hoped that," "It is possible that," and the like, the other by way of a kind of "objectification" of the predicate through the use of categories, such as the category of substance. Furthermore, Kant argues that in the case of judgments that express possible knowledge the relationship between the modal notions and the categoreal notions is even closer than an affinity in the results. The type of possibility that he associates with the real objects of knowledge is constituted by the presence of the objects at some time, and each category—each concept of an object as something in which descriptions can be combined—is a concept that gives conceptual definition to a temporal determination of the object. In this way Kant goes as far as it is possible to go in the direction of a collapsing of the conditions for reference into the conditions for description. But because he does not complete that collapse of the two sets of conditions for judging, he finds himself in opposition to a very common doctrine in the contemporary logic of science.

When the forms of intuition are *not* distinguished from the categories of understanding, then evidence of apparent inconsistency between two sets of observations will have to be interpreted in a way that does not permit the two sets of observations to be about the same kinds of objects. In this way, the identity of some object of reference is made to depend upon the way the object is categorized. One expression of this very common idea is given in Peter Winch's claim that "To notice something is to identify relevant characteristics, which means that the noticer must have some *concept* of such characteristics; . . ."[10] This view of the matter leads Winch to postulate a peculiar problem for students of other cultures. Since the student may not share the relevant categories and concepts, he cannot be assumed to notice the same objects. Kant discussed the same issue and explicitly rejected Winch's position. Kant tells us that if a savage who is unfamiliar with houses were to

[10] Peter Winch, *The Idea of a Social Science and Its Relation to Philosophy* (London, 1958), p. 85.

see a house in front of him, he would have just the same object represented before him as a man who recognizes it in a definite way as a human dwelling. Yet as regards the form the cognition of one and the same object is different in the two men. For the savage the cognition of the house is mere intuition, while for the other it is intuition and concept together.[11]

We can anticipate that Kant, who believed very strongly in the possibility and the importance of progress in the sciences, would have reacted in the same way to contemporary views about the impossibility of comparing views from different periods in the history of science. The possibility has been denied in one contemporary school in the history of science. The ground of the denial is the view that the subject matter of different theories is determined by the content of the theories or by the deductive relationships between the terms within each theory. If that were so, then we could not say that Newton gave us a better understanding of something than Aristotle provided. Newton simply changed the subject. But of course, if the underlying view were true it would apply equally to the various statements in the history of science itself and we could not talk about theory-succession itself in an unequivocal way—or in a way that presupposes that there is only one time in which the changing scientists and their theories can be described as being.

One of Kant's strengths as a philosopher of science is that he worked out an answer to these paradoxical and perhaps self-contradictory views about the logic of cognition. The paradox results from a simple conflation of the forms of reference and the categories of description. The fact that the paradox has appealed to a strain of romanticism or a strain of Hegelianism in the modern soul does not make the basis for the paradox a sound one. Kant's defense of the autonomy of the forms of intuition confirms the robust good sense with which Wallace Stevens concluded his poem, "So and So Reclining on Her Couch". Much of Stevens poetry and prose was preoccupied with Winch's paradox, and in this particular verse the poet indicates how the subject of the poem "floats in the contention, the flux/between the thing as idea and/The idea as thing," but his final thought is very unromantic and non-Hegelian. He returns from Quine and Winch to Kant:

But one confides in what has no
Concealed creator. One walks easily
The unpainted shore, accepts the world
As anything but sculpture. Good-bye
Mrs. Pappadopolous, and thanks.

[11] *Gesammelte Schriften*, IX, p. 33.

APPENDIX

LOGICAL FORM IN CRITICAL PHILOSOPHY

There are substantial chunks of Kant's argument in the first *Critique* which can only be assessed if we are able to compare his views on logical form with views that are today accepted as sound, or at least as reasonable. One way to make this comparison is by noting the role that Kantian principles had in the historical development of post-Kantian logic—that is to say, in the genesis of views that are widely accepted today.

The major principles that will govern an approach that is in the Kantian spirit can be deduced from his conception of logic as one of the sciences of criticism. The fact that it is a *science* of criticism tells us that whatever is true for a science is true for logic. Now we know that for Kant there is only as much of science in a given discipline as there is of mathematics in it. Hence, the first general principle governing the Kantian approach to problems in logic will be to seek to introduce the concepts and methods that will make logic (or an important part of logic) into mathematical logic. The fact that for Kant logic is a science of *criticism* tells us that the fundamental *fact* for this discipline is the fact that we have a conscience, or a consciousness of things that we ought to do and ought not to do. Hence, the second general principle governing the Kantian approach to problems in logic will be to define the fundamental concepts of logic in a way that will reflect our consciousness that there are good and bad ways of conducting ourselves in the area that logic is concerned with.

What is that area? What are the fundamental acts of the understanding that are subject to logical review and control? Kant's official answer is that all the acts of the understanding can be reduced to the acts of judgment. The concept of logical form is a concept that enters the *Critique* in connection with the analysis of the form of judgments. However, the subsequent development of Kantianism in logic—notably in C.S. Peirce's application of the major principles gleaned from Kant—followed the route suggested by Kant's distinction between analytic and synthetic knowledge. On this view, the fundamental datum for logic is the fact that some reasoning is good and some reasoning is bad. The concept of logical form enters into the basic or elementary theory of pure deduction as part of the effort to give an account of this fact that some purely analytic connections of propositions are good and some will not withstand criticism—as a process that involves the possibility of review and control in the light of general standards.

If we construe the act of reasoning as an operation of the mind performed upon one series of propositions to yield a further proposition, then the mathematical approach to the definition of the distinction between good and bad reasoning will obviously turn to the question of whether that operation can be defined as some appropriate mathematical function. If we consider particular propositions in all their limitless diversity, the task is hopeless for a mathematical logic. But if we determine that only the truth or falsity of the constituent propositions can affect the goodness or badness of the reasoning—the reasoning being bad if it leads us from truth in the premises to falsity in the conclusion and otherwise being good—we can define the function over those limited aspects of propositions, namely their truth and falsity. By considering the function to be one that assumes values in the same domain, we are naturally led to the view that the goodness of a deduction in the elementary theory of the subject consists in the fact that when this function is applied to the premises and the conclusion of the reasoning (when these are considered in respect to their possible truth or falsity) the function always yields truth in the case that the reasoning is good but otherwise sometimes yields falsity. All that remains for the elementary part of deduction is to construct the function to fit our intuitions about the goodness or badness of a small number of examples of reasoning that we are aware of as examples of good reasoning and bad reasoning. The standard definition of the function in question—the so-called material conditional—can be deduced from this array of information. All the other concepts that enter into the discussion of logical form in the elementary theory of deduction can be defined by means of the material conditional, which is usually expressed as "if . . ., then . . .". For example, negation can be defined by "if P, if P, if P . . ." or by "if P, then f" (where f is some particular falsehood).

The preceding account of the definition of the material conditional—an account which stresses that it is defined to satisfy our critical instincts about good and bad reasoning—gives a sketch of the actual development of this concept in the work of Peirce. Also it must be pointed out that it results in an explanation of the material conditional with which modern logicians are thoroughly familiar. For example, E.W. Beth's *Formal Methods* gives a very

clear discussion of the details of the deduction of the definition of the conditional. Nevertheless, students of logic are not usually given any insight into
this historical background to the concept or to this way of explaining its
truth-table definition. Instead, they are typically given to believe that the
notion has been introduced to translate the meaning of individual propositions
in English—sometimes with the suggestion that the translation closes a
"truth-value gap" in these sentences. The results are usually not very satisfactory from a pedagogic point of view. If the student who objects to the truth-
table that defines the material conditional can be brought to see that it is
defined as it is in order to fit his logical conscience in particular cases (via the
mathematical approach to the definition of good reasoning), he can be brought
to accept it as an illustration of how the two fundamental principles of a
Kantian approach to logical form are bound to get applied.

In summary, then, the Kantian idea of logical form is that it is an element
in a proposition which expresses a fundamental act of the understanding.
This idea is not a fashionable idea in modern logic and will be scouted by
some modern logicians as unintelligible nonsense. However, the idea guided
the actual genesis of the modern, elementary theory of deduction in Peirce
and, as in Beth, the idea can be employed to motivate the basic definitions in
that theory. Hence, it is not a wholly worthless idea.

INDEX OF NAMES